Turning Points in Play Therapy and the Emergence of Self

by the same authors

Play Therapy Dimensions Model
A Decision-Making Guide for Integrative Play Therapists
Lorri Yasenik and Ken Gardner
ISBN 978 1 78592 990 8
eISBN 978 1 78450 579 0

of related interest

Narrative Play Therapy
Theory and Practice
Edited by Aideen Taylor de Faoite
ISBN 978 1 84905 142 2
eISBN 978 0 85700 333 1

A Manual of Dynamic Play Therapy
Helping Things Fall Apart, the Paradox of Play
Dennis McCarthy
ISBN 978 1 84905 879 7
eISBN 978 0 85700 644 8

Inclusion, Play and Empathy
Neuroaffective Development in Children's Groups
Edited by Susan Hart
Foreword by Phyllis Booth
ISBN 978 1 78592 006 6
eISBN 978 1 78450 243 0

TURNING POINTS IN PLAY THERAPY AND THE EMERGENCE OF SELF

Applications of the Play Therapy Dimensions Model

Edited by
LORRI YASENIK and KEN GARDNER

Jessica Kingsley Publishers
London and Philadelphia

First published in 2019
by Jessica Kingsley Publishers
73 Collier Street
London N1 9BE, UK
and
400 Market Street, Suite 400
Philadelphia, PA 19106, USA

www.jkp.com

Copyright © Jessica Kingsley Publishers 2019

Front cover image source: Shutterstock®. The cover image is for illustrative purposes only, and any person featuring is a model.

All rights reserved. No part of this publication may be reproduced in any material form (including photocopying, storing in any medium by electronic means or transmitting) without the written permission of the copyright owner except in accordance with the provisions of the law or under terms of a licence issued in the UK by the Copyright Licensing Agency Ltd. www.cla.co.uk or in overseas territories by the relevant reproduction rights organisation, for details see www.ifrro.org. Applications for the copyright owner's written permission to reproduce any part of this publication should be addressed to the publisher.

Warning: The doing of an unauthorised act in relation to a copyright work may result in both a civil claim for damages and criminal prosecution.

Library of Congress Cataloging in Publication Data
A CIP catalog record for this book is available from the Library of Congress

British Library Cataloguing in Publication Data
A CIP catalogue record for this book is available from the British Library

ISBN 978 1 78592 388 3
eISBN 978 1 78450 747 3

Printed and bound in the United States

All pages marked with ⤓ can be downloaded at www.jkp.com/catalogue/book/9781785923883 for personal use with this programme, but may not be reproduced for any other purposes without the permission of the publisher.

Contents

Acknowledgements 7

Introduction 9
Lorri Yasenik and Ken Gardner, Rocky Mountain Play Therapy Institute

1. Turning Points and Understanding the Development
   of Self Through Play Therapy 15
   Lorri Yasenik and Ken Gardner

2. Emergence of Self through Learn to Play Therapy 43
   Karen Stagnitti, Deakin University

3. Just Like a Kid! Adlerian Play Therapy 59
   Terry Kottman, The Encouragement Zone

4. "You can be the door": Establishing Safety and Facilitating
   Growth of Personal Identity with a Traumatized Child . . . 83
   Eileen Prendiville, Children's Therapy Centre

5. Turning Points in Treating Complex Trauma in Carlos,
   a Foster Care Child 103
   Athena A. Drewes, Astor Services for Children and Families

6. Shame Can Get Stuck in Your Throat: The Rise of
   Consciousness for Five-Year-Old Freddy 125
   Paris Goodyear-Brown, Nurture House

7. Corrie and the T-Rex: Courage Reclaimed 147
   Linda E. Homeyer, Texas State University

8. Acknowledging the Unexpressed beneath Trauma: An Encounter of Subjectivities through Play Therapy. 161
Carolina S. Araya, Magdalena S. Oyanedel, and Francisca Jenschke Smith, Metáfora Centre

9. The Therapeutic Dance: The Role of Affective Synchrony in Guiding Therapists When to Lead and When to Follow in Psychotherapy with Traumatized Children 187
Katherine Olejniczak, Psychology and Play Therapy Australia

10. The Container: Piecing Together a Life Story. 207
Adriana Sorbo, Private Practice, Valerie Kendall, Private Practice, and Cassandra White, Private Practice

11. To Kill or Not to Kill While Figuring Out How to Love Me Forever: A Child Loves Her Play, Not Because It's Easy, But Because It's Hard 223
Theresa Fraser, Wilfrid Laurier University

12. Symbolic Solutions: Establishing a Sense of Safety for Relationship Repair 237
Sonia Murray, Play Therapist

13. From Isolation to Invigoration: Five Canadian Play Therapists Share an Emergence of Selves through the Power of Finding Belonging in a Professional Community 255
Irene A. Barrett, Registered Psychologist, Bruce A. Beaudet, Clinican, Katharine Chapman, Clinical Social Worker, Dana Diamond, Registered Play Therapist, and Tammy Reis, Play Therapist

14. Discussion and Summary. 273
Lorri Yasenik and Ken Gardner

The Editors 283

The Contributors 285

Appendix A: Degree of Immersion: Therapist Use of Self Scale . . . 291

Appendix B: Supervision Form for Therapist Use of Self: Degree of Immersion for Next Session Plan 302

Subject Index. 305

Author Index. 310

Acknowledgements

We want to express our gratitude to the contributors. Many of you are our dear colleagues with whom we study each year as part of the International Play Therapy Study Group. We also want to acknowledge and welcome new contributors to our field, who we have had the pleasure to work with during training and practice.

INTRODUCTION

——— LORRI YASENIK AND KEN GARDNER ———

This edited book is meant for students, supervisors, instructors, and advanced play therapy practitioners. Anchored by an integrative decision-making framework, the Play Therapy Dimensions Model (Yasenik and Gardner, 2012), each contributor uses the model to illustrate turning points in the play therapy process. Additionally, the impact of the therapist's use of self on the emergence of the child's self is examined through detailed case analyses.

A main premise of the book is that effective clinical practice requires a thorough understanding of the ways in which turning points surface in the play therapy process, and how factors such as the therapist's use of self contribute to significant movement in therapy. The notion of a therapeutic turning point is not new to the literature on adult psychotherapy. Turning points have been examined for specific clinical issues such as suicide (De Leo, 2010), as well as critical turning points in psychotherapy through detailed retrospective reviews of classical cases in psychotherapy (Schoenewolf, 1990). Unfortunately, the examination of this construct is noticeably absent in the play therapy literature.

To establish a foundation for the reader, Chapter 1 breaks down the concept of a turning point into four main forms or subtypes, augmented by case vignettes to illustrate the underlying characteristics of each type of form. As discussed in Chapter 1, one form of turning point is indicated by a change in thought, behavior, affect, and/or understanding about something. When examined from a play therapy perspective, especially taking into consideration child development and the importance of the emergence of self, other unique forms of turning points must also be considered, such as the emergence of a level of awareness not previously available to a child. Whether a rise in awareness or consciousness occurs at a symbolic or verbal level, its significance lies in the fact that it is something that is useful in the process of change, either in a global sense or in a micro sense.

The play therapist is often the facilitator of turning points and an important partner in the evolutionary journey with the child. To strengthen the practitioner's understanding and ability to monitor use of self, contributors explore specific turning points in their clinical cases by using a detailed self-reflective tool—the Degree of Immersion: Therapist Use of Self Scale (Appendix A). This tool, which is introduced in Chapter 1, has been used extensively by play therapy practitioners since first published as part of the Play Therapy Dimensions Model. It has been updated here for use by the expert clinicians contributing to this book and is available to download from www.jkp.com/catalogue/book/9781785923883. The reader is encouraged to make use of this tool to enhance their clinical practice.

Another premise of the book is that the *development of self* is a central construct to all restoration, growth, and change. To exemplify this point, a range of referral issues are examined through various models of play therapy including Adlerian, child-centered, prescriptive, integrative, and the Intersubjective and Relational Psychoanalysis approach. Other clinical paradigms are also represented such as the Embodiment-Projection-Role (E-P-R) developmental paradigm (Jennings, 1999), the Learn to Play Therapy approach (Stagnitti, 1998, 2016), and the Flexibly Sequential Play Therapy model (Goodyear-Brown, 2010).

To set the stage for subsequent discussions and case illustrations, Chapter 1 provides an overview of important concepts and research on the development of self, including work by developmental/self-concept specialists such as Susan Harter (2012). Making use of developmental frameworks, as well as other theoretical constructs, each expert discusses specific markers that reflect shifts and/or growth in the child's development of self. This discussion is particularly valuable for practitioners and instructors alike, as it occurs in the context of case examples ranging in age from early to late childhood, and with various presenting concerns such as developmental challenges, complex relational trauma, and sexual abuse.

To guide the reader, Table I.1 provides an overview of each chapter, identifying the primary referral issue, the age of the child, the primary theoretical orientations adopted by the clinicians, and the phase and/ or length of therapy. While most chapters provide a summary table outlining the identified turning points, there are a few exceptions to this format. Chapter 5 presents an integrative perspective on the treatment of complex trauma through a composite case to represent the symptom phenomenology as well as intervention strategies, which included parent-child work. To orient the reader, primary phases of treatment are examined along with exemplary turning points. Chapter 10 offers a shift in perspective by exploring "stuck points" in the play therapy process, offering an understanding of how therapists are challenged to work within complex systems and must harness their creativity. Chapter 13 breaks away from the conceptualization of clinical cases by examining the play therapist's development of the professional self. Specifically, this chapter explores contextual barriers to the development of the professional self, along with factors that contributed to growth.

Table I.1 Chapter summary

Chapter	Primary referral issue and age of child	Theoretical orientation	Phase/length of therapy
2	Four years old; specific language impairment	Learn to Play program	
3	Eight years old; behavioral issues	Adlerian	1.5 years; school-based counseling
4	Five years old; complex trauma	Humanistic; integrative; E-P-R	73 sessions
5	Four years old; complex trauma	Integrative	95 sessions
6	Five years old; sexual abuse	Flexibly Sequential Play Therapy	16+ sessions
7	Three years old; sexual abuse	Adlerian; trauma informed	19 sessions—disclosure and treatment
8	Four years old; sexual abuse	Integrative; Intersubjective and Relational Psychoanalysis	Disclosure and initial treatment

cont.

Chapter	Primary referral issue and age of child	Theoretical orientation	Phase/length of therapy
9	Seven years old; trauma	Integrative; trauma informed	42 sessions/two years
10	Six years old; complex trauma	Integrative; trauma informed	+20 sessions
11	11 years old; relational trauma	Integrative; trauma informed	
12	9–14 years old; relational trauma; sexual abuse	Integrative	Long-term 100+ sessions

How to use the material in this book

Ideally, the reader would benefit from first reading Chapter 1, "Turning Points and Understanding the Development of Self through Play Therapy," as it provides an overview of the Play Therapy Dimensions Model, the Degree of Immersion: Therapist Use of Self Scale, and, most importantly, the underlying constructs of turning points and emergence of self. However, each chapter stands alone and can be read separately from the other chapters to focus on a specific model or approach, or referral issue. To assist the reader, most chapters conclude with a summary table that chronologically identifies turning points according to the stage in the therapy process, the quadrant(s) in which each turning point occurred (as identified by the Play Therapy Dimensions Model), and factors that contributed to the turning point, particularly the therapist's use of self. The summary table alone will assist the play therapy practitioner in their case conceptualization skills.

Play Therapy Dimensions Model (Yasenik and Gardner, 2012) is a helpful companion and can be read as a follow-up to this book. Like the original work, the current edited book will appeal to those working at both ends of the play therapy spectrum, from the development of basic play skills to the resolution of complex clinical issues through high levels of awareness and advanced play skills, cognition, and language. Throughout, the book highlights the special turning points that happen all along the growth pathway.

Note
The names of clients who appear within case studies or examples have been omitted or changed for confidentiality reasons. Some case studies are based on composite case material.

References
De Leo, D. (2010) *Turning Points: An Extraordinary Journey into the Suicidal Mind.* Bowen Hills: Australian Academic Press.
Goodyear-Brown, P. (2010) *Play Therapy with Traumatized Children: A Prescriptive Approach.* Hoboken, NJ: Wiley Publishing.
Harter, S. (2012) *The Construction of the Self: Developmental and Sociocultural Foundations* (2nd edn). New York: Guilford Press.
Jennings, S. (1999) *An Introduction to Developmental Playtherapy.* London: Jessica Kingsley Publishers.
Schoenewolf, G. (1990) *Turning Points in Analytic Therapy: From Winnicott to Kernberg.* New Jersey: Jason Aronson Inc.
Stagnitti, K. (1998) *Learn to Play: A Program to Develop the Imaginative Play Skills of Children.* Melbourne: Coordinates Publications.
Stagnitti, K. (2016) Play Therapy for School-Age Children with High Functioning Autism. In A. Drewes and C. Schaefer (eds) *Play Therapy in Middle Childhood.* Washington, DC: American Psychological Association.
Yasenik, L. and Gardner, K. (2012) *Play Therapy Dimensions Model: A Decision-Making Guide for Integrative Play Therapists.* London: Jessica Kingsley Publishers.

TURNING POINTS AND UNDERSTANDING THE DEVELOPMENT OF SELF THROUGH PLAY THERAPY

LORRI YASENIK AND KEN GARDNER

The emergence of self in play therapy

What is meant by the emergence of self? There are many writers past and present who have examined the concept of self (and use of self) in the psychotherapy literature (Baldwin, 1987; Bragan, 1996; Erwin, 1997; Gergen, 1996; Hobson, 1985; Khan, 1997; Wosket, 1999). Consciousness is related to degrees of self-knowledge and self-awareness and most, if not all, therapies are interested in self-development, self-agency, self-efficacy, and self-awareness, even if the focus is not primarily on "talk" as the main form of intervention. James's (1990) theory, which was re-embraced during postmodernism, is viewed once again as a current important construct (Harter, 2012). The idea of the I-self as knower, the Me-self as known, and multiple Me-selves as part of self-development is closely related to turning points in play therapy. How are these concepts related? Of considerable importance is self-understanding through narrative and autobiographical memory, which is what Harter (2012) refers to as a rudimentary story of the self. Beginning at the age of approximately two years, children start to form a sense of continuity of self over time of which autobiographical memory is part (Nelson, 2003). The development of language and the use of personal pronouns (and by about three and a half years of age the development of past tense) allows young children to expand the ways of thinking and talking about the I-self and elaborates a categorical (and continuous) knowledge of the Me-self (Bates, 1990; Miller *et al.*, 1990). Parents and caregivers are critical in a child's development of the autobiographical self and personal narratives. This leads to a representational self (Nelson, 2003) that in turn allows for shifts and change therapeutically, allowing for turning points in self-understanding.

Adult self-theories cannot be compared to the self-theories of the developing child based on numerous cognitive limitations. Harter (2012) notes:

> That is, the I-self, in its role of constructor of the Me-self, does not, in childhood, possess the capacities to create a hierarchically organized system of postulates that are internally consistent, coherently organized, testable or empirically valid. In fact, it is not until *late adolescence* if not early adulthood that the abilities to construct such a self-portrait potentially emerge. (p.9, original emphasis)

Harter (2012) therefore argues for the analysis of I-self at various stages of development, because the I-self impacts the emergence of the Me-self. The focus on developmental changes also allows the therapist to address levels of differentiation and integration (two levels of self-theory). Through differentiation, increasing cognitive abilities will help the child to differentiate experiences. Through integration, higher order generalizations can be made about the self as related to traits and abilities.

It is important for play therapists to have good observation skills in following and supporting the emergence of consciousness in play therapy. An awareness of the indications of the presence of the I-self in play therapy is a part of the foundation upon which change and growth occurs.

Turning points in play therapy

What might we observe when identifying a turning point in therapy? The adult literature reflects on the following possible ways to explain a therapeutic turning point: review of the goals of therapy to identify a relief of symptoms and change in an emotional state; difference in a person regarding their before and after therapy experience; a sudden dramatic improvement; chemistry between a therapist and client; the transference and countertransference therapist/client relationship; growth in the therapist having an impact on the growth in the client; and a sudden transition from a maladaptive coping style to a more integrated adaptive state (Stone, 2015). The psychotherapy and psychoanalytic literature also focuses on classic cases and reviews the turning points of both the therapists and the patients (Schoenewolf, 1990). In Schoenewolf's *Turning Points in Analytic Therapy: From Winnicott to Kernberg*, there are references to a child client's turning points. Erikson, for instance, is described as working with a three-year-old girl through non-directive play. Erikson (although not known for play therapy) asserted that spontaneous play was self-curative and he looked for play activity that signaled a change in behavior and emotion. In a similar vein, Winnicott is described as making use of his authentic self in his work with a nine-year-old boy. His authenticity with this child led to a major turning point in his relationship with the child and in his career. It was soon after his experience with this child that he wrote a paper on "Hate in Countertransference" in 1947. The paper described the importance of a therapist being able to hate his patients objectively. Others viewed Winnicott as making use of his authentic self.

A turning point may come in many forms and in multiple ways in the play therapy room. Landreth (2002) notes that it is not typical for children to demonstrate big, sudden change with "insightful breakthroughs" in play therapy. Therapeutic growth is described as a slow process. Landreth comments on the possibility that the therapist, in an attempt to hasten a child's growth and change, may resort to trying one technique after another and not remain consistently "with" the child. Landreth points out:

> Children's nonverbal behavior can provide significant cues to understanding the totality of their way of behaving or functioning and useful information in understanding the therapeutic process in play therapy. Change is occurring in hundreds of little ways, and the therapist just has to look for those indications of the process of change. (2002, p.353)

One way of looking at a turning point is what Landreth (2002) describes as a therapeutic "first." Look for small firsts such as the child's expanded use of space, proximity to you as the therapist, a shift in use of materials, an emotional change, limit-setting no longer being necessary, the development of new play themes, or an elaboration of a play theme and the child stopping a repetitive play theme. Turning points may occur in a moment in time, during a single session, or over many moments in time and many sessions. There is little disagreement in the therapy literature that there is high importance placed on the therapist/client relationship and that relational factors also contribute to a turning point.

Consideration was given to categories in which a play therapist may identify a turning point. Through case review and observation of video examples of play therapy sessions, four main contributing areas emerged. These areas interrelate with the development of self and self-understanding. The identified areas of consideration may offer the play therapist a way to more easily observe a type of turning point, and once observed, the therapist may choose to make use of themselves in a particular way to support and stay "with" the child client. An explanation of the *four types* of turning points and supportive case examples are provided below.

The four types of turning points
Turning point type 1: a change in thought, behavior, affect, or understanding about something

Changes in thought are observed by way of an increase in cognitive ability in relation to patterns of thought, sequencing of thoughts and ideas, cognitive understanding of an aspect or many aspects of a situation, and/or problem-solving capacities through symbolic and/or verbal representations. Sometimes a change or elaboration of a way of thinking about something can also lead to change in behavior or the way a person feels about something, which leads to an overall expanded understanding of something. Other times, a repetitive behavior such as aggression in therapy can lead to a change in affect alone. A behavioral expression can, for instance, invite an integrative experience of aggression accompanied by anger.

- Justin was three and a half years old and in foster care. He presented as delayed in speech and was not yet toilet trained. He engaged the play therapist by grunting and pointing to indicate his need for various objects. Once the objects were made available, he dumped them into the sandtray. This happened session after session. His play appeared chaotic and disorganized in that his actions with the objects were related to dumping (with little to no purposeful manipulation) and then the session would end. It was noteworthy that what looked like chaos was always contained in the sandtray. After about the fifth session, still using no words, Justin repeated the dumping action but left a small space in the corner of the tray. He then pointed to a small child figure and placed it in the corner. He pointed to a doll house and then a rubber bird. He then took the bird and placed the child character on top of the bird and flew the two over to the doll house, child character on top of the bird. He placed the child character in the house and chose two adult figures to also place in the doll house. He placed the figures in proximity to one another and then flew the child character back to the corner in the sandtray. Order had appeared out of disorder. It seemed that Justin's play behavior had changed to incorporate something happening in his real life: the beginning of home visits. His play behavior demonstrated his new understanding and sequential ability to represent this change in circumstances.

Turning point type 2: the emergence of a level of awareness not previously available to a child; something that is useful in the process of change either in a global or micro sense

Between the ages of 18 and 27 months a child begins to refer to the self as "I," "me," "my," and "mine" (Bates, 1990; Miller *et al.*, 1990). Language begins to assist a child to think and talk about the I-self and expands their knowledge of the Me-self. Self-concept is viewed as a collection of beliefs about oneself and helps to answer the question of "who am I?" The "I-self" becomes the observer that becomes aware of the "Me-self" which is being observed. James (1892) viewed the "I-self" as a function of the development of self-awareness. Self-awareness develops first from a physical self-awareness and evolves to the use of verbal descriptions including self-references about self-behaviors and values. Children who are in therapy are likely to have had interruptions to their emerging complexity of the I-self/Me-self process. It is through providing materials and distance from the discomfort of the potentially negative appraisals from the I-self to the Me-self that allow children to recover and positively shift their schematic representations of self and others. Experiences and feelings can be disclosed through metaphor and ordered and re-ordered. It allows the I-self (the informer of Me-self) to watch and engage without immediate ownership. During therapy, it is often noted that children will shift between referring to experiences and feeling states using a third person reference (he, she, or it) and using the pronoun "I," which is more closely and consciously demonstrating a level of self-awareness and ownership. When this occurs, it signifies a turning point in the process as more insight becomes available to the child.

- Ten-year-old Jennifer was in the middle of a high-conflict divorce. She drew many pictures of choice that depicted happy scenes. Although her parents continually tried to get her to align with each of them against the other, Jennifer remained positive and loyal in her depictions of family and in her comments about each of them. When offered the possibility to identify how difficult it could be to be "in the middle" between two people she loved, Jennifer appeared unaware or unwilling to consider the pressure she was under. Others such as the school and her gymnastics teacher noticed (because the parents would often fight at transitions in front of others), and Jennifer would later become sullen and withdrawn. Jennifer, although using a reasonable defense mechanism, did not appear happy or empowered to her teachers. Out of respect for Jennifer's way of managing her feelings, the play therapist asked her to engage in a number of different types of "happy" activities in designing sand scenes and in art-making. One day, Jennifer sat down in front of the sandplay shelves where hundreds of symbols were lined up. She reached over and picked up a mesh-looking item and began to give it shape. She pulled its edges until she created a round sphere and placed it in the sandtray. She then pulled out a small figure of a girl and placed it inside the sphere. "There," she said. "That's me, and I am trapped in this cage and can't breathe because they can't stop arguing over me." She then chose two cats and placed them close by, looking in. "These are my cats and they are just watching what is happening. They are my friends and they know what is going on." This was the first time Jennifer entered into a metaphor that more directly depicted her situation. She brought herself into the scene through the direct use of the "Me-self" and the "I-self" indicating a greater awareness and consciousness in the play therapy session.

Turning point type 3: a moment in time where the child makes use of themselves or play objects in a way previously not observed, such as a change in the drive and direction of the play or the positioning of themselves in the play

Mastery play, safe play, highly ordered play before disorder, or highly disordered play before order are all examples of types of play that may be observed where a change in drive and direction occurs.

Mastery play is often thematically repetitive where the child may use characters or engage in role play to practice or engage in a variety of empowerment experiences and re-enactments. This can include being a superhero, a wise wizard, an expert, an omnipotent parent, a magician, or a fairy, to name a few. The child plays out themes of power and control and problem-solving and draws on inner knowledge and strength—mostly in metaphor, but sometimes alternating between the externalized characterization and the self. The onset of mastery play is often a signal of a turning point in the play therapy.

Highly ordered or constricted play may be observed just prior to a shift towards more disordered and chaotic play. The drive towards disorder is often necessary to reorganize traumatizing and/or abuse experiences. The child may set the stage for containment before the "undoing." During the chaotic play phase things can be in disarray, possibly reflecting past confusing and disordering experiences. Through the chaos phase, the child may be able to express a number of dissociated parts of an abusive experience, for instance. This turning point offers a way to put things out that were previously tightly held or dissociated from the child's conscious awareness.

Some children may begin by demonstrating high levels of chaos in their play. This can look like dumping things in piles, moving quickly from one thing to another, short play sequences with no real identified theme, aggressive play when engaging with a variety of play materials, and/or demonstrating through role play or other play materials a lack of order, problem-solving, or overall safety. A turning point may be noted when this type of play becomes more ordered and play materials are used to sequence a story or an experience.

A shift from safe play may also be indicative of a turning point. As is demonstrated below in the case of Patty, some children will engage in play that is seemingly normative with little or no sign of themes related to their presenting issues. This can include engaging in drawings and activities that are always thematically happy or perfect, only wanting to play games with rules in a repetitive way, or engaging in talking and avoiding any expressive activities, to name a few. A change in the drive or direction of the child's play toward something more expressively diverse or inclusive of multiple feeling states or themes is another observable turning point in play therapy.

- Patty was a quiet, reserved seven-year-old girl who had witnessed domestic violence. Patty's play was generally devoid of any distress or aggression. She liked to play games with rules and build houses and roads with Lego. She did not typically use family figures or any other family-like figures such as animal families. She loved to create things and then move on to something else in the playroom such as using the white board to draw hearts or to play darts or ball games. During one session where Patty was playing magnet darts, she began to increase her intensity and demonstrated her strength at hitting the board. She then became more random in her throwing and purposefully threw her dart at the play therapist who was retrieving her dart after taking a turn. The therapist made a comment indicating she was hit: "Oh that one hit me!" This action led to Patty running over to the puppet stand and choosing an alligator puppet with sharp teeth. She then threw a small kitty puppet to the play therapist. The play therapist barely had a chance to put the puppet on before the alligator was biting and hurting the kitty. This marked a new use of self in play for Patty and launched a different direction in play from this session forward. Patty began to "show and express" the violence she had witnessed, and she became the aggressor, placing the play therapist in the victim role. Through the play metaphor, Patty was able to begin to disclose the powerlessness of her position in her family by projecting the victim role onto the therapist.

Turning point type 4: a change in what is illuminated or seen in the play; a change in the way of viewing self or others

Self-concept in children is made up of self-schemas (internal model of self-assessment), a form of self-knowledge which is a cognitive description of one's self that is consistent and applicable to a child's current attitudes and dispositions (Ayduk, Gyurak and Luerssen, 2009). It relates to personality, skills and abilities, hobbies, physical characteristics, and so on and is a collection of schemas. In some instances, children present in therapy with what Harter (2006) notes as an "impoverished self." This can be due to attachment issues, poor parenting, or abusive parenting where there has been a failure of the caregiver(s) to assist the child through a co-construction process to develop a positive, rich, and coherent self-narrative. Some caregivers have provided distorted, untrue narratives for children about themselves resulting in children incorporating an unauthentic false-self. Individual differences in children can also contribute to a false-self construct, as some children are highly sensitive and over-identify external input in a negative manner. A change in the way a child views the self or others during play therapy is another important turning point in the process.

> Bart, 11 years old, was a highly sensitive child who had been picked on and targeted by tougher peers for years. Bart presented with low self-esteem and a lack of self-confidence. For many sessions, Bart deferred all decision-making to the therapist. He did not engage at all in any play-based or expressive activities without clear direction. When he did engage, he asked for permission or direction throughout the activity. Observing this pattern, the play therapist decided to lead Bart in a metaphorical activity where he was asked to choose a character or object to represent himself. Bart chose a small rabbit. Next, the therapist asked Bart to choose objects of protection and place them all around the rabbit. Bart chose a number of glass stones and followed the therapist's directions. The therapist then lay down on the floor and looked carefully over at the rabbit and asked Bart to join her. The therapist instructed Bart to look for holes through which something or someone could get through to the rabbit. Together, they looked for any opening areas that were not closed and protected by the glass stones. Bart added more glass stones in a circular manner around and around

the rabbit. Next the therapist asked Bart to choose objects that might attack the rabbit and place them all around the outside of the glass stones. Now Bart was engaged. He found threatening-looking animals and weapons and placed them all around the outside of the protective stones. "The protective stones look strong," said the therapist. "They are!" said Bart. "These ones think they are strong [pointing to the aggressive animals], but they are wrong." Bart chose some weapons to attack back and placed them near the rabbit. Now the rabbit figure was utilized by the therapist, and the therapist asked what the rabbit could see. "A bunch of mean stupid kids," said Bart on behalf of the rabbit. "Do they know how smart the rabbit really is?" asked the therapist. "Nope. They think he is stupid, but he's not," said Bart. "Does anyone know how smart he really is?" asked the therapist. "Yeah, his teachers know," said Bart. Bart continued to work with the rabbit and increased his positive regard for this little, yet fast, smart animal. He began to use intermittent statements where he referred to the rabbit as him. A turning point was noted in the positive view of self as smart and strong and the aggressive characters as stupid and less powerful over time through the use of the rabbit as a symbol of self.

An integrative conceptualization framework: the Play Therapy Dimensions Model

How does the play therapist know when a child is progressing in play therapy? Many practitioners state they may never really know which variables contribute to a child's reorganization or re-processing and some might state it is not possible, or even necessary, to know. Yet, the manner in which the therapist and child share the therapeutic space is central to most models of play therapy. Recognizing the complexities inherent in the client-therapist-treatment interaction, Schaefer (2003) encourages the practitioner to look at underlying change mechanisms. An integrative approach to therapy moves the practitioner in this direction as this approach is generally considered to be a purposeful weaving of theory, techniques, and common factors identified across therapies (Norcross, 2005). Although adopting an integrative approach places the decision of how best to work with the child/client upfront, Garfield (1994) noted that practitioners who described their work as integrative, following what was best for the child, in fact made use of differing decision-making processes and differing theories and techniques from one another. This runs the danger of becoming what eclecticism has been criticized for, namely being "a hodgepodge of inconsistent concepts and techniques" (Smith, 1982, p.802). Integrative play therapists and supervisors have an inclusive integrative framework that helps articulate decision-making and supports practitioner understanding of the complex moment-to-moment interaction that occurs in the therapy process. This was the main impetus for developing the Play Therapy Dimensions Model in 2004, and updating it in 2012 (Yasenik and Gardner, 2004, 2012).

One theoretical approach to integrative decision-making, "bounded rationality," takes note of the practical limitations for therapists such as resources, time, and knowledge (Gigerenzer, 2001), and emphasizes the need to describe timely ways to gather information and make decisions. Bounded rationality theory supports the development of techniques, habits, and standard operating procedures to facilitate decision-making. The theory also sheds light on the cues therapists use to consider one direction over another in their work with clients. In short, this approach stresses the need to know *where* to focus and parameters for determining *when* or *why* to use certain techniques or interventions. The Play Therapy Dimensions Model (Yasenik and Gardner, 2012) is consistent with a bounded rationality approach to conceptualization as it offers the play therapist decision-making structures for looking at the interaction of client-therapist-treatment factors. An examination of this interaction is accomplished by conceptualizing the play therapy process according to two primary dimensions: directiveness and consciousness. This integrative approach also provides a process-oriented framework, offering guidance for tracking important change mechanisms.

The two dimensions: directiveness and consciousness

As represented in Figure 1.1, the two primary dimensions—directiveness and consciousness—intersect, forming four quadrants: Quadrant I: Active Utilization; Quadrant II: Open Discussion and Exploration; Quadrant III: Non-intrusive Responding; and Quadrant IV: Co-facilitation. Each of the four quadrants is identified by the therapist's activities and the child's direction and level of consciousness during the play therapy session. Depending on the case conceptualization, and theoretical approaches taken by the play therapist, a therapist might choose to focus therapy activities primarily in one quadrant. Alternatively, there may be numerous indicators that suggest movement amongst the four quadrants would support the child's integration or processing of events. Consistent with an integrative approach, there is no prescribed order for movement between the quadrants. Furthermore, movement may occur within a session, across sessions, or as the therapy process evolves. As will be illustrated in the case of Sammy, the conceptualization of the two primary domains, and the resulting four quadrants, assists the therapist in navigating the complex client-therapist-treatment interactions to best tailor the treatment approach.

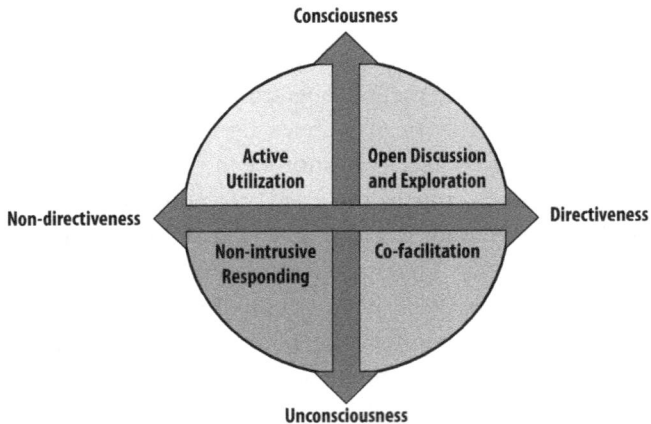

Figure 1.1 Play therapy dimensions diagram

The directiveness dimension is perhaps the most familiar dimension to play therapists, regardless of their theoretical orientation. This dimension represents the therapist's activity with respect to the degree of immersion in the play. The term immersion refers to the manner in which the therapist enters and actively takes part in the play. At the far left side of this dimension the therapist is tracking the play through observation and reflection, and is not involved in interactive play with the child. At the far right side of this dimension, the therapist has entered the play as a co-facilitator, and is actively taking part in elaborating and extending the play.

The non-directive side of the directiveness continuum is most clearly evidenced in the child-centered approach to play therapy.

However, close inspection of child-centered approaches suggests that variations exist in the way contemporary experts (Guerney, 2001; Landreth, 2002; VanFleet, Sywulak and Sniscak, 2010; Wilson and Ryan, 2005) think about certain strategies and non-directive skills. Accordingly, some non-directive/child-centered play therapists weave back and forth along the directiveness dimension, at times following the child's lead and direction in the play, but also taking the lead momentarily and then returning the lead to the child.

On the right side of Figure 1.1 the therapist would be viewed as fully immersed as evidenced by the child *and* therapist's involvement in a play activity structured by the therapist. Adlerian play therapy (Kottman, 2003), for example, demonstrates movement along the directiveness dimension. Initially, the Adlerian play therapist may work with a child non-directively and, over time, take on a more directive position, structuring the process by modeling and teaching prosocial skills to aid the child in connecting with others. Examples of therapeutic activities include family drawing techniques, asking the child questions about early recollections, helping the child gain personal insight, and the use of metacommunication (where the therapist makes a direct interpretation about an observed interactional pattern). Other structured theoretical approaches to play therapy include gestalt play therapy (Oaklander, 2003), Theraplay® (Munns, 2000), ecosystemic play therapy (O'Connor, 1997), Cognitive-Behavioral Play Therapy (Knell, 1999, 2003), and prescriptive play therapy (Schaefer, 2003). Practitioners using these approaches make decisions about the *degree* of directiveness at any given time during the therapy process and may be seen as more or less immersed in the play process with the child. When examining the degree of *directiveness*, the practitioner must remain mindful that relationships are two ways or mutually influenced. Although there are times when the child is driven to choose and direct the play activity, there may be times when the child becomes immobilized and looks to the therapist to provide structure or direction.

The consciousness dimension reflects the child's representation of consciousness in play activities and verbalizations. For the integrative play therapist that seeks to understand the unique needs of each child, and respond in an intentional manner, there is great value in conceptualizing movement along this dimension. For example, an understanding of child moderating factors, such as the nature and strength of the child's defenses and the child's worldview, is critical when helping a child to reorganize or make sense of a disturbing experience (Yasenik and Gardner, 2012). This work may be accomplished at a lower level of the child's self-awareness, through the play metaphor, or at a higher level of awareness, through a process of interpretation or open discussion. Depending on the therapist's understanding of the child's defenses and need for distance from the issue, the therapist might weave up and down this dimension, at times bringing issues into higher levels of conscious awareness through interpretations or restatements of affect. Alternatively, the therapist could remain working at the symbolic level, staying within the play metaphor, and gradually elaborate the play to assist in the child's drive to gain mastery and reorganize the experience.

By examining indicators of shifting levels of self-awareness, the therapist can gauge the child's readiness to incorporate information and affect at higher levels of consciousness, on a moment-to-moment and/or session-by-session basis. At times, a child may use play scenarios and objects in a less conscious and more symbolic or metaphorical manner, representing lower levels of self-awareness, likely because they need distance and protection from troublesome thoughts or feelings. However, the therapist might also observe brief shifts in play, where the play is accompanied by verbalizations, representative of the I-self reflecting on the Me-self. This is a noteworthy turning point as it signals that the child is working with a higher level of conscious awareness.

Children need to be viewed from a developmental perspective when considering movement along the *consciousness* dimension. Each child will present with a different capacity for conscious self-awareness. For instance, the very young child's language and cognitive schemas are still developing and symbolic play may sometimes occur solely at the experiential level. At other times, play may be at the semi-conscious level, where the child is making use of symbols to organize cognitive schemas and assimilate new possibilities into a past representation, which leads to potential growth and change. Consideration of the degree of consciousness represented in a given play therapy session is critical as the play therapist tracks the child's process.

The therapist's knowledge of coping strategies used by children who have experienced traumatic events or life-threatening experiences is critically important when conceptualizing movement along the consciousness dimension (Yasenik and Gardner, 2012). In particular, play therapists must exercise sound clinical judgment when making decisions about facilitating greater degrees of conscious representation of dissociated thoughts and feelings. Pynoos and Eth (1986), in their study of children who had witnessed homicide, observed a range of coping strategies/defenses: repression, fixation on the trauma, displacement, denial-in-fantasy (child imagines a positive experience rather than the traumatic one), and identification (child identifies themselves with a parent or helper figure). Overall, play therapists must use developmentally anchored observations when considering the level of *consciousness* in the play, paying particular attention to the capacity of the child to move in the direction of increased conscious awareness.

The consciousness dimension is therefore a primary area of concern for the play therapist. Directive play therapists may choose to name possible feelings, behaviors, and future actions during a play session or they may structure play activities for the child, as related to the interrupting events. Those working on the lower end of the consciousness continuum would not interrupt the child's process; rather they would follow the child's lead and trust the inner drive of the child to reorganize their experiences without using interpretive comments to bring the issues to conscious awareness. Neither approach is wrong. Taking a bounded rationality approach, the Play Therapy Dimensions Model encourages play therapists to answer the when, why, and how (directed by knowing and observing the child) when facilitating greater degrees of consciousness.

The four quadrants

The quadrants provide an organizing structure for case conceptualization. Rather than anchoring each quadrant name to a specific theoretical model of play therapy, quadrant titles highlight elements of client-therapist-treatment interactions, as conceptualized by the two primary dimensions, directiveness and consciousness. For example, when working in Quadrant III: Non-intrusive Responding, the therapist is less immersed in the play, the child leads the play, and the therapist acts as a *non-intrusive* responder.

On the far right-hand side of the directiveness dimension, but occurring below the mid-point on the consciousness dimension, is Quadrant IV: Co-facilitation. When working in this quadrant the play therapist enters the play, either at the invitation of the child, or because the therapist has observed a number of themes or patterns and makes a decision to test a hypothesis or elaborate the play by inserting comments, actions, or soft interpretations in the context of the play. The therapist becoming more immersed in the play would seem familiar to those working from an Adlerian approach, where emphasis is placed on an egalitarian relationship in which there is a sense of shared power and responsibility (Kottman, 2003). To maintain this relationship, the therapist may enter and elaborate the play after tracking a number of patterns and themes in the child's play. The degree of therapist immersion increases considerably in Quadrant IV compared to Quadrant III. This signifies that the therapist's role shifts from a non-intrusive responder to that of an active participant.

Children's play can be observed as naturally co-facilitative. During cooperative play each child adds to and elaborates their playmate's ideas, affect, themes, and characterization of objects and dramatic representations. A story line evolves, and children may project into it new themes, conflicts, or resolutions. Children's play is naturally interactive and relational, which makes it fun. When working in Quadrant IV, the therapist remains in the fantasy and symbolism of the child's play and may be seen engaging in activities such as introducing new characters (not directed for use by the child) such as helper figures, helpless figures, or using more than one character to demonstrate a child's inner conflict.

In the upper left corner of Figure 1.1, Quadrant I: Active Utilization is identified. This quadrant, being on the non-directive side of the diagram, is distinguished from Quadrant III (which is also on the left side of the diagram) due to the use of brief, intermittent interpretive comments initiated by the therapist that may facilitate conscious responses from the child. That is, during the play process a therapist may choose to expand the play metaphor by making reflective/interpretive comments about what is occurring in the child's metaphorical play, thereby extending the thematic play into higher levels of conscious awareness. Typically, active utilization is entered into in a brief, time-sensitive manner.

Quadrant I will be familiar to therapists who believe in using interpretive comments to help children reorganize dissociated affect or to work through material in a more conscious manner. Psychodynamic theorists and Jungian analytical play therapists (Peery, 2003) support the notion that children project internal energy onto play objects whether they are consciously aware of it or not. Viewing the play objects or materials as symbolizing internal energy, the therapist may choose to make use of an interpretation. For example, Jungian play therapists will identify conscious and unconscious influences and may at times make interpretive comments and identify observed themes in the play. The concept of deintegration would be considered and the therapist may explore possible regression to access deeper unconscious material. Although some play therapy theories fully explore the levels of consciousness in therapy, others may not. The degree to which consciousness is acknowledged and explored is a decision-making factor for all play therapists.

Interpretations are typically offered in a quick manner and the therapist may not expect it to lead to an open discussion of the issue at hand, unless the child is ready or inclined to continue in this way. Interpretations can occur with varying levels of "distance." For example, a therapist may make an interpretation about an underlying need or motivation of a character. At other times, the therapist may make a more direct interpretation, linking the play scene to what the child has experienced. O'Connor (2002) notes the strong correlation between children's mental health and their use of language. In part, the child's ability to use language as a bridge from action to symbol to thought, as well as language's central function in emotional self-regulation, suggests that language should play a central role in the treatment process.

Mills and Crowley (1986), drawing on Ericksonian theory, refer to the term "utilization" as being a profound respect for the validity and integrity of the child's presenting behavior. Central to the technique of utilization is the discrete set of skills and abilities to observe, participate in, and reframe what the child presents. In play therapy, active utilization signifies that the therapist brings forward key elements of the child's play into the realm of conscious awareness by offering a verbal, interpretive context to explore and potentially resolve specific issues.

Quadrant II: Open Discussion and Exploration is located in the upper right corner of Figure 1.1. A therapist working in this quadrant would be observed as initiating and structuring play activities relative to the child's presenting problem by introducing the child to concrete, highly conscious activities such as board games with problem-solving activities or other psychoeducational, skill-building interventions. Additionally, the therapist is viewed as primarily using a developmentally sensitive, cognitive play therapy approach, in which they engage in open discussions and conscious processing of the child's presenting issues.

The therapist may choose to work in this quadrant when a child needs more structure, feeling language, or if the child has been unable to reorganize a traumatic event through the normal course of play. Greenspan (1997) stresses that problem-solving follows an emotional pathway and it is not until a child arrives at an intuitive, emotionally mediated response or idea that *feels* right that they will be able to make use of the resolution. Accordingly, the play therapist must understand that the playing through until it *feels right* is part of the healing process. This understanding, and the skill set required to carefully pace the introduction of material at higher levels of consciousness, distinguish the cognitive and directive play therapist from other therapists not trained in the therapeutic powers of play.

It must be emphasized that the model is not prescriptive and does not presume that movement must occur within a single session. Rather, the model invites the therapist to view the play therapy process on a moment-to-moment basis and see therapeutic activities as dynamic, based on a number of factors such as the stage of the therapeutic process, responses of the child to the therapist's use of self, the child's play skills, and the child's drive and direction in therapy.

The four quadrants help play therapists organize and identify how they are intervening with child clients. Furthermore, from a supervision point of view, supervisors can help supervisees begin to answer the *who, what, when, and why* by examining movement in the therapy process.

Degree of Immersion: Therapist Use of Self Scale
Knowing one's self is an essential underpinning of clinical work, particularly with children as one's inner self is instantly awakened and

present during play therapy. Not only must the play therapist constantly work on knowing the self, they must also use self-understanding in the most appropriate and meaningful way, therapeutically. The Degree of Immersion: Therapist Use of Self Scale was developed to strengthen therapist understanding and awareness of the impact the use of self has on child clients and to support appropriate decision-making. The authors have used this scale extensively as part of the supervision process since it was originally developed in 2002. Based on feedback from supervisees and colleagues, the scale has been modified; the current version appears in Appendix A.

As one might appreciate, this is a challenging concept to address in supervision, made even more difficult because it is necessary to define specific therapist behaviors that represent use of self. Additionally, for each behavior it is necessary to identify the degree to which the therapist's self was involved or immersed and, most importantly, what the observed impact on the child or therapy process may have been. This follows from the basic assumption that it is the child's needs that drive the therapy process. Higher levels of immersion are not necessarily better. Instead, the degree and type of immersion must be carefully examined for each child, as well as in relation to the overall therapy process.

To explore the degree to which a therapist is immersed in the play, four main categories of immersion are rated: 1. Verbal Use of Self; 2. Emotional Use of Self; 3. Physical Use of Self; and 4. Self-System. These categories are broken down into components to identify specific forms or examples of immersion. After each rating the supervisee is to provide three clinical indications of the effectiveness of their use of self. When used regularly in supervision, the immersion scale keeps supervisees on track by continually reflecting on the interaction between them and the client.

Understanding what happens in the therapy space enhances therapist attunement to the child and strengthens decision-making. In many cases, it also supports the therapist's awareness of certain markers of transference and countertransference, and the impact of these issues on the play process. To assist in the supervision process a Supervision Form for Therapist Use of Self: Degree of Immersion for Next Session Plan is provided in Appendix B. This form provides a structure for the supervisee and supervisor to discuss and target specific ways to make use of the self in upcoming sessions. It is also available to download from the JKP website.

CASE STUDY: TRACKING THERAPIST IMMERSION AND IMPACT ON TURNING POINTS

The case of Sammy, a seven-year-old boy referred due to the sudden and intense onset of obsessive-compulsive disorder (OCD) symptoms, illustrates clinical decision-making based on the Play Therapy Dimensions Model. It also underscores the importance of tracking therapist use of self, linking this to a significant turning point in the therapy process.

Upon referral, his parents described Sammy as an outgoing and energetic young boy who enjoyed school and sporting activities. Sammy was also a child who freely moved about his community to play with friends. Over the previous three weeks, Sammy's parents noted a series of unusual and concerning behaviors such as Sammy "collecting" weeds each time he went outside and picking up garbage off floors and secretly placing these same items in his room. Consultations with a pediatrician that had known Sammy and his twin brother for numerous years led to a psychiatric referral and placement on a lengthy wait list. Sammy's parents realized they could not wait any longer when one night at bedtime Sammy reported that he had been collecting leaves and placing these in his room so that his parents could never move. Subsequent to this revelation, Sammy's parents observed that he would cover his head with a hat or hood whenever he went outdoors. When questioned, Sammy explained he was afraid of going outside because he couldn't stop looking for leaves to pick up. In tears, Sammy remarked that he was going "crazy" and worried his friends would find out and make fun of him. A week later, Sammy asked his parents if they would cover his eyes and ears when he was outside so he couldn't hear the leaves. In desperation, and good judgment, Sammy's parents offered support to contain his "urges." For example, they provided Sammy with a cell phone so he could take pictures of garbage, instead of picking it up and bringing it home. They also provided containers for his room, with the understanding that once these were full they must be emptied.

Regarding family history, one parent noted she was diagnosed with OCD at age 11, while the other parent experienced mild-to-moderate issues with anxiety throughout his teenage years. Given the therapist's previous experience working with children and adults with rapid onset of OCD symptoms, he asked about possible exposure to the streptococcal virus, or "strep throat," which has been linked to a condition referred to as Pediatric Autoimmune Neuropsychiatric Disorder Associated with Streptococcus (PANDAS). Briefly, it is thought that the body's immune reaction to infection, not the strep infection itself, causes the symptoms, which can be tic symptoms or OCD symptoms characterized by rapid onset with the potential to worsen considerably over a brief period of time. As might be expected, there is a range of possible co-morbid behaviors or symptoms including emotional lability, age-inappropriate behaviors such as bedtime rituals, and frequent urination. A throat swab test for strep is often the starting point for diagnosis; however, blood testing for a specific antibody is often required. Complicating matters is the fact that PANDAS is not the only immune system disease that may cause these symptoms to appear.

Sammy's parents were strong advocates and worked through several referral sources to connect with an out-of-town medical expert on PANDAS. Based on results from a throat swab and blood tests, the medical expert determined that Sammy had PANDAS and an antibiotic was prescribed. Unfortunately, the first type of antibiotic had minimal impact and Sammy's symptoms worsened. Within a week, a different antibiotic was tried and some of Sammy's symptoms softened. However, by the time Sammy came to the therapist's office, he entered bundled in layers of clothing and was unable to remove his two hats and scarf to greet the therapist. His parents reported that the night before the appointment Sammy was overwhelmed with worry and took five hours to settle for bed.

OCD is commonly viewed as a neurobiological problem where the client is often best supported by cognitive-behavioral approaches that focus on new ways to think about and respond to thoughts and urges. Through exposure and response prevention, the child is supported in experiencing an OCD thought or urge without trying to neutralize it with a ritual. Sammy's parents were ahead of the game, so to speak, and had purchased a children's book on OCD in which OCD is externalized as a "pest" and a psychoeducational approach is taken to help the child understand what is happening in their brain. Concrete, step-by-step strategies on how to stand up to OCD are also outlined. Sammy's parents reported that Sammy made it through the first three or four pages before protesting that the book didn't help. The book was well constructed, conceptually, and had all the requisite components for this type of intervention. Unfortunately, Sammy couldn't identify with the behaviors portrayed in the book and certainly had no sense of connection to the drawing or characterization of OCD as a "pest." In short, the characterization or externalization of OCD, as well as the narrative, was likely too "sensorally dry," a term Sunderland (2000) uses to describe therapeutic or literary stories for children using "everyday" language that is not engaging for children. Instead, Sunderland stresses that the primary psychological message needs to empathize with the child and, in turn, the child's imagination needs to be activated in order to stay with the "too difficult" feelings.

Sammy and his parents had essentially been involved in Quadrant II: Open Discussion and Exploration prior to entering the first session, by discussing OCD symptoms and brain functioning. However, working at this level of consciousness seemed to have activated Sammy's fears and defenses. Given Sammy's recent worry that his friends would think him "crazy," it was likely he did not have the ego strength to directly explore what was happening to him. Even though we, as therapists, like to think that therapeutic stories automatically provide "distance" from thoughts that are upsetting or disturbing to the child, this is not always the case. There really seems to be an "art" to creating stories with distance and what Mills and Crawley (1986) refer to as therapeutic potency.

Given this backdrop, the therapist decided to play out the story by entering Quadrant IV: Co-facilitation. Briefly, after a stressful introduction to the therapist, with acknowledgment by Sammy's parents that they had looked together at a book on OCD that discussed how children's brains can get "stuck," the therapist invited Sammy to the playroom to join in a target game using special Nerf "zappers" to shrink "Mr. Sticky." Sammy peeked out from his scarf asking, "What kind of zappers do you have?" The answer was obvious! The therapist replied, "Only specially designed zappers because Mr. Sticky is very tricky, and he has been giving me tricky/sticky feelings!" Sammy immediately asked where the zappers were, which in short order led to an introduction and brief tour of the playroom.

Upon entering the playroom, Sammy immediately went to the Nerf zappers and found some foam darts. The therapist drew up his Mr. Sticky on a whiteboard, and mentioned a few tricky thoughts and rules that Mr. Sticky made for him. The invitation to help zap and shrink the therapist's Mr. Sticky was immediately met by Sammy grabbing another zapper and repeatedly zapping Mr. Sticky, erasing his parts each time the zapper dart stuck to him. Referring to the Degree of Immersion: Therapist Use of Self Scale (Appendix A), the therapist made moderate use of his physical self (3.1 Physical Self: rating 3—Moderate), in terms of physical movement and level of physical energy. This was energetic play, and Sammy's response was rated as Moderate-to-High, as he actively participated and added verbalizations, sometimes remarking that he "hated" Mr. Sticky. Regarding the therapist's emotional use of self, a moderate level of emotional intensity was placed into reflective/tracking statements and animating the sounds and words of Mr. Sticky (2.1 Emotionality: rating 3—Moderate). While it would be tempting to have structured the play so that we were easily beating or overpowering Mr. Sticky, this was unlikely the schema or worldview that Sammy held regarding power and control over his symptoms. Instead, emphasis was placed on knowing about the kinds of sneaky tricks and rules Mr. Sticky was capable of, thereby making it hard for him to hide from us anymore. Upon reflection, the therapist's emotional self was also present and somewhat activated during this session. In reviewing section 2.2 of Appendix A, the Emotional Self scale was rated as a 2-to-3, with an awareness of personal feelings of anger and frustration surfacing for the therapist. These feelings were of course projected toward Mr. Sticky, and it was felt that the purposeful use of self in this instance supported Sammy's engagement in the process as well as self-expression. Accordingly, Sammy's response was rated as Moderate as he was observed voicing feelings of frustration and anger toward Mr. Sticky. Sammy was not simply modeling or copying the therapist's words or actions. Rather, Sammy used colorful language and added specific contextual cues, indicating he was finding his own voice to talk back to Mr. Sticky.

In the next session, Sammy showed interest in exploring the sandtray, which led to an invitation to make traps for Mr. Sticky and essentially give him a taste of his own medicine. Sammy readily joined this activity, constructing an elaborate series of traps and choosing a character to represent Mr. Sticky. To test the traps, he asked the therapist to take on or become Mr. Sticky, issuing the dare to Mr. Sticky to "just try to escape." This play segment wove back and forth between Quadrant III: Non-intrusive Responding and Quadrant IV: Co-facilitation. At times, Sammy was fully in charge and directing actions and verbalizations, while at other times the therapist made brief forays with Mr. Sticky to see if the traps were indeed present or strong. The therapist's responses can be seen as a means of soft hypothesis testing, checking whether there is a sense of strength or containment present, as previously this would not have been part of Sammy's worldview or schemas about his ability to have power, control, or protection. These activities are represented in Appendix A: 1.4 Interpretations. In this case, a rating of 3—Moderate—was given as soft hypotheses were formed and used through characters, while remaining within the play metaphor. It was Sammy who ultimately directed this play segment, as the therapist often checked in with Sammy, using the whispering technique, to get direction for what Mr. Sticky should say or do. Although the therapist and Sammy were clearly involved in metaphorical play, Sammy was working at a level of self-awareness. At times Sammy made reference to behaviors and situations he had directly experienced. Understanding this, the therapist's use of self, both emotionally and physically, remained in the moderate range, so as not to further activate Sammy's fragile defenses.

A turning point occurred in the following session when the therapist asked if Sammy might be interested in making a "super trap" for Mr. Sticky. Sammy eagerly replied that he already had something in mind. The therapist wondered if the trap would be strong enough to keep Mr. Sticky from making them follow one of his tricky rules, such as picking up and keeping garbage. Sammy was certain it could and immediately started to place fences as barriers in the sand, dug bottomless holes, and wetted portions of the tray to form quicksand. Once the traps were in place, Sammy and the therapist left the room to discuss their plan. With parent support, it was agreed that they would each bring a snack bar into the room, eat it in front of Mr. Sticky, and then throw the wrapper on the floor. They also devised a plan of what they would say to Mr. Sticky if he said they had to pick up the wrappers and take them with them. Essentially, they were ready to leave Mr. Sticky trapped, unwilling to listen to his rule, and even leave him in the playroom with the garbage on the floor. Sammy was fully engaged and participated in this "caper." While there was a moment of hesitation when he closed the playroom door to leave Mr. Sticky and the garbage behind, it was clear that he now had greater strength and resolve to stand up to Mr. Sticky. In this session, the therapist's use of tracking and reflecting statements was in the Moderate-to-High range. The spotlight was placed on what Mr. Sticky might be thinking or saying as well as tracking and reflecting Sammy's non-verbal and verbal responses. Additionally, Moderate-to-High levels of emotionality were used to convey or lend a certain degree of emotional intensity to the play, otherwise this could end up being a "hollow victory." The therapist's physical self was also accessed throughout this play segment, in a manner keeping with the overall intensity and thematic nature of the play.

In future sessions, several other noteworthy turning points surfaced in which exposure and response prevention activities occurred in a playful but direct manner. For example, the therapist and Sammy had leaf smashing or crunching "competitions" against Mr. Sticky, held outside during the fall. Sammy also devised an obstacle course outdoors, complete with traps for Mr. Sticky, in which he strategically placed items of garbage for himself and the therapist to run over, stomp on, or tear up. These activities involved high levels of emotionality and physicality, which contributed to therapeutic potency. As a backdrop to the therapy process, it was clear that the course of antibiotics was effective in reducing some primary and secondary symptoms. Within a few months Sammy was once again actively exploring his community and enjoying school and sporting activities.

The turning point captured in this case study is primarily the first type: a change in thought, behavior, affect, or understanding. However, as therapy progressed, there were turning points where an emergence of a level of awareness (not previously available to Sammy) occurred as a result of the "I-self" reflecting on or observing the "Me-self."

This case also highlights the importance of tracking therapist use of self, in concert with the child's observed reactions or response.

When accessing the therapist's self, even at low or moderate levels, a high degree of self-awareness is required, which is not easily obtained as the therapist is also immersed in the play. Access to supervision and feedback is essential for this reason, and this is examined further in Chapter 14.

References

Ayduk, O., Gyurak, A., and Luerssen, A. (2009) Rejection sensitivity moderates the impact of rejection on self-concept clarity. *Personality and Social Psychology Bulletin 35*, 1467–1478.

Baldwin, M. (1987) The use of self in therapy. *Journal of Psychotherapy and the Family 13*, 7–16.

Bates, E. (1990) Language about Me and You: Prominal Reference and the Emerging Concept of Self. In D. Cicchetti and M. Beeghly (eds) *The Self in Transition: Infancy to Childhood*. Hillsdale, NJ: Erlbaum.

Bragan, K. (1996) *Self and Spirit in the Therapeutic Relationship*. London: Routledge.

Erwin, E. (1997) *Philosophy and Psychotherapy*. London: Sage.

Garfield, S.L. (1994) Eclecticism and integration in psychotherapy: Developments and issues. *Clinical Psychology: Science and Practice 1*, 123–137.

Gergen, K. (1996) The Healthy, Happy Human Being Wears Many Masks. In W.T. Anderson (ed.) *The Fontana Postmodernism Reader*. London: Fontana Press.

Gigerenzer, G. (2001) The Adaptive Toolbox. In G. Gigerenzer and R. Selten (eds) *Bounded Rationality: The Adaptive Toolbox*. Cambridge, MA: MIT Press.

Greenspan, S.I. (1997) *The Growth of the Mind and the Endangered Origins of Intelligence*. Cambridge, MA: Perseus Books.

Guerney, L. (2001) Child-centered play therapy. *International Journal of Play Therapy 10*, 2, 13–31.

Harter, S. (2006) The Self. In W. Damon and R. Lerner (eds) and N. Eisenberg (vol. ed.) *Handbook of Child Psychology. Vol. 3: Social Emotion, and Personality Development* (6th edn). New York: Wiley.

Harter, S. (2012) *The Construction of the Self: Developmental and Sociocultural Foundations*. New York: Guilford Press.

Hobson, R.F. (1985) *Forms of Feeling: The Heart of Psychotherapy*. London: Routledge.

James, W. (1892) *Psychology: The briefer course*. New York: Henry Holt.

James, W. (1990) *Principles of Psychology*. Chicago: Encyclopedia Britannica.

Kahn, M. (1997) *Between Therapist and Client: The New Relationship*. New York: Freeman.

Knell, S.M. (1999) Cognitive-Behavioral Play Therapy. In K. O'Connor and C. Schaefer (eds) *Play Therapy Theory and Practice: A Comparative Presentation*. New York: Wiley.

Knell, S.M. (2003) Cognitive-Behavioral Play Therapy. In C.E. Schaefer (ed.) *Foundations of Play Therapy*. New Jersey: John Wiley and Sons, Inc.

Kottman, T. (2003) Adlerian Play Therapy. In C. Schaefer (ed.) *Foundations of Play Therapy*. New York: Wiley.

Landreth, G. (2002) *Play Therapy: The Art of the Relationship* (2nd edn). New York: Brunner-Routledge.

Miller, P.J., Potts, R., Fung, H., Hoogstra, L., and Mintz, J. (1990) Narrative practices and the social construction of self in childhood. *American Ethnologist 17*, 292–311.

Mills, J. and Crowley, R. (1986) *Therapeutic Metaphors for Children and the Child Within.* Philadelphia, PA: Brunner/Mazel.

Munns, E. (2000) Traditional Family and Group Theraplay. In E. Munns (ed.) *Theraplay: Innovations in Attachment-Enhancing Play Therapy.* Northvale, NJ: Aronson.

Nelson, K. (2003) Narrative and Self, Myth and Memory: Emergence of the Cultural Self. In R. Fivush and C.A. Haden (eds) *Autobiographical Memory and the Construction of the Narrative Self.* Mahwah, NJ: Erlbaum.

Norcross, J.C. (2005) A Primer on Psychotherapy Integration. In J.C. Norcross and M.R. Goldfried (eds) *Handbook of Psychotherapy Integration* (2nd edn). Oxford: Oxford University Press.

Oaklander, V. (2003) Gestalt Play Therapy. In C.E. Schaefer (ed.) *Foundations of Play Therapy.* New Jersey: John Wiley and Sons, Inc.

O'Connor, K. (1997) Ecosystemic Play Therapy. In K. O'Connor and L. Braverman (eds) *Play Therapy Theory and Practice: A Comparative Presentation.* New York: Wiley.

O'Connor, K. (2002) The value and use of interpretation in play therapy. *Professional Psychology: Research and Practice 33,* 6, 523–528.

Peery, C. (2003) Jungian Analytical Play Therapy. In C.E. Schaefer (ed.) *Foundations of Play Therapy.* New Jersey: John Wiley and Sons, Inc.

Pynoos, R. and Eth, S. (1986) Witness to violence: The child interview. *Journal of the American Academy of Child Psychiatry 25,* 3, 306–319.

Schaefer, C.E. (2003) Prescriptive Play Therapy. In C.E. Schaefer (ed.) *Foundations of Play Therapy.* New Jersey: John Wiley and Sons, Inc.

Schoenewolf, G. (1990) *Turning Points in Analytic Therapy: From Winnicott to Kernberg.* New Jersey: Jason Aronson, Inc.

Smith, D. (1982) Trends in counseling and psychotherapy. *American Psychologist 32,* 752–760.

Stone, M.H. (2015) *Turning Points in Psychotherapy.* Accessed on 03/08/2018 at www.freepsychotherapybooks.org/product/494-Turning-Points-in-Psychotherapy

Sunderland, M. (2000) *Using Storytelling as a Therapeutic Tool with Children.* Milton Keynes: Speechmark Publishing Ltd.

VanFleet, R., Sywulak, A., and Sniscak, C. (2010) *Child-Centered Play Therapy.* New York: Guilford Press.

Wilson, K. and Ryan, V. (2005) *Play Therapy: A Nondirective Approach with Children and Adolescents* (2nd edn). Philadelphia, PA: Elsevier.

Winnicott, D.W. (ed.) (1947) Hate in Countertransference. In *Through Paediatrics to Psychoanalysis.* New York: Basic Books.

Wosket, V. (1999) *The Therapeutic Use of Self: Counselling Practice, Research and Supervision.* London: Routledge.

Yasenik, L. and Gardner, K. (2004) *Play Therapy Dimensions Model: A Decision-Making Guide for Therapists.* Calgary, AB: Rocky Mountain Play Therapy Institute.

Yasenik, L. and Gardner, K. (2012) *Play Therapy Dimensions Model: A Decision-Making Guide for Integrative Play Therapists.* London: Jessica Kingsley Publishers.

2

EMERGENCE OF SELF THROUGH LEARN TO PLAY THERAPY

—— KAREN STAGNITTI ——

Case introduction

Billy was unsure of what to expect when he came into the play therapy room. He was quiet and watched himself in the two-way mirror. He was anxious and appeared to "float" into the room with no interest to socially engage with his mother or myself, although he glanced at his mother from time to time. Billy was four years old. He had been diagnosed with specific language impairment (SLI). His speech pathologist noted delays in language and poor social interactions with peers. On the *Diagnostic and Statistical Manual of Mental Disorders* (DSM-5) (American Psychiatric Association, 2013), children with specific language impairment are included in the broad category of language disorders. Children with SLI score "below age-expectations on standardized language measures" which cannot be explained by "cognitive, neurological or hearing problems" (Jester and Johnson, 2016, p.25). These children also have delays in pretend play; for example, they have problems initiating play, have limited play scripts, and engage in earlier forms of pretend play than age-matched peers (Jester and Johnson, 2016). Billy attended a mainstream preschool in the local area; however, his teacher noted that he played by himself and mainly observed other children. If children approached him to play, they could not understand what he was saying and often drifted away to other activities, leaving Billy alone. Consequently, due to his language and play difficulties together with information from his preschool teacher, his speech pathologist had recommended the family seek out Learn to Play Therapy (Stagnitti, 1998, 2016).

Before Learn to Play Therapy began, the first meeting with Billy and his mother was to establish Billy's spontaneous pretend play ability. The Child-Initiated Pretend Play Assessment (ChIPPA) (Stagnitti, 2007) was used to do this. A sheet had been thrown over adult-sized chairs (called a "cubby house" in Australia, "wendy house" in the UK, and "fort" or "house" in Canada). This created a space that suggested "play". The play materials for the first session of the ChIPPA had been placed on the floor. These play materials were a truck and trailer, fences, animals, a wrench, and small non-gendered doll. As Billy was anxious and this was his first time, my emotional use of self was low (Appendix A: 2.1 Emotionality) with few verbal comments apart from pointing out the toys on the floor and inviting Billy to "play whatever he would like". My physical use of self was also low (Appendix A: 3.1 Physical Self), as I kept a distance from Billy to allow him to settle into the room and feel accepted as he was. After 10 minutes, Billy sat on the floor and began playing with the toys. After 15 minutes, I told Billy that was all the time we had to play with these toys and I had some other toys to play with. I replaced the toys with the unstructured play materials from the ChIPPA. My observation of Billy's play ability during this first session noted that he did not engage with any characters in the play, he could logically sequence three to four actions of play from time to time, he did not use objects as symbols in play (such as a box for bed), and he could not play for 30 minutes. His play showed no narrative or cohesive story. His mother noted that she had not seen him pretending to eat or drink (body-related scripts in play), nor did he play out events from his daily life (such as shopping, going in a car). He did not emotionally engage in the play and did not speak during the play assessment. His emerging sense of self appeared weak. Observation of his play ability guided my decisions on the play activities that may engage Billy and would be appropriate for his level of play ability.

Theoretical orientation

Understanding the development of pretend play and how this impacts on a child's ability to engage in their world is a strong underpinning framework in Learn to Play Therapy. Pretend play involves the imposition of meaning onto play materials, actions, and the play scene. This ability to impose meaning has been referred to as meta-representational thought (Leslie, 1987), symbolic thinking (Kelly and Hammond, 2011), and thinking beyond the literal (Stagnitti, 2010). Meta-representational thought and symbolic thinking have been conceptualized by Tessier *et al.* (2016) as "play [having] a central role in the discovery and understanding of mental and internal reality as distinct from external reality" (p.61). This differentiation between internal and external reality leads to a child being able to understand that they can represent thoughts and mentalize (Tessier *et al.*, 2016). Pretend play, in particular, is crucial to this development as the defining feature of pretend play is the ability to use symbols in play, impose meaning to attribute properties, and refer to absent objects (Hughes and Leekam, 2004; Leslie, 1987). For the majority of children, pretend play begins from 12 months of age, and play behaviours, such as pretending to drink from an empty cup, reflect body scripts (Stagnitti, 2009). From two to three years of age pretend play scripts reflect the daily life of the child, and short logical sequential actions show an increasing complexity of organization of a child's play (Stagnitti, 2009). This time of development in play also coincides with the I-self's awareness of the Me-self as the child is able to describe the self (Harter, 2012). From ages two to four years, this description of the self is most likely to be based on a description of the child's activities and skills for boys, and description of the self in terms of social and relational activities for girls (Harter, 2012). This heightened sense of self-awareness during the ages of two to four years, where children can act out life events in their play and use symbols in play, is argued by Tessier *et al.* (2016, p.61) to "contribute to the development of an internal autobiographical narrative". Harter (2012) notes that a child's autobiographical narrative during this time is also informed by parents, for example a parent showing pictures to their child of the child engaging in activities, or talking to the child about where the child has been and what was seen. I would also argue that play scripts reflecting the child's daily life provide evidence of how the child expresses their growing sense of their autobiographical narrative.

In Learn to Play Therapy, the power of pretend play is understood to underpin and integrate the child's sense of self through the child's increasing ability to impose meaning through play. By representational thought and the imposition of meaning within the play, the child shows narrative understanding (Nicolopoulou and Ilgaz, 2013), creativity (Hoffmann and Russ, 2012; Russ and Wallace, 2013), problem-solving (Hoffmann and Russ, 2012), social competence (O'Connor and Stagnitti, 2011), metacognition (Whitebread and O'Sullivan, 2012), understanding of context and language (Kirkham, Stewart and Kidd, 2013; Stagnitti and Lewis, 2015; Westby, 1991), reasoning (Whitebread *et al.*, 2009), and emotional understanding and self-regulation (Elias and Berk, 2002; Hoffmann and Russ, 2012; Whitebread *et al.*, 2009).

Vygotsky believed that children developed mental ability when they engaged in pretend play (Vygotsky, 1966, 1997). He also acknowledged the social and cultural influences on how people construct their world and argued that capable peers and adults could influence development positively (Vygotsky, 1997). Hence, co-facilitation of the play by the therapist with the child is a core process within Learn to Play Therapy.

Learn to Play Therapy is also underpinned by humanistic theory, based on Rogerian theory, where the child is approached as a capable being who is able to solve their own problems and there is acceptance of the child at every point in time (Axline, 1974). The establishment of a warm relationship is central to therapeutic engagement (Axline, 1974) as this establishes a sense of safety. Seven of the eight basic principles of Axline (1974, p.73) are central to Learn to Play Therapy and the therapeutic engagement between the therapist and child. These principles are: establish a warm relationship, acceptance of the child, child is free to express feelings, therapist recognizes those feelings, the child can solve problems, therapy is at the pace of the child, and limitations are established only for the safety of the child. Creating a safe environment for the child where the child feels safe, together with a warm therapeutic relationship between the therapist and the child, and presenting play activities within the capabilities of the child, create an environment where the child can joyfully engage in the play. Joyfully engaging in play is true play (Stagnitti, 2017). The child's emotional engagement in pretend play stimulates the limbic and cortical regions of the brain (Stagnitti, 2017) which results in the release of hormones such as dopamine, opioids, and oxytocin (Sunderland, 2007). This release of hormones results in feelings of pleasure (Sunderland, 2007), which in turn brings a deeper engagement in play.

Case study conceptualization

Billy was two to two and a half years delayed in his play, with the larger delays being in his ability to symbolize with objects (that is, use objects in substitution, such as use a box for a car), and in play scripts. Symbolizing with objects is predictive of language and narrative (Stagnitti and Lewis, 2015). He could play in short bursts with familiar toys; however, he did not represent home scripts, such as cooking and eating, in his play. He was anxious and not confident when in unfamiliar situations and relied on his mother as a stable base when he came into the playroom. On the continuum of non-directive – directive on the Play Therapy Dimensions Model (PTDM; Yasenik and Gardner, 2012), Learn to Play Therapy always begins in Quadrant IV: Co-facilitation. The therapist co-facilitates the play by introducing play activities and modelling play beside the child. In Learn to Play Therapy parents are encouraged to join in the therapy sessions as building the parent's capacity to understand their child's play and how to engage with their child in play is an important part of the therapy (Stagnitti, 2014). The full involvement of parents in therapy has been shown to yield larger effect sizes (.59) than no or partial caregiver involvement (.33) in therapy (Lin and Bratton, 2015). Billy's mother, Maureen, was concerned about his lack of social engagement with his peers and his lack of self-regulation. For example, Billy had not had a friend come to his place to play and he could become frustrated very easily. His frustration resulted in him yelling and throwing objects and screaming and crying uncontrollably.

In the playroom, children with specific language disorder present as angry. Their manipulation of the play materials is rough, and aggressive play is observed with children crashing objects, and "injuring" the dolls or teddies. I surmise that the built-up anger comes from frustration in their verbal and social interactions with others. Billy's preschool teacher noted in their report that Billy experienced not being understood by peers and feeling rejected as peers walked away from him or did not reciprocate verbal interactions. Accepting these children for who they are and respecting their ability are not common experiences for these children.

I believe that facilitating a child's pretend play ability will stimulate language, narrative understanding, social awareness, symbolic thinking, and self-regulation because, in engaging a child in pretend play, areas of the brain related to language, narrative, theory of mind, and self-regulation are activated (Kuhn-Popp et al., 2013; Lewis and Carmody, 2008; Whitehead et al., 2009). To be effective, however, necessitates a child's emotional enjoyment in play as emotional engagement precedes shifts in play ability (Sherratt and Donald, 2004; Stagnitti and Casey, 2011). Eberle (2014) and Gaskill and Perry (2014) also argue that for "true" play to occur, the child must experience joyful pleasure. For Billy, engaging him in joyful and pleasurable play activities would not only establish trust, an important theme in play (Ryan and Edge, 2011), but was also important for increasing his capacity and involvement in play.

Play activities are chosen that match the child's developmental play abilities. For Billy, this meant choosing play activities at the developmental ages of 18 months to two years. Selecting play activities that matched Billy's play age respected Billy for who he was and where he was in his understanding of his world. He could engage with these activities and understand what to do. Starting therapy at the level of Billy's understanding of play would also reduce his anxiety as the play activities were not challenging in the early stages of therapy. These activities would be more complex as therapy progressed, together with shifts in my use of self. These shifts in use of self and turning points for Billy are now detailed below.

Therapy process: turning points and emergence of self

The reasons why children have not developed complex play skills are varied. Reasons range from environmental and emotional circumstances (such as abuse or neglect) (Cooper, 2000), to diagnosis or developmental delay, for example children with autism (Stagnitti, 2016), to no known reason. However, play ability is not dependent on diagnosis (Emblen, 2014), and each child's play ability needs to be ascertained before Learn to Play Therapy can begin. The principles of therapy are: accept the child for who they are, understand the play ability of the child, gain the child's focused attention, use variation and repetition within play activities, talk about the play as play progresses, engage with the child emotionally, and allow opportunity for the child to self-initiate. In the first therapy session, the choice of play activities was informed by the play assessment and by Billy's sense of self, that is, he "floated" into the room and did not seem aware of what was going on around him. Taking into account his play level and weak sense of self, I chose play activities that were at the sensory-motor level to late toddler stage of play. In the first therapy session, I had low verbal use of self (1.1 on the Immersion scale), with emotional use of self being higher at moderate (2.3 on the Immersion scale) with high levels of physical engagement in the play (3.5 on the Immersion scale). I introduced the first play activity (working in Quadrant IV of the PTDM—at the base of the quadrant), and while responding to Billy's emotional state, I started to play. The first play activity was a sensory motor activity together with the early pretend play ability of decentration (that is, sense of other outside of the self). This activity was also chosen to engage Billy, create an atmosphere of non-judgment, and to provoke his emotional engagement in the play. I chose a catching ball activity where I use a large soft doll with long arms. The doll was holding the ball (thus an active agent in the play that introduces the concept of decentration). The doll threw the ball to Billy. I did this slowly. Billy missed the ball and picked it up and threw it back. My large doll scrambled to catch the ball and missed. It then wobbled over to the ball, picked it up, and threw it back at Billy. Billy had focused attention during this time, watching the doll. He caught the ball this time and threw it back. This time the doll made a noise, "Oohh", and I said, "She missed it." Billy smiled at this. The doll threw the ball back to Billy. This time he threw it hard. My doll caught it and made another noise, "Aww". Quickly she threw it back to Billy. I was increasing my physical involvement in the play as Billy maintained his focus and continued to smile. Billy threw the ball, which went to another part of the room. My doll raced over to get it and Billy giggled. She then said, "Got it." She threw the ball to Billy. Billy caught the ball and looked at my face. I moved the doll in front of my face to encourage him to engage directly with the doll. Lewis and Carmody (2008) note that other-related play (e.g. doll-related play) is when the child imposes meaning and thoughts on something or someone outside of themselves. This has been argued to be a sign of theory of mind (Lewis and Carmody, 2008). Developmentally this is also a higher level of play than self-related play (Westby, 1991). For children with difficulties in play, I have found that, starting at other-related play first, children can engage in play more easily before I take the play to the self-related play of themselves eating, drinking, and sleeping. One possible reason for this is that when children play with an object outside of themselves it is external; they can see it. Seeing play actions imposed on an object externally, and for the child to actively impose these actions, may help them to then internally represent the action when they can do it on themselves. During the ball catching with the doll, Billy became more and more boisterous and, in response, the doll then started to try to get the ball before Billy did. She even climbed on his back. He responded with delight. He was fully engaged in the play. When he tired of this activity, I introduced an eating activity with wooden fruit and a wooden cutting knife. Using the knife children could "cut" the fruit, which was in two pieces held together by Velcro. Billy, being emotionally engaged, moved onto this activity straight away and started cutting the fruit. The large doll that was used in the ball catching sat at the table and ate the fruit pieces as he cut them. He laughed at her but didn't eat the pieces himself. Other play activities for this session were: pushing trucks around the room, dancing the doll while Billy played music, and driving smaller cars to a wooden garage to get petrol. During this first session, I directed and introduced all the play activities, while responding to Billy as to the length of time he engaged in the activity. In the first sessions of Learn to Play Therapy, the therapist is cognizant of the child's play ability level and uses this session to not only establish a warm relationship with the child but also to observe the child's play to confirm or refine the child's play ability and how they respond and engage in play.

Turning point 1: I'm happy to come and I know I'm here

By the third session, Billy was running in front of his mother to get to the playroom. He was happy to come. His emotional engagement in the play and his sense of safety were established. Emotional engagement is important neurologically because if children do not experience joy in play, it is not true play (Eberle, 2014; Gaskill and Perry, 2014). The sense of wellbeing, through the surge of oxytocin and dopamine, comes with interactive play with others that is enjoyable (Sunderland, 2007). The depth of the emotional engagement of the child in play has been found to increase the depth of the child's focused attention in play in the next session as well as increase play ability (Stagnitti and Casey, 2011).

As Billy's enjoyment to come continued, the complexity in the play activities increased. In the first session minimal toys were used and play scripts that reflected everyday life activities in the home were the focus. During this time, I was responding to him using variation in the play activity (such as pretend the tea was too "hot"; or building up blocks in different configurations) to extend his play as well as using repetition to extend the time of his involvement in the play. I also used repetition and variation within the play activity to either extend or simplify the play, in response to Billy's engagement in it. Billy began to initiate his own play ideas within the session. As Billy did this, my reflecting and tracking statements moved from moderate to high (1.2 on the Immersion scale), and restating content moved from low to moderate (1.3 on the Immersion scale). His play became more aggressive during these stages of play as he expressed himself emotionally through the play. Cars would crash, small figurines would get hurt, and buildings would be destroyed. His play was rough and loud, and during these times reflecting and tracking and restating content moved from moderate to high. I was moving therapeutically from directing all the play activities to responding to his needs in play, even if this resulted in me not utilizing any or some of the play activities I had planned for the session. I was now sitting comfortably with uncertainty, in that I did not know what play activities would evolve during the play sessions. At this stage, Billy started to initiate the construction of play scenes and the use of symbols in his play.

Turning point 2: I did that!

A lot more play materials were being used in the sessions as Billy's play ability became more complex. The second turning point came at the end of one session where he had planned and built a road system and then created trees out of blocks and green feathers. He carefully placed the trees beside the road. At the end of the road, he built a large block construction. Cars then drove up and down the road and occasionally he knocked over a tree, which he would choose to leave or re-build. At the end of the session, his mother commented on the play scene and indicated that she would like to take a photo to show his dad. He squatted beside his roads, trees, and tall buildings and his mum took several photos. His body straightened, his chin lifted, and he looked again at what he made with a sense of pride. He had created this! I had responded and co-facilitated but only on his direction. It was the first time I saw a shift in his self-awareness. His I-self had a sense of agency where he had a conviction that he had control over his actions as he had thought about how to build this play scene (Harter, 2012).

Turning point 3: this play script goes on all session

From turning point 3, Billy took over the play for most of the session. I now moved between Non-intrusive Responding (Quadrant III in the PTDM) and Co-facilitation (Quadrant IV in the PTDM). While I had planned play activities, these were only utilized in response to Billy and where he took the play. In response to Billy, my therapeutic self was holding the play. I was responding to Billy in the play, observing his play ability and deciding, in the moment, whether to stay quiet, to co-facilitate the play, to challenge his play by bringing in a more complex play skill, or extending his play by suggesting a new idea. In this stage of therapy, I was more physically distant from Billy with my physical use of self now being moderate. There were times in the play when Billy was on the other side of the room from me and I couldn't see what he was doing. He was working on his ideas in play and he was relying less on me. My emotional use of self at this stage moved from moderate to high as I intensely observed his play to reflect and track or restate content.

At this time, Billy's play activity extended for the whole session. His play had developed to include a variety of play materials and several characters. He took over the room with his created play scene. The scene started with Billy fixing cars. I gave him a small block to use as a phone, in case he needed to call me. He concentrated on fixing, then he called me as he needed roads. I handed him the roads. We built them together on his instruction. I was engaged in reflecting and restating content. He built two houses. Then he decided that there was a party at one of the houses. So we needed to make food from play dough. There was lots of food. During this time he indicated that we needed to go shopping to buy more food because many people were coming. As the people came to the party, some of the cars crashed and rolled over. He asked for the doctor's kit and attended to the people. Eventually all the people, except one, made it to the party. They ate all the food, they danced, and then they went home. He was exhausted. He had played without reducing his pace of play for the full session.

His play had long sequences of actions and many characters who interacted with each other. He had problems in his play and he used symbols in his play. He was deeply involved in the play. As his play skills became more complex, play was cathartic for Billy. His pent-up feelings of frustration and anger had been released in a safe place (Drewes and Schaeffer, 2014).

Turning point 4: I stopped

While his play ability was increasing in complexity, his aggressive play was reducing. However, there were still scenes where he crashed everything. In one such session, he had built several houses, having brought the blocks in trucks from across the room. He decimated the first house, then my figurine talked to him about needing another house. My verbal use of self was low (1.1 on the Immersion scale) as I stayed in the play, holding him. He built the next house, then he crashed it down with a truck. There was chaos. Then he decided to build another house. It was a larger house. My figurine was in this new house cooking. Billy was on the other side of the room and drove the truck towards this third house. He moved menacingly towards this new house. My figurine (low verbal use of self—1.1 on the Immersion scale) was worried about the truck coming. She said she was cooking dinner and if the truck crashed into her house there would be no dinner for anybody and everyone would be hungry. The figurine was scared. She was worried. What would happen if she couldn't make dinner? She would have no food; she would not have a house. Billy moved the truck back and forth and back and forth. My emotional use of self was high (2.1 on the Immersion scale). He moved the truck strategically close to the house with a grin and then stopped one centimetre from the wall, just near where my figurine was standing. My figurine was relieved. She still had a house and she could cook dinner and her family could eat. From this session, his aggressive play decreased in the sessions.

Turning point 5: I'll explain it another way

Billy continued to develop complexity in his play. In the Learn to Play Therapy sessions, I was now opening up my cupboards so he could see all my toys. He chose what he wanted to play with. He could now cope with lots of play materials. He created play scenes that covered the room. I was now attuned to his speech and could understand most of what he was saying. If I couldn't understand it, his mother would indicate what he was meaning.

His sense of self was emerging. The next turning point occurred during a session where the room had been set up with roads, buildings, and figurines, and the scene also included a large car mat. He was narrating the story that was unfolding in the play, and at a critical point in the story he turned and looked at me and spoke. From his non-verbal stance, this was a critical piece of information that I should know about. Usually when this occurred in therapy, I would wait to see what actions would occur next in the play to understand the context, or my figurine would say something like, "You show me. I'll follow you." However, on this occasion, none of these options was viable. He was verbalizing the story to me without the accompanying play actions. He was in the metaphor with imposed meaning. I could not understand what he was saying (nor could his mother). This is the type of situation which would have caused him anger, pain, and frustration. I tried to work out what he wanted but I couldn't. I asked him to repeat the word three times. He paused, looked at me, tilted his head, stared at me knowingly, and then re-phrased. It was a knowing "She doesn't know what I'm saying. I'll try another way." I still couldn't understand, so he re-phrased again—to no avail. Then, without pause, he continued by re-directing his play and taking charge, accepting that I couldn't understand what he was saying. His emotional state remained calm. His I-self was evaluating his Me-self and he was capable.

Turning point 6: this is my world here

In his last session, Billy built houses for animals. Then he built a house that had a boy and girl. As he narrated his play, I was moving between Quadrant III and Quadrant IV, with reflecting and tracking and restating content (1.2 and 1.3 on the Immersion scale) being high. Internally, I was hypothesizing that the boy was himself and the girl was his mother and they were safe in the house. Then he introduced a third doll who stood outside the house. The boy figurine said to this doll, "You are the mum. You can come in here with us." I was passive as I realized what he had created was his view of the playroom. The emotional impact for me was large; however, I stayed attuned to him and incongruent with myself. In the playroom he was safe. It was a secure place where his mother was welcome to come and there were no dangers.

Billy was imposing meaning and going beyond the literal in his play now, as he used symbols, attributed properties to objects, referred to absent objects, and created figurines and characters. He regulated his emotional self. Over the sessions, his mother had been involved in the play on his direction. Sometimes he would include his mother in his play and other times she sat and watched. Over the sessions his mother came to realize how important she was in the life of her son and his emotional wellbeing (Sunderland, 2007). At home she was an advocate for play spaces, play materials, and time to play. Billy's growing play ability had, I believe, now given him the tools to build his emerging sense of self and his autobiographical narrative, which was of someone who could cope with people not understanding every word he said, because he was a capable person.

Turning points summary

Stage in process	Quadrant	Turning points	What contributed to the turning point?
Play assessment The therapist's understanding of the child's play ability as a starting point in engagement in play activities	QIII		
Therapy Session 1 Focus on engaging the child in play. Engaging the child's interest. Creating a sense of safety and acceptance. Play is physically demanding	QIV		• Laying the ground for development of the therapeutic relationship
Sense of safety and joy established. Introduction of decentration (sense of other) through the play. Play is physically demanding	QIV	1. I'm happy to come and I know I'm here	• Child experiencing safety and his emotional engagement in play is one of joy and pleasure • This lays the ground for development of therapeutic relationship and underpins "true play"

cont.

Stage in process	Quadrant	Turning points	What contributed to the turning point?
Engagement as a co-facilitator of play but a clear stepping back and responding to the child. Increasing comfort with uncertainty as child begins to take the lead in play	QIV but initiated by the child	2. I did that!	The child experiences a sense of pride and experiences himself as capable: • He is initiating play and extending his play • He uses symbols in play
A move from directing play activities to holding the child in the play. Therapeutic decisions about when to be passive, to challenge, and extend or simplify the play	QIV initiated by the child	3. This play script goes on all session	• The child's ability to self-initiate play, to engage emotionally in the play, to use symbols in play, and begin to impose meaning on play • The child's ability to take in a whole play scene because of an increasing understanding of the play narrative
Staying in the metaphor with using the figurines to hold the child in the play and re-direct	QIII, QIV initiated by the child	4. I stopped	• The child's increasing ability to engage in complex play together with an emerging sense of self and control—play is cathartic • Increasing ability to regulate emotionally
Holding the child in play with increasing physical distance. Being attuned to the child's play and shifts in the child's play	QIV initiated by the child	5. I'll explain it another way	• Child's emerging sense of self and awareness of others • Ability to regulate emotions
Holding the child in the play. Attuned to changes, reflective statements, empathic reflections	QIV initiated by the child with weaving into QIII	6. This is my world here	• Through an increasing ability to play metaphorically, the child expresses feeling subconsciously

References

American Psychiatric Association (2013) *Diagnostic and Statistical Manual of Mental Disorders* (5th edn). Arlington, VA: American Psychiatric Association.

Axline, V. (1974) *Play Therapy*. New York: Ballantine Books.

Cooper, R. (2000) The impact of child abuse on children's play: A conceptual model. *Occupational Therapy International 7*, 4, 259–276.

Drewes, A.A. and Schaefer, C.E. (2014) Catharsis. In A.A. Drewes and C.E. Schaefer (eds) *The Therapeutic Powers of Play* (2nd edn). New Jersey: Wiley.

Eberle, S.G. (2014) Elements of play: Toward a philosophy and definition of play. *Journal of Play 6*, 2, 214–233.

Elias, C. and Berk, L. (2002) Self-regulation in young children: Is there a role for sociodramatic play? *Early Childhood Research Quarterly 17*, 216–238.

Emblen, T. (2014) Development of play profiles: Influence of disability on children's play. Unpublished masters research thesis, Deakin University, Geelong, Australia.

Gaskill, R. and Perry, B.D. (2014) The Neurobiological Power of Play: Using the Neurosequential Model of Therapeutics to Guide Play in the Healing Process. In C. Malchiodi and D.A. Crenshaw (eds) *Play and Creative Arts Therapy for Attachment Trauma*. New York: Guilford Press.

Harter, S. (2012) *The Construction of the Self: Developmental and Sociocultural Foundations* (2nd edn). New York: Guilford Press.

Hoffmann, J. and Russ, S. (2012) Pretend play, creativity, and emotion regulation in children. *Psychology of Aesthetics, Creativity, and the Arts 6*, 175–184.

Hughes, C. and Leekam, S. (2004) What are the links between theory of mind and social relations? Review, reflections, and new directions for studies of typical and atypical development. *Social Development 13*, 590–619.

Jester, M. and Johnson, C.J. (2016) Differences in theory of mind and pretend play associations in children with and without specific language impairment. *Infant and Child Development 25*, 1, 24–42.

Kelly, R. and Hammond, S. (2011) The relationship between symbolic play and executive function in young children. *Australasian Journal of Early Childhood 36*, 21–27.

Kirkham, J., Stewart, A., and Kidd, E. (2013) Concurrent and longitudinal relationships between development in graphic, language and symbolic play domains from the fourth to the fifth year. *Infant and Child Development 22*, 297–319.

Kuhn-Popp, N., Sodian, B., Sommer, M., Dohnel, K., and Meinhardt, J. (2013) Same or different? ERP correlates of pretense and false belief reasoning in children. *Neuroscience 248*, 488–498.

Leslie, A. (1987) Pretense and representation: The origins of "theory of mind". *Psychological Review 94*, 412–426.

Lewis, M. and Carmody, D. (2008) Self-representation and brain development. *Developmental Psychology 4*, 5, 1329–1334.

Lin, Y.-W. and Bratton, S.C. (2015) A meta-analytic review of child-centred play therapy approaches. *Journal of Counseling and Development 93*, 45–58.

Nicolopoulou, A. and Ilgaz, H. (2013) What do we know about pretend play and narrative development? A response to Lillard, Lerner, Hopkins, Dore, Smith and Palmquist on "The impact of pretend play on children's development: A review of the evidence". *American Journal of Play 6*, 55–81.

O'Connor, C. and Stagnitti, K. (2011) Play, behaviour, language and social skills: The comparison of a play and a non-play intervention within a specialist school setting. *Research in Developmental Disabilities 32*, 1205–1211.

Russ, S. and Wallace, C. (2013) Pretend play and creative process. *American Journal of Play 6*, 136–148.

Ryan, V. and Edge, A. (2011) The role of play themes in non-directive play therapy. *Clinical Child Psychology and Psychiatry 17*, 3, 354–369.

Sherratt, D. and Donald, G. (2004) Connectedness: Developing a shared construction of affect and cognition in children with autism. *British Journal of Special Education 31*, 1, 10–15.

Stagnitti, K. (1998) *Learn to Play: A Program to Develop the Imaginative Play Skills of Children.* Melbourne: Coordinates Publishing.

Stagnitti, K. (2007) *The Child-Initiated Pretend Play Assessment.* Melbourne: Coordinates Publishing.

Stagnitti, K. (2009) Children and Pretend Play. In K. Stagnitti and R. Cooper (eds) *Play as Therapy: Assessment and Therapeutic Interventions.* London: Jessica Kingsley Publishers.

Stagnitti, K. (2010) Helping Kindergarten Teachers Foster Play in the Classroom. In A. Drewes and C. Schaefer (eds) *School Based Play Therapy.* New York: Wiley.

Stagnitti, K. (2014) The Parent Learn to Play Program: Building Relationships through Play. In E. Prendiville and J. Howard (eds) *Play Therapy Today.* London: Routledge.

Stagnitti, K. (2016) Play Therapy for School-Age Children with High Functioning Autism. In A. Drewes and C. Schaefer (eds) *Play Therapy in Middle Childhood.* New York: American Psychological Association.

Stagnitti, K. (2017) A Growing Brain—A Growing Imagination. In E. Prendiville and J. Howard (eds) *Creative Psychotherapy: Applying the Principles of Neurobiology to Play and Expressive Arts-Based Practice.* Oxford: Routledge.

Stagnitti, K. and Casey, S. (2011) Il programma *Learn to Play* con bambini con autismo: Considerazioni pratiche e evidenze. *Autismo Oggi 20,* 8–13.

Stagnitti, K. and Lewis, F.M. (2015) The importance of the quality of preschool children's pretend play ability to the subsequent development of semantic organisation and narrative re-telling skills in early primary school. *International Journal of Speech-Language Pathology 17,* 2, 148–158.

Sunderland, M. (2007) *What Every Parent Needs to Know.* London: Dorling Kindersley.

Tessier, V.P., Normandin, L., Ensink, K., and Fonagy, P. (2016) Fact or fiction? A longitudinal study of play and the development of reflective functioning. *Bulletin of the Menninger Clinic 80,* 1, 60–79.

Vygotsky, L. (1966) Play and its role in the mental development of the child. *Voprosy Psikhologii 12,* 62–76.

Vygotsky, L. (1997) *Thought and Language* (A. Kozulin, trans.). Cambridge, MA: The MIT Press.

Westby, C. (1991) A Scale for Assessment of Children's Pretend Play. In C. Schaefer, K. Gitlin and A. Sundgrund (eds) *Play Diagnosis and Assessment.* New York: Wiley.

Whitebread, D. and O'Sullivan, L. (2012) Preschool children's social pretend play: Supporting the development of metacommunication, metacognition, and self-regulation. *International Journal of Play 1,* 197–213.

Whitebread, D., Coltman, P., Jameson, H., and Lander, R. (2009) Play, cognition, and self-regulation: What exactly are children learning when they learn through play? *Educational and Child Psychology 26,* 40–52.

Whitehead, C., Marchant, J., Craik, D., and Frith, C. (2009) Neural correlates of observing pretend play in which one object is represented as another. *SCAN 4,* 369–378.

Yasenik, L. and Gardner, K. (2012) *Play Therapy Dimensions Model: A Decision-Making Guide for Integrative Play Therapists.* London: Jessica Kingsley Publishers.

3

JUST LIKE A KID!

Adlerian Play Therapy

—— TERRY KOTTMAN ——

Case introduction

Lonny was eight years old when I met him, but I had heard him at the school where I volunteer my play therapy services. I had heard him for at least a year and a half before we actually spent any time together. When I say "I had heard him..." I mean that literally—I had heard him yelling and screaming about once or twice a day, sometimes for an hour or even two at a time—in his classroom, in the hallways, on the playground, in the office. Sometimes I even saw him—writhing around on the floor in his classroom, in the hallways, on the playground, in the office, yelling and screaming. When I asked the school counselor about him, she said, "He hits... other kids, teaching associates, even the principal. He never smiles, he never makes eye contact, and he acts like a very, very angry old man, not a little kid. We are at our wits' end. No one knows what to do to help him."

So, I had heard Lonny, seen him, even heard about him, but until that day in January, I had never met him. Lonny stood between me and the door of his classroom when I stopped in to drop off one of my "play kids" after our session. He kept his eyes trained on the ground, all hunched over on himself, looking like a little old man, and mumbled, "Hey, play lady, would you play with me?" (Wow—I hadn't thought about this before I started writing the case study, but it might just be his "Turning point 1," so I will wait to tell you the rest of the story in the section on turning points.)

In this chapter, I will describe how I used Adlerian play therapy (AdPT) (Kottman and Meany-Walen, 2016, in press) to (a) build a relationship with Lonny; (b) discover his patterns of seeing himself, the world, and others; (c) explore his ability to interact with others, his capacity for dealing with stress, and his desire for and competence in self-regulation; (d) help him gain insight into some of his maladaptive patterns of thinking, feeling, and behavior; and (e) help him experiment with more appropriate ways of interacting with others, communicating his needs to others, dealing with stress, and self-regulating. I also worked with the school personnel to help them learn different ways of thinking about and interacting with him. Starting at about the twentieth session, Lonny's grandmother consented to have an occasional consultation session with me to help her begin to understand him better and learn more ways of interacting with him.

Lonny and I worked together for a year and a half in "school time" in a process designed to build upon our relationship to help Lonny learn better ways to deal with the neglect and trauma he had experienced from birth to age six, living with his drug-addicted, physically abusive parents; having his parents go to jail and lose their parental rights; being temporarily placed in foster care; and moving in with his grandmother. During this time of our evolving connection, as his sense of self developed Lonny learned to be flexible with his own rules, pay attention to his needs and recognize that he could ask for his needs to be met, recognize that others had needs too and that he might need to accommodate them, tolerate delay and frustration, deal with changes in routine, survive having other people in his personal space, and calm himself down when he started to feel agitated. More importantly, he learned to like himself, and he learned to be a kid.

Theoretical orientation

[Play] should be seen as educational aids and as stimuli for the child's psyche, imagination and life skills. Every game is a preparation for the future... In observing children at play, we can see their whole attitude towards life; play is the utmost importance to every child. (Adler, 1927/1998, p.83)

Adlerians believe that individuals are (a) socially embedded and (b) goal-directed, and (c) have a need to belong and gain significance (Adler, 1927/1998). They also believe that people's perceptions of reality are subjective, in that they filter how they interpret what happens to them through their own unique perceptions of themselves, others, and the world. Because people respond to situations and relationships as if these perceptions are true, the therapist must discover clients' filters in order to understand what is going on with them. People's behaviors are goal directed, with the aim of reaffirming to themselves what they already believe about themselves, others, and the world; but they are often unaware of their goals. Adler (1927/1998) stressed that people develop "lifestyle" (beliefs about self, others, and the world and the patterns of thinking, feelings, and behaving based on those beliefs) during their early years based on their interpretation of their early experiences and interactions. Sometimes, these beliefs are positive and encouraging; and other times they are self-defeating and discouraging. "We must look at things from the children's point of view if we want to know why they act as they do" (Adler, 1927/1998, p.33). Adler viewed individuals as striving towards a sense of connection with others and the world (social interest), and Adlerians believe this sense of connection is the key ingredient in mental health (Adler, 1956).

Adler wrote much about the importance of play and childhood but did not work directly with children. In the mid-1980s, wanting to find a way to work therapeutically with children that was congruent with my own beliefs about how people grow and change, I developed AdPT. AdPT is a comprehensive, developmentally responsive approach to counseling children that integrates Adler's Individual Psychology concepts and strategies with the process of play therapy—using toys, play, art, metaphor and storytelling, game play/adventure techniques, sandtray experiences, and dance/movement to learn about, communicate with, and educate child clients (Kottman and Meany-Walen, 2016). One of the hallmarks of AdPT is the therapist's use of self to "read" what individual clients need and custom-design the interaction in play therapy sessions. This can include adjusting the specific play modality (toys, puppetry, art projects, storytelling, game play/adventure techniques, sandtray experiences, and/or dance/movement), showing interest in topics that are compelling to the client (literature, television, movies, video games), matching the client's usual mode of communication (direct or metaphoric), and using attunement to the client to manage the pacing of sessions and the course of the therapeutic process. By paying attention to what clients naturally use to express themselves, how they play, and what is happening in the rest of their lives and by attending to their own affective reaction (Appendix A: 2.2 Emotional Self) and physiological sensations (Appendix A: 4.1 Embodiment) in response to clients, the therapist fine-tunes how to interact with and react to them.

As with traditional Adlerian theory, AdPT follows four phases of counseling: Phase 1, building an egalitarian relationship with the client; Phase 2, investigating the client's lifestyle; Phase 3, helping the client gain insight into their lifestyle; and Phase 4, reorienting/re-educating the client. These phases are not discrete, in that they often overlap, depending on the needs of the client and the circumstances of the therapy. The therapist might use interventions from all four of the dimensions of play therapy described by Yasenik and Gardner (2012) in all of the phases, depending on what comes up in the sessions (see Appendix K in Kottman and Meany-Walen, 2016 for a checklist of specific skills used in each of the phases).

In Phase 1 (which can last anywhere from a single session to nine or ten sessions), the play therapist works collaboratively with clients in order to build a warm, consistent, and accepting therapeutic relationship, sharing leadership of the session with clients (Kottman and Meany-Walen, 2016). The therapist actively interacts with the client (Appendix A: 3.1 Physical Self), and the main components of the therapist's interaction consists of tracking, reflections of feelings, and restatement of content (Appendix A: 1.2 Reflecting and Tracking Statements, 1.3 Restating Content, and 2.1 Emotionality). While most of the therapist's interventions during this phase fall into Quadrant III: Non-intrusive Responding, there are times when the therapist believes it is appropriate to shift into Quadrant II: Open Discussion and Exploration, either because the presenting problem seems to require an open discussion and exploration, or the client seems more comfortable with direct conversations, rather than metaphoric communication. Even in the first phase, there are times when the Adlerian play therapist might decide to metacommunicate, which is the AdPT version of interpretation (Appendix A: 1.4 Interpretations), which would be Quadrant I: Active Utilization or Quadrant IV: Co-facilitation. Metacommunication can involve several types of interpretation—reflection of the client's non-verbal reactions, of secondary gain, or of "hidden" issues underneath the client's behavior; linking thoughts, feelings, and behaviors within and across sessions; and bridging to patterns of thinking, feeling, and behaving in the "real" world outside the playroom (Kottman, 2011; Kottman and Meany-Walen, 2016). While metacommunication usually happens during Phase 3 as a way of helping the client gain insight into their lifestyle, there are times when it is appropriate to share interpretations during the first phase. For instance, if the therapist notices that the client has a habit of self-defeating behavior, they might tentatively point out that pattern in an early attempt to help the client begin to catch themselves in the process of the habit manifesting itself. Again, the therapist custom-designs the method of metacommunication delivery for specific clients. With clients who are likely to be able to "hear" interpretations that are more direct, the therapist would use direct interpretations that would fall into Quadrant I, and with clients who need a softer approach to interpretations, the therapist's responses would tend to fall into Quadrant IV.

During Phase 2 (which usually lasts from three to six sessions), the play therapist uses a variety of techniques to gather information about the client's lifestyle—playing active games and tabletop games with the client and inviting the client to use art, sandtray techniques, movement, dance, and music activities (Kottman and Ashby, 2015; Kottman and Meany-Walen, 2016, 2017). The therapist observes the patterns of the child's free play and play themes and the child's interactions with important adults, including the therapist, the parents, and teachers (if possible). It is also helpful to use questioning strategies with the child. The therapist weaves questions into the fabric of the interaction with the child, sometimes asking them directly and sometimes asking indirectly in the context of the child's metaphor. The therapist can also use metaphoric techniques and storytelling to ascertain information about how the child views self, others, and the world; forms and maintains relationships; solves problems; and so forth. The majority of therapist interventions in this phase fall into Quadrants II, III, and IV (Yasenik and Gardner, 2012). Information of particular interest includes the family atmosphere, family constellation, and functioning at life tasks; personality priorities; mistaken beliefs; Crucial Cs; goals of misbehavior; assets; and lifestyle convictions, mistaken beliefs, and private logic (Kottman and Meany-Walen, 2017). During this phase, the play therapist works to develop a systematic conceptualization of the client's lifestyle and a treatment plan that guides the rest of the therapeutic process (for more information on this process, see Chapter 8 and Appendix G in Kottman and Meany-Walen, 2016).

During Phase 3 (which can last anywhere from 3 to 20 sessions), the therapist uses activities and opportunities that present themselves in session to facilitate the client gaining insight into their emotional, cognitive, attitudinal, and behavioral patterns. While the therapist continues to use a limited number of skills from Phase 1 (e.g. tracking, reflecting feelings, etc.) and Phase 2 (questioning, doing art, sandtray activities, etc.), most of the therapist responses during this stage will consist of metacommunication about (a) a single event, behavior, or interaction and/or the meaning of a specific event, behavior, or interaction; (b) a pattern within a session or across sessions; (c) a pattern in the playroom that extends to other situations or relationships outside the playroom; or (d) a lifestyle theme or conviction, mistaken beliefs, or private logic (Appendix A: 1.4 Interpretations), which would be Quadrant I: Active Utilization or Quadrant IV: Co-facilitation. The therapist will also usually use at least one of the following metaphoric techniques: (a) an extension of one of the client's metaphors, (b) custom-designed therapeutic metaphors, (c) mutual storytelling, or (d) bibliotherapy (Quadrant IV). These metaphors can be in the form of puppet shows, drawings or crafts, role plays, stories, sandtrays, and/or movement/dance intervention. With some clients, a direct approach of open discussion (Appendix A: 1.1 Here and Now Discussion; Quadrant II) is a more appropriate way to help them gain insight than a metaphoric intervention. The therapist's degree of immersion (in terms of the emotional and physical use of self) varies from client to client, depending on the therapist's understanding of what a particular client needs at that moment, which would rely, at least in part, on the therapist's embodiment of their self-system.

Phase 4 can last anywhere from 3 to 20 sessions. The focus in Phase 4 is on reorienting and re-educating the client—helping the client develop more adaptive patterns of thinking, feeling, and behaving; facilitating shifts in the client's beliefs about self, others, and the world; and fostering skills for appropriately interacting with others and solving problems (Kottman and Meany-Walen, 2016, 2017). In this phase, the therapist either helps the client use play activities, metaphors, and direct conversation to generate strategies for (a) capitalizing on their personal assets; (b) improving functioning at one or more of the life tasks; (c) fostering improvement in

Crucial Cs; (d) moving toward healthy functioning in personality priorities; (e) shifting from goals of misbehavior to more positive goals; (f) substituting positive convictions for mistaken beliefs and common sense for private logic; (g) reducing self-defeating behaviors and learning positive behaviors; and/or (h) increasing abilities in needed skills (e.g. social skills, negotiation skills, communication skills, assertiveness, taking appropriate responsibility for behavior, etc.) as appropriate. If the client does not have the internal resources to generate these strategies, the therapist sets up play experiences designed to teach them to the client and provide opportunities for the client to practice them in sessions. The therapist may even invite a classmate, friend, or sibling into play sessions for the purposes of having the client practice these newly acquired skills. Interventions in Phase 4 would fall into Quadrants I, II, and IV. After the client has mastered these strategies in play sessions, when possible, the therapist also asks other people in the client's life (parents, teachers, spouses) to help the client practice outside the sessions.

Adlerian play therapists also work with the important adults in the child client's lives whenever possible (Kottman and Meany-Walen, 2016, 2017, in press). Because Adlerians believe that people are socially embedded and cannot be understood in isolation, parents or other important adults (such as teachers) are invited to be involved throughout the process of working with child clients. They are invited to provide information about their relationship with the child, the child's history, current functioning, and changes. The play therapist builds relationships with these important adults and coaches them in strategies that can encourage positive change for the child. (See Appendices I and J in Kottman and Meany-Walen, 2016 for the specific skills used in AdPT parent and teacher consultation.)

Case study conceptualization

Although Phase 2 is officially the phase for gathering information to go into the case conceptualization, I actually begin the conceptualizing from the first time I hear about (or hear, in this case) the client. As I worked with him in Phase 1, I observed his behavior with me and in his interactions with others at the school; talked with his teachers, the teaching associate assigned to him, and the school counselor; and interviewed his grandmother as the prelude for moving into the formal lifestyle assessment process in Phase 2. During Phase 2, I gathered more information about him and his patterns as I began to form a mental picture of him and his life. His presenting problem was clearly observable—he was manifesting externalizing behavior problems, including defiantly and uncooperatively interacting with others, especially authority figures and peers; being physically aggressive; refusing to do school work; and having frequent tantrums (which included the aforementioned yelling, screaming, and thrashing) when things did not follow a predictable routine. He had lived with his parents until, at six years old, he was taken into foster care because of his parents' drug abuse and their physical abuse of him. He had spent a brief period of time in foster care and was currently living with his maternal grandmother, Mrs. K. Although Mrs. K. gave me permission to work with him at the school and answered some initial questions about Lonny's early life in a phone conversation, she was initially unwilling to engage in ongoing consultation with me because she reported having few problems with him at home. Because of this reluctance on her part, I had to rely heavily on my own interactions with and observations of Lonny and information I gathered from school personnel as I formulated my conceptualization of what was going on with him. I usually organize my ideas using a conceptualization and treatment planning form for the AdPT process (see Appendix G in Kottman and Meany-Walen, 2016). The following is an example of how I could use this form to gather my thoughts about Lonny in a systematic conceptualization and guide to treatment planning.

Family constellation/psychological birth order position

Lonny was his parents' only child and believed that he had caused many of the problems they had. Part of this was a typical reaction of an only child to a family problem (they tend either to blame themselves or tell themselves the problem is everyone else's fault), and part of it was a message his parents conveyed to him by saying things like "Before we had you, things were fine" and through their physical abuse of him. His reaction to being an only child and being unjustly accused of and physically punished for "ruining" his parents' lives resulted in him trying to protect himself by shifting the blame to others for any problems he experienced at school. Partly because of him being an only child and partly because of his parents' preoccupation with illegal substances, he was accustomed to being self-entertaining and was not comfortable being around other children. His foster care placement failed after just one month, partly because Lonny did not handle being with other children who had the same high level of needs he had, which reinforced his perception that he could not get along with others.

Family atmosphere

The atmosphere in Lonny's family with his parents was very chaotic. There were no rules or structure in place and, even when his parents made a rule, they enforced it seldomly or inconsistently. He reported being punished by his parents for things he did not do, which reinforced his tendency to deny responsibility. The physical abuse from his parents contributed to his violent reaction to anyone approaching him too closely when he was feeling dysregulated—he was trying to protect himself by striking out before anyone else had a chance to hurt him. Lonny had lived with his grandmother, a self-reported "very strict disciplinarian," for two years when I met him. Based on my interaction with her and Lonny's reports, Mrs. K. seemed very rigid, with an inflexible structure for routines and many rules for everyday activities and for living a "good life" and being a "good person." Lonny seemed both to crave and chafe at the structure in his grandmother's house. While he reported knowing that she loved him, he was afraid of her, even though she threatened punishment more than she delivered it, and the corporal punishment she administered never reached the level of physical abuse. His fear of her reinforced his tendency to avoid taking responsibility for his behavior by blaming others. Both of these family atmospheres seemed to contribute to his rigid need for structure and his propensity to react with a "meltdown" when the things he expected to happen did not happen or there was a change in the classroom routine.

Functioning at life tasks (family, school, friendship, self, and spirituality)

Lonny seemed to be struggling with all five of the life tasks. Although he was very intelligent, he was behind academically, partly because he had missed much of the foundation for education while he was living with his parents and because he was gone from the classroom quite a bit when he was having a tantrum. His special education teacher reported he could do a surprising amount of his work on grade level but was very reluctant to try novel assignments. Lonny was having difficulties making friends at school. Most of the other children in his class were nervous about playing with him because when they got too close to him, he often reached out and hit them. He blamed others for his behavior and demanded that children play what he wanted to play the way he wanted to play. As for the family life task, as stated in the previous two items, he was not sure what his place with his grandmother was. Though she reported that she did not have many behavior problems with him, he reported being "not sure she was going to keep" him. He did, however, have a relatively positive relationship with several of his uncles, who often invited him over to their houses to play video games with them (though I got the idea that Mrs. K. didn't know that part). Lonny did not seem to like himself much, verbalizing many negative comments about his looks, his behavior, his personality, and his abilities. While his grandmother was a devout woman, and demanded that he attend church, he expressed dislike for sitting still and listening to sermons at church and reported he wasn't sure "why God made" him the way he was, so he was clearly having difficulty with the spirituality life task.

Goal(s) of misbehavior (attention, power, revenge, and proving inadequacy)

Lonny seemed to have two goals of misbehavior: power and proving inadequacy. He had had too much power when he lived with his parents and his position with them gave him the idea that he could not trust adults to keep him safe and that he needed to control things. When he could not control things he became afraid, which led him into reacting in anger and temper flares (and yelling and screaming). He did not willingly share power, although he seemed to flourish in having age-appropriate limited power in his relationship with his grandmother. Academically and in peer relationships, he seemed to be set on proving his own inadequacy. He refused to try to do any school work that he wasn't sure how to do, and he was reluctant to try to make friends, saying things like "I can't do it, so why even try when I would fail?" This had become a self-fulfilling cycle, with him re-proving what he already believed about himself and his abilities.

Assessment of Crucial Cs (connect, capable, count, courage)

Unfortunately, Lonny had not mastered any of the Crucial Cs. He was struggling to connect, did not believe he was capable, knew he did not count and did not make a contribution, and was unwilling to try new things without a guarantee of success. In thinking about how to use a triage method of deciding which one to begin to foster first, I decided that if he could connect with others and believe he counted, the other Crucial Cs of capable and courage would follow. He had already started working on connecting with me as his first turning point, inviting me to play, and I was going to extend our connection by being a person who did not buy into any of the negative things he believed about himself and did not judge or distance myself when he was having a meltdown. As a part of my helping foster his belief that he counted, I always used my emotionality and emotional self to express how excited I was when he joined me in the playroom and, in order to give him a way to contribute to the school, we sometimes spent five minutes of our sessions picking up litter on the playground. As he got more comfortable with me, I asked him who he liked best of all the people who worked at the school. As a result of that conversation, I inquired whether several members of the school staff (the secretary, the nurse, and the janitor) would be willing to include him in their jobs whenever possible. This would work on both connect and count simultaneously.

Personality priorities (comfort, control, pleasing, superiority)

Obviously, Lonny's primary personality priority was control. He wanted to have control of everything and everyone because he felt very anxious when he was not in control. Because he felt that he needed control, he tried to make sure that no one could control anything he did. (The ironic thing was that, many times, he told people that they had to do things because "that's the way my gram does them.") His secondary priority was comfort—he was easily overwhelmed by anything that felt like pressure or stress. He wanted to make sure that things were comfortable and stress-free. Unfortunately, he found any situation in which he did not have control stressful, which resulted in his temper flares, which in turn increased his stress (and increased the stress of everyone else in the school).

Assets

With children who manifest externalizing behavior problems, it is essential for me to have a list of their assets, including the things I like about them as a way to counteract the negative impact of their acting-out behavior on me. Lonny was funny (when he was relaxed), smart, perceptive about other people, generous, and thoughtful. He was also incredibly artistically talented, spending much of the time he was avoiding school work drawing on his assignments. I wanted to reinforce all of these assets.

Lonny's lifestyle convictions

I am dumb, powerless, worthless, unwanted… *I must be in control.*

Others are unpredictable, uncaring, out to hurt me, unsafe… *Others must be controlled because otherwise they will hurt me, pushed away before they hurt me.*

The world/life is scary, unpredictable, dangerous, unfair, never easy or fun.

Based on these convictions/perceptions/beliefs/feelings, my behavior must be controlling, overpowering others to make sure they cannot control or hurt me.

Self-defeating/useless behavior you want to change

This included being rigid and insisting that there was only one way to do things, hitting other children and school personnel, having meltdowns every time something did not go the way he thought it should go, controlling how he played with others, giving up on school work, and refusing to try new things or make changes.

Skills the child needs to learn
These included becoming aware of his own emotional and physiological reactions to situations and learning to clearly communicate his feelings and needs to others in socially appropriate ways, becoming more flexible and willing to try new things, developing coping strategies for when things did not unfold the way he thought they should, and learning anger management strategies.

Therapy process: turning points and emergence of self
Turning point 1: an invitation to play
Now, believe it or not, I get this kind of solicitation from children at the school on a pretty regular basis, so I have a standard answer that I give to kids who ask if they can come and play with me. (How can you not get a reputation for being a fun person who folks want to hang out with in an elementary school when you are the only grownup there who plays with kids on a regular basis?) I told him that I would love to play with him and that we needed to talk to Ms. J., the school counselor, so we could figure out when I could start seeing him and that Ms. J. would have to ask his grandmother for permission for me to work (oh, I mean play) with him. He started to look angry because I wasn't doing what he wanted when he wanted it, and I said, "I really do want to play with you. And we have some rules we have to follow." He took a small breath and said, "Okay, as long as you are going to play with me just as soon as you can." I took that for his first turning point—him recognizing that he needed help, believing that someone else could maybe be helpful to him, asking for that help, and then being willing to wait even though he wanted to start right away.

After Ms. J. got permission from Lonny's grandmother for me to work with him, I called her to try to set up some parent consultation. She was willing to tell me some information about Lonny, but chose not to set up regular consultation, saying that she really didn't have a problem with him other than the school calling her all the time and telling her to come and get him because he could not stay at school when he was "acting up." (As time passed and the school called her less, she indicated that she was willing for me to call her occasionally to update her, which I used to subtly make some suggestions about being a bit more flexible and giving Lonny some choices about chores and other things at home.)

The following week, I started working with Lonny. As part of my Quadrant II orientation to the way I work, in the first session I almost always tell children that in our playing sometimes they get to be the boss and sometimes I get to be the boss. When I said this to Lonny, his body tensed up and he turned his back to me, saying, "I thought the kids got to be the boss when they played with you." Sensing that this was important to him, I replied, "Well, with some kids, I usually want to do exactly what they want to do, so it works out that we do what they want to do most of the time, even when I am the boss." He seemed to relax a bit and said, "Can that happen with me?" My answer of "I think we can do that for a while until you feel more comfortable and safe in here" seemed to satisfy him. I had an intuition that he would have difficulty switching who was in charge mid-session, which is what I do with most child clients, so I suggested that we alternate being in charge of a whole session, so he would be in charge of what we were going to do during the first session, then I would be in charge of what we were going to do during the second session, and so on. His mumbled response "But we are going to pick the same things for at least a while, right?" and my affirmative reply seemed to satisfy his need for control.

For the first three sessions, he came in to the playroom, got the Uno deck from the shelf, sat down, and dealt the cards—without making eye contact the entire time. Uno was the only thing he was willing to do, so I chose it as my activity too. He always dealt the cards ("I am really good at shuffling and handing out the cards"), and he always had the first turn ("I am the youngest, so I have to go first"). He insisted we play by the rules his grandmother made (e.g. having the youngest player deal, dealing seven cards to each player, drawing an unlimited number of new cards until you get a card you can play, etc.), saying repeatedly, "This is the only way to play. My gram says it is." He would not make eye contact with me as we played, just focusing on the cards. Sensing that he was still unsure that I was a safe person, I carefully gave him his distance, not getting too physically close to him and not doing anything to pressure him to make eye contact or "let me in" in any way. I also recognized that he needed to feel in control in the playroom, so I did not challenge him on any of his rules (or his grandmother's either). Because of what I was seeing and feeling,

I almost exclusively stayed in Quadrant III: Non-intrusive Responding for this part of the therapy, which led to…

Turning point 2: ignition—eye contact

At the beginning of the fourth session, he came in, looked me in the eye (still no smile or any indication that he was glad to be there), got the Uno deck from the shelf, sat down, made eye contact again, dealt the cards, made eye contact again, and said, "You can go first this time." I was very excited by all this and wanted to jump up and down for joy. However, I knew he would not handle this level of emotionality on my part, and so I restrained myself (with a lot of effort). As we continued in this vein, taking turns being first and just chatting a small bit as we played, he began to relax in our sessions. As time passed, with us taking turns shuffling, dealing, and being the first to go, we continued to play by his gram's rules. Although we were playing together, I continued in Quadrant III for most of my responses to him, occasionally straying into Quadrant IV by pointing out (during the sessions in which I was "the boss") that some of the kids I played with had different rules for how to play Uno (e.g. dealing more than seven cards, fewer than seven cards, only drawing one card when you don't have any cards you can play). I knew I was planting seeds for helping him move toward being more flexible. Truthfully, I expected it to be a long time before those seeds sprouted, especially since, when I suggested that we could maybe change the rules we followed when we played, he either ignored me or vehemently denied that we could do such a thing, until…

Turning point 3: changing the rules, part 1

In session 9, Lonny said, "If we did change the rules, what would we change?" At my suggestion that we could change the number of cards we dealt, having more than seven cards each, he said, "Let's try six instead. That way if we don't like it, we can get another one." And we were off to the races. At first, we could only change the number of cards we dealt, but then gradually changed several different rules for playing. We did this for eight sessions, with Lonny winning almost every game—not because he was cheating; he was just a better strategist than me. When we had first started play, he had no reaction to winning. Beginning with this rule-changing section of our work together, initially every time he won, he just had a little secret smile, but after several sessions, he started having a small party when he won—smiling and doing a little celebration dance. (I was pretty excited about him showing such enthusiasm because, up to that point, no one in the school had seen him expressing anything but unhappy emotions. However, staying attuned to his reactions to other people's emotionality, I reined in my own emotionality because he seemed to find other people expressing strong emotions difficult.) After six weeks of this, he occasionally told me that he was sorry that he always won, and I always lost, even asking me one day whether it hurt my feelings, or I got angry when he won. In response, I told him that I was very impressed by his abilities (working to build his Crucial C of capable) and that I enjoyed the pleasure of his company so much (building his Crucial Cs of connect and count) that I never minded when he won. Because he seemed curious about this, I shifted into Quadrant II and initiated an open discussion and exploration of feelings and why people feel certain ways and how different people express their feelings in different ways—this also allowed me to begin to ask some Phase 2 questions about his family and his relationships with people at the school as a means for furthering my understanding of his lifestyle. Our conversation also allowed me to sneak in some Phase 4 teaching about ways to handle strong emotions and stress-management skills, talking about what I did to self-regulate when I did feel angry or sad. Integrating some strategies from Phase 3 (helping the client gain insight), we talked about families, feelings, self-management, and things that bugged us as we played. At the end of the school year, Lonny asked if he could see me again the following year. He came in to our first session in the fall having decided that, even if I didn't mind losing, he wanted me to win sometimes, leading to…

Turning point 4: changing the rules, part 2

In session 21 (our first session of the new school year), Lonny announced that we were "going to make a *big* rule change…just don't tell my gram." He said he had thought a lot over the summer when he hadn't gotten to see me about how to "make things fair." He had decided that he was going to deal a different number of cards to me than he dealt to himself. He assured me that "this isn't cheating.

It's just fairer this way." We experimented with numbers over several sessions, figuring out that I won every once in a while if he started with ten cards and I started with six, so we played that way for several sessions. I began to notice that, often in our sessions, Lonny seemed a bit bored with playing Uno, but even when I pointed this out to him (using Phase 3, Quadrant IV responses such as metacommunication) and gave him the choice of Uno and another game or activity when it was my turn to "be the boss," he insisted he wanted to continue to play Uno until…

Turning point 5: expanding our Uno universe

Before I went to his classroom to get Lonny in session 23, I put the game Uno Attack on the table where we had been playing. (If you don't know Uno Attack, quick, run out and buy it—the game is great for working on so many different goals in play therapy; Petersen and Kottman, 2017.) When we walked in and he saw the card dispenser, he wanted to know what it was. I told him to get ready for a surprise (just to warn him that something new was going to happen, since, historically, his reaction to change had been kind of radical), and pressed the button so that cards flew out of the dispenser. He backed up a bit and actually reached out to hold my hand, saying, "Whoa! What *is* that?" When I explained it was another kind of Uno game and asked if he wanted to play it, he said, "*No way!* That thing is too wild!" We played "regular Uno" that entire session with him seeming to be increasingly disconnected from the game, but more than willing to engage in conversations about other topics related to his lifestyle and his emerging insight into his patterns, including beginning to develop some friendships at school and in his neighborhood, his teacher smiling at him more often, and managing to stop himself from having a meltdown during the week despite the fact that several people had "invaded my personal space." (Basically, he was switching things up, moving us into Quadrants I and II as Phase 3 continued with him gaining insight into his own patterns of thinking, feeling, and behaving and moving toward Phase 4 where he would learn and practice new, more adaptive ways of thinking, feeling, and behaving.)

The following week, as we walked into the playroom, he grabbed the Uno Attack card dispenser from the table and said, "Want to get wild?" We played Uno Attack for several weeks after that, continuing to talk as we played, with me also using metacommunication to point out ways he was beginning to make changes in his patterns of thinking, feeling, and behaving during the game and then when he brought things up that were happening outside the sessions (combining elements of Quadrants I, II, and IV as a transition to Phase 4). At his request ("Let's do something different—got any other ways to play Uno?"), we even tried playing Uno Spin for several sessions. While we played, he sometimes talked about the video games he was playing with his uncles at their houses. He seemed particularly interested in "Plants vs. Zombies," describing the various plants and zombies and their unique attributes and abilities. He had, by this time, moved into being able to verbalize many of his feelings and expressed frustration with my lack of knowledge about "Plants vs. Zombies."

By this time in the therapeutic journey, many of the really difficult behaviors he had been manifesting at school had diminished. He had stopped yelling and screaming when he was upset, even though he continued to have small meltdowns when things did not follow a predictable routine; he had gotten more tolerant of having people in his personal space, though not if he felt truly threatened by them; and he was more willing to try new activities and academic assignments. However, he was still highly anxious, showing more "normal" signs when he felt out of control (wringing his hands when other children were not interested in playing what he wanted to play, needing to have his school supplies lined up in a certain way, rocking in his chair during tests). He seemed more aware of the feelings he was having but was still struggling with articulating those feelings and asking others for help. While several children were willing to play with him on the playground or work on assignments with him as a partner, the children in his class were still a bit hesitant because he had not given up quite a few of his tyrannical ways and he would not/did not know how to cooperate with others on getting a goal accomplished. I was pleased by the progress, as were his teacher, the other folks who worked with him at the school, and his grandmother (who was very happy to stop getting quite so many phone calls from the school). Given this progress and my feel for how relaxed and comfortable he was with me in our sessions, I felt that it was time to "up our game" a bit, moving into the reorientation/re-education phase (Phase 4) of the AdPT, so in session 30, when it was my turn to suggest what we were going to do during the session, I told him that I was struggling actually visualizing the characters from "Plants vs. Zombies." I mentioned that I had several clients who were interested in "Plants vs. Zombies," and even though I knew a lot about some video games because my son is/was a gamer, I did not know that game and wanted to learn. I had heard he was an amazing artist and asked if he would be willing to skip playing Uno that week and draw pictures of the characters from "Plants vs. Zombies" on the white board. I was nervous about this rather radical departure, but, having checked with my own self-system, I believed he was ready to make a change. And, hip hooray, he was, which triggered…

Turning point 6: plants and zombies

Lonny spent the next several sessions drawing characters on the white board and explaining how each of the characters moved and what powers they had. He even demonstrated how each of the zombies ambulated, and we began to play the characters, alternating being the zombies and acting out what each of the plants did to protect themselves from the zombies. Because I wanted to give him a chance to practice recognizing his own feelings and being able to take the emotional perspective of others, we took turns being plants and zombies—the plants defending themselves (without touching the zombies) while the zombies lurched menacingly at the plants, all while labeling the feelings that both sets of characters might be feeling. I metacommunicated about how important it was for everyone to be able to keep themselves safe and that there were many ways to do it, and I did some bridging to other ways folks could keep themselves safe in situations at school and outside the school (Quadrants I and IV).

This was going so well, I decided to come up with a way to help him practice expanding his ability to be flexible. I suggested we could make up our own plants and zombies and add to the pantheon of characters available by drawing them and then inventing ways for the plants to defend themselves during session 36, and, initially (of course), he was appalled, saying, "That's just not how it goes. You can't just invent your own characters." When I pointed out that was how they got invented in the first place ("Well, at some point, *somebody* made them up"), he looked thoughtful, but did not take up my suggestion until…

Turning point 7: let's get inventing!

Session 37 started with Lonny saying, "Did someone really make up the plants and the zombies?" I talked to him about how artists and video game designers had the job of inventing characters and making up stories for video games. He told me that he would like to do that when he grew up, and when I suggested we could start working on his future job during our sessions, he grabbed the markers and some paper and said, "Let's get inventing!" We spent several sessions developing new plants and zombies—making up ways for the plants to keep themselves safe and the zombies to do things that were threatening to the plants, using art and movement to fully bring our creations alive. We bounced back and forth between Quadrant II and Quadrant IV, moving in and out of the metaphor provided by "Plants vs. Zombies," practicing ways to label our feelings in both roles, experimenting with ways to manage our anxiety when we were plants, talking about things that might be scary to each of us outside the playroom, and brainstorming ideas about how to keep ourselves safe. After several sessions of this, Lonny surprised me when he said, "Hey, I have a friend who likes 'Plants vs. Zombies' too. I have been showing him some of my moves. His name is Jin Soo, and he is in my class." This was the segue into...

Turning point 8: "Can he come and play with us?"

Since I had already decided that our next (and final) step in the therapy process would be to include a second child in our session so that Lonny could practice his newfound social skills and anxiety management with another child, I wanted to jump up and down and sing for joy as I casually said, "Well, we will have to ask Ms. J. to ask your teacher if it's okay with her and then ask his parents if it's okay with them for him to come and play with us. Shall we go and do that now?" He thought that was a splendid idea, so we asked the school counselor if she would get permission for his friend to come and play with us. The next week (session 47), Jin Soo joined us in the playroom, and we spent the next two or three sessions playing "Plants vs. Zombies." As we played during session 49, Jin Soo remarked that he wasn't very scared about zombies, but he was "totally freaked out" by "Five Nights at Freddie's" (FNAF) (another very frightening computer game that is highly popular with elementary-age children, especially those who have experienced trauma) (Kottman *et al.*, 2017). Although Lonny had not actually played the game, he had seen some clips of Let's Plays on YouTube, and he mentioned that he was having some nightmares about being chased by animatronics (scary characters from FNAF). When I suggested we could pretend to be characters from FNAF as a way to practice naming our feelings, using our anxiety management tools, and working as a team to keep ourselves safe, he was very excited to do that. We continued to play together until the end of the school year, with him getting better each day. We even wound up cooperatively playing "the real" "Plants vs. Zombies" on my tablet during some of our sessions, but that is a story for another time.

By our termination, Lonny was a different boy than the one who originally invited me to play with him. While he was still anxious, he had developed coping strategies to handle most situations without becoming too dysregulated. He was more flexible in his thinking and behavior and understood that there was more than one way to do things; he had stopped hitting other children and school personnel and having meltdowns at school; and he had learned to share power with teachers and other students. Although he sometimes still doubted his capabilities and was not completely sure that he counted, all four of Lonny's Crucial Cs had improved. He now demonstrated courage in being willing to try on school work and new experiences; he was much more able to make positive connections with adults and other children; he was more confident in his abilities, especially for creativity and doing art projects; and he knew there were areas in his life where he made a contribution, especially at home with his grandmother and with his uncles. He had increased his awareness of his own emotional and physiological reactions to situations, was learning to clearly communicate his feelings and needs to others in socially appropriate ways, and had demonstrated that he could and would apply several different anger management strategies in situations with peers and teachers. And, most importantly, he was no longer an angry old man. Lonny had begun to smile and laugh and play—just like a kid.

Turning points summary

Stage in process	Quadrant	Turning points	What contributed to the turning point?
Even before session 1 (Phase 1 of AdPT)	QII	Asking for what he needed directly and being willing to negotiate the timing	• Truthfully, I am not sure. I have a feeling it was my reputation with the other children in the school as being someone who cares about kids and is safe
Session 4 (Phases 1 and 2 of AdPT)	QIII	Making eye contact and letting me go first	• Using my emotionality and my emotional and physical self to guide my attunement with him and his need for control which created his experiencing of being in control while sharing a tiny bit of power with me • His growing sense of the Crucial C of connect with me and his feeling as though he would be able to have most of the power in our sessions
Session 9 (Phases 2 and 3 of AdPT)	QI	Showing a willingness to change the rules by which we played	• Continuing to use my own emotionality and my emotional self and physical self to guide my letting him stay in control, combined with my occasional interpretive comments and tentative deliverance of invitations to try a different way of doing things and his willingness to take my invitations as permission rather than pressure
Session 21 (after summer vacation) (Phase 3 of AdPT)	QI, then QIV	Initiating a change in the rules so that they were fairer so that I would win occasionally	• The continuing emergence of his self-confidence and willingness to share power in sessions, activated by my willingness to let him have the majority of the power, along with my stated desire for sharing power between the two of us, plus his growing sense of his own values and the importance of fairness

Session 24 (Phase 3 of AdPT)	QII, then QI and QIV	Being willing to play a game that was very much out of his comfort zone	• My introducing him to the idea that we could branch out and try a game that was considerably less controlled than the game we had been playing, but without pressure to play it—him feeling that he was truly in control of whether we shifted to a different game or not • His growing self-confidence and belief in his own ability to self-regulate even when something was not in his control and his willingness to expand our sharing power in new ways, along with his increased level on all four of the Crucial Cs
Session 30 (Phases 3 and 4 of AdPT)	QI and QIV	Shifting from game play into imaginative play, art, and movement	• His growing ability to be flexible and increased willingness to share power and have events unfold without having the need to completely be in control of his surroundings and other people
Session 37 (Phase 4 of AdPT)	QII and QIV	Being willing to take the psychological and artistic risks of creativity and imagination	• Lonny's desire to express himself creatively combined with his wish to learn more about expressing his feelings and about taking someone else's perspective • His increasing belief in his ability to keep himself safe and ask for his needs to be met in appropriate ways and his continued growth in the Crucial Cs of courage and capable
Session 47 (Phase 4 of AdPT)	QI and QIV, with a bit of QIII	Requesting a playmate in the playroom and being willing to share my attention without feeling threatened and to share power with another child	• Lonny's continued growth in his recognition that he did not always have to be in control, his enhanced confidence in his ability to communicate appropriately with peers, his sense of self-assurance in his relationship with me, and the progress in his awareness that he knew how to keep himself safe and had tools he could use to cope with his own anxiety • His improvement in the Crucial Cs of count and capable

References

Adler, A. (1956) *The Individual Psychology of Alfred Adler: A Systematic Presentation in Selections from His Writings.* Edited by H.L. Ansbacher and R.R. Ansbacher. New York: Harper & Row.

Adler, A. (1998) *Understanding Human Nature.* Oxford: Oneworld. (Original work published in 1927.)

Kottman, T. (2011) Adlerian Play Therapy. In C. Schaefer (ed.) *Foundations of Play Therapy* (2nd edn). New York: John Wiley.

Kottman, T. and Ashby, J. (2015) Adlerian Play Therapy. In D. Crenshaw and A. Stewart (eds) *Play Therapy: A Comprehensive Guide to Theory and Practice.* New York: Guilford Press.

Kottman, T. and Meany-Walen, K. (2016) *Partners in Play: An Adlerian Approach to Play Therapy* (3rd edn). Alexandria, VA: American Counseling Association.

Kottman, T. and Meany-Walen, K. (2017) *Treatment Manual for Adlerian Play Therapy.* Unpublished. Available upon request from the first author.

Kottman, T. and Meany-Walen, K. (in press) *Doing Play Therapy: From Building the Relationship to Facilitating Change.* New York: Guilford Press.

Kottman, T., Petersen, N., Kottman, J., and Lavenz, E. (2017) *How to Talk so Gamers Will Listen and Listen so Gamers Will Talk: Using the Language of Video Games in Play Therapy and Counseling.* Cedar Falls, IA: Author.

Petersen, N. and Kottman, T. (2017) *Using Tabletop Games in Play Therapy.* Cedar Falls, IA: Author.

Yasenik, L. and Gardner, K. (2012) *Play Therapy Dimensions Model: A Decision-Making Guide for Integrative Play Therapists.* London: Jessica Kingsley Publishers.

4

"YOU CAN BE THE DOOR"

Establishing Safety and Facilitating Growth of Personal Identity with a Traumatized Child

—— EILEEN PRENDIVILLE ——

Case introduction

Tony was the only child I ever met in the play therapy room who brought a suitcase of toys, his own sealed drink, and a sealed biscuit to his first session. This chapter presents and explores a humanistic and integrative psychotherapy process with this five-year-old boy (called Tony for the purposes of anonymity), who had experienced chronic sexual abuse by multiple perpetrators, including his father, from the time he was a toddler. Tony attended 73 sessions of child psychotherapy, over two and a half years, with play therapy being the medium. Over this period Tony regained a strong sense of self, the capacity to have joy in his day-to-day life, became more self-aware, developed maturity, and moved toward healthier and more satisfying ways of being. His stress response system became regulated and his capacity to self-soothe became very strong. He learned to avoid being triggered by innocuous sensory input by engaging his higher brain functions and focusing on safe stimuli and making use of reassuring self-talk. Most importantly of all, he learned to live with spontaneity in the present without being constantly triggered by reminders of his tragic past. He returned to the normal developmental pathway.

Theoretical orientation

The humanistic and integrative modality is underpinned by a commitment to working with the whole unique child: all elements of the self—mind, body, and spirit. With children, in keeping with developmentally appropriate practice, the process relies on the power of the therapeutic relationship and the therapeutic powers of play (Schaefer and Drewes, 2014), rather than focusing on identified problem behaviors. Tony's presenting symptoms, which will be described later, can be best understood in terms of an over-active stress response system and an inability to stay within his window of tolerance (Siegel, 2012) due to the persistent levels of terror he had experienced in the past and which had now become his base state (Perry, 2006). In short, Tony continued to experience the world as a terrifying place and the people within it as untrustworthy and dangerous. In subscribing to humanistic philosophy, reflected in the core principles of non-directive play therapy as put forward by Axline (1947), I trust that the child's behavior, including presenting problems, can be understood in the context of their drive for self-actualization. I believed that Tony's ability to use his cognitive functions to measure safety was sorely restricted; his way of being in the world was governed by his lower brain regions, and his window of tolerance was very narrow. He alternated between states of hyper- and hypo-arousal. The lower brain regions assess safety based on physiological sensations; safety is measured on a somatic level. Tony's ventral vagal system was dysfunctional and his physiological reactions consistently led him to experience the world as a scary place. He strove to achieve some control over his overwhelming emotions. Some of his symptoms, e.g. sexualized behavior, communicated his confusion in relation to the inappropriate experiences that he had been subjected to. He had been given an inappropriate social role that negatively impacted his personal identity.

I accept child clients as they are, not attempting to treat or remove presenting symptoms, but trusting that the therapy process can provide a relationship and environment in which the difficulties can be resolved and the core wounds healed. Change becomes possible when the person and their status quo are witnessed, accepted, and explored, within a relationship where the social engagement system (Porges, 2011) is activated and when both hemispheres of both brains are engaged and working in partnership. I believe that therapist use of self and a capacity for informed decision-making are central to this process. I do not rely on a single model. Instead, I combine two or more theories as a coherent whole at times, while also utilizing various models as judged appropriate for the client at the particular moment in time. I also rely on a neurobiological understanding of both normal development and the impact of trauma in making clinical decisions.

> The key to therapeutic intervention is to remember that the stress response systems originate in the brainstem and diencephalon. As long as these systems are poorly regulated and dysfunctional they will disrupt and dysregulate the higher parts of the brain. All the best cognitive-behavioral, insight-oriented, or even affect-based interventions will fail if the brainstem is poorly regulated. (Perry, 2006, pp.38–39)

In sessions, it is very common for me to be fully engaged on a physical and emotional level. I am regularly an active participant in the child's role play scenarios. Other than making tracking comments (generally in the very early sessions) and reflecting content and emotions (at any stage in the process), when I engage verbally during the session it tends to be what I surmise is the internal state of a character, in either projective play or role play, rather than trying to engage the child in a conversation. Referencing the Degree of Immersion: Therapist Use of Self Scale (Appendix A), I would often be more immersed in the play, emotionally and physically, periodically utilizing reflective interpretative statements (Appendix A: 1.4 Interpretations). However, unless the child initiates a direct conversation, I try to ensure that my verbalizations do not disrupt the play, although I do use commentary to influence static play or looping play. In addition, when the child has achieved some level of integration and it is apparent that they are somewhat aware of how their play might relate to their lived world experiences, I will make brief linking interpretative comments with the aim of facilitating the child in achieving greater levels of awareness.

I pay deep attention to my internal emotional state (Appendix A: 2.2 Emotional Self) and physiological sensations (Appendix A: 4.1 Embodiment) and consider how I can make use of these aspects of self to support the child's process. When assigned a role, especially one that is in relationship with a role taken by the child, I allow myself to fully engage with the role as I believe that my experience within this role will allow me to embody emotions, thoughts, and sensations that are familiar to the child and over which they are attempting to gain empowerment.

Case study conceptualization

Tony presented with many troubling symptoms and some strong resiliency features; he was very withdrawn and exhibited extreme clinginess to his mother, who was deeply attuned to him and with whom he had a secure attachment relationship. This relationship, along with the working-in-partnership approach that we adopted, was one factor that greatly enhanced Tony's ability to engage in and make use of the psychotherapeutic space and assisted Tony in achieving integration and developing mindsight (Siegel, 1999): the capacity to look within and recruit higher brain areas to override stress signals emanating from the limbic area and brainstem.

When referred, Tony had very high levels of anxiety and a visible startle response to unexpected or loud noises. He greatly feared and resisted physical contact, even within a caring context; his physiological responses led him to resist what he most needed—healthy and soothing touch. His sleep was very disturbed by frequent nightmares and night terrors and he had recently started sleepwalking. He was masturbating excessively and engaged in inappropriate sexualized behavior. It later emerged that he was engaging in literal, static, post-traumatic play at home in which he recreated a specific traumatic scene (Gil, 2006; Prendiville, 2014; Terr, 1983).

Despite his negative experiences with his father and others, this little boy had a strong positive relationship with his mother who responded appropriately to his disclosures and had taken all possible measures to secure his current and future protection. This was very important; Tony was lucky in that his mother was very attuned to him and was totally committed to supporting his recovery. She was also willing to engage in the many battles that ensued in her efforts to prevent her son having access visits with the main perpetrator. This was no easy task—but that story is not for here.

The E-P-R paradigm and overcoming trauma linked to child sexual abuse

I believe that the child's play in therapy can often be best understood in the context of the Embodiment-Projection-Role (E-P-R) developmental paradigm identified by Dr. Sue Jennings (1999) and further developed by myself (Prendiville, 2010, 2017b, pp.22–23). Jennings (1999) suggests that there are three main play categories: embodiment, projective, and role play. Children progress through these stages sequentially, each being significantly influenced by the previous stage and the degree of maturity already achieved. However, all stages remain active so that when a child begins to engage in role play they still engage in both projective and embodiment play also. As adults we also engage in embodiment, projective, and role activities.

I propose (Prendiville, 2010) that each stage is directly linked to separate stages in the process of personal development:

- physical identity—embodiment play: understanding "me" as a separate person

- emotional identity—projective play: understanding personal thoughts, feelings, and intentions and becoming aware of "other" as not sharing all our perceptions

- role identity—dramatic and role play: learning to have relationships and develop empathy by developing the ability to see the world from another person's viewpoint.

Each of these stages relies on the foundations laid within the previous stage/s. Emotional development will be hampered by the inability to read one's own body cues that arise from disruption during the embodiment stage. The capacity to develop empathy will be thwarted by deficiencies in physical and emotional identity.

Should a child experience neglect or trauma, their development may be interrupted and distorted as the usual achievements associated with one or more stages are compromised. Trauma and prolonged stress may interfere with the satisfactory development of physical, emotional, and role identity and can manifest in difficulties in the child's relationships and play capacity. This will be influenced both by the stages of development previously achieved, the degree to which each has been successfully integrated, and by the timing and nature of the trauma (e.g. if it directly confused or harmed the child on a physical, emotional, and/or inappropriate role level). Adults who experience trauma will also be affected on these three levels and this will be likewise influenced by their earlier experiences at each level so that adult trauma may damage something already achieved (e.g. reduce the ability to trust rather than prevent the capacity to trust from developing).

Invasive trauma—including physical or sexual abuse, neglect, or medical interventions that cross the body boundary—is likely to distort physical identity and interfere with the person's capacity to feel safe on a somatic level. Developmental trauma of this nature can also contribute to a lack of coordination, sensory dysfunction, lack of awareness of bodily sensations, and difficulties with personal boundaries. Of critical importance is the need for psychotherapists to recognize that the child exhibiting difficulties with trust, with assertiveness—saying yes and no—and having poor body image and low self-esteem may well be struggling with physical identity issues that cannot be resolved purely with cognitive-based approaches.

Confusing experiences interfere with emotional identity, and can lead to a persistent sense of being overwhelmed, a lack of clarity, inability to form a coherent narrative, and difficulties with sequencing, memory (including intrusive recollections), and making sense of physiological sensations and understanding emotions.

Being assigned inappropriate roles within relationships distorts the development of role identity and can lead to difficulties with relationships, understanding the thoughts and feelings of others, and developing empathy, and ultimately a propensity to take on inappropriate roles in relation to others.

Therapy process: turning points and emergence of self

Experiences of sexual abuse impact on all three areas in the E-P-R paradigm. The content of Tony's play, recurring play themes, and his verbalizations helped me to understand how he had been traumatically impacted by his experiences and shone a light on his evolving understanding of these experiences. There were several significant turning points during Tony's therapy process that can be linked to changes in his sense of physical, emotional, and role identity and his development of self.

I used the Therapeutic Touchstone (Prendiville, 2014) approach in Tony's first session, partially as a way to demonstrate trustworthiness and secondly to provide a coherent narrative of Tony's story by telling him a simplified version of his own story, in a carefully structured, age-appropriate way (Play Therapy Dimensions Model Quadrant II: Open Discussion and Exploration). My experience is that using the touchstone story enables the child to engage more fully in the therapy at an early stage, invites them to introduce relevant play safely, and eliminates much of the need for limit-testing. I also use this story to clarify my role and my approach. Tony was very relieved that he would be "the boss of the play" and that I had one big rule—the safe rule—that nobody would get hurt in the playroom. He was not totally convinced that I was telling the truth when I explained that I would not be asking him questions. After hearing the story, in the company of his mother, Tony and I entered the playroom as he announced that he was planning to "play and play and play."

Initially, Tony focused his attention on sorting the toys he had brought in his suitcase. He soon dressed up as a workman who was gathering tools (and a megaphone and clock) to "fix things." I was enlisted as a postal worker to deliver mail to the workman. Disorganized projective play was evident (e.g. the family with no name and some furniture being placed in the doll house but not engaged with), as was randomized presentation of what seemed to be personally relevant play (Norton and Norton, 2008)—the introduction of a doll who could not sleep, was very frightened, and cried bitterly. Tony was preoccupied with cleanliness and had to change the painting water after every dip of the brush.

I believe that the way the child plays in the first session tells me something about where they experience most difficulties and distress in their world if I stay in Quadrant III: Non-intrusive Responding (Yasenik and Gardner, 2012) throughout this session. Tony was not going to take any risks and there was no way he was going to trust me, my toys, or any food items I might provide! I surmised that his biggest challenge was in the areas of trust and that this underpinned his significant difficulties with relationships and with organizing his thinking. I expected that his early role play would highlight his relationship struggles, that themes to emerge in his projective play would show more clearly the nature of the confusion he was struggling with, and that later embodiment play would plant the seeds for core recovery. I was interested to see what use he might make of me in this process.

The early, mainly non-directive, Quadrant III (Yasenik and Gardner, 2012) sessions were very intense, linked to repetitive rituals, themes of being dirty (baby dolls cannot be made clean despite constant washing), portrayal of huge confusion and need for control (bags of small toys and junk being brought in for me to sort throughout the sessions), and a lack of theme development; there were many play scenes that were disrupted just as the scene was set up. Both play and stories were disorganized. For example, Tony stated, "Once upon a time there was a lady bug and there was teddy bears hidden in the sand and then they had a fight and then they heard a giant's leg. The end."

In role play, Tony always took the more powerful role and I was regularly the maid, servant, or slave. In these roles I had to be almost robotic in my subservient demeanor and comply fully with all demands while presenting a pleasant, upbeat, smiley, and jolly persona. This emotional and physical use of self was exhausting but gave me great insight into the position that was familiar to Tony and that he was trying to gain mastery over it by giving me his experiences in play. His way of coping, to suppress and ignore his own impulses and merge with the powerful other in situations of danger, was apparent.

Turning point 1: you can be the door

Interestingly, as safety was established, the need for confluence diminished, themes of conflict emerged, and battles commenced. This gave us the chance to check our protection and led into a session when Tony decided to draw images from nightmares. He set us up in the playhouse, both wearing shields, helmets, body armor, and disguises and securing window locks to make this safe. This was our first turning point as Tony decided on my precise role in this session: "You can be the door." Thus, I became part of the safe container that enabled him to begin to explore his deepest fears while I was entrusted to keep the "scary people" out. The context of "just playing" enabled him to stay engaged in meaningful contact with me (Kestly, 2014; Panksepp, 1998, p.283; Porges, 2011, pp.276–277; Prendiville, 2017a, p.9) as he began to build his emotional digestive system, participate in emotionally corrective experiences, and gain empowerment over the feelings that had previously caused him to dissociate or become hyper-aroused. He began to know himself more fully and build an identity that was separate from those that had abused him.

Tony's worldview was changing and his capacity for hope was being reignited. This was linked to my initial (repeated) task of sorting toys and junk and bringing order. Initially I had to do this in the role of "maid" but later we were both engaged in this as "sister and brother." My commentary during these tasks generally focused on how big a mess there was but also how confident I was that "even very big messes" could be sorted. I wove my way between Non-intrusive Responding, Co-facilitation, and Active Utilization (Yasenik and Gardner, 2012) so as to leave Tony in the lead but allow me to make comments that I felt applied to the here and now (my sorting task) and would have relevance in challenging what I saw as Tony's confusion and belief that his own situation might be beyond repair. I remembered back to the initial session when he had introduced the idea of the workman and my role in that session of delivering mail to the workman. Tony's response to my purposeful use of self seemed to be that of tentatively communicating a shift in his limiting belief in his own play and beyond.

Tony's therapeutic progress was supported by his wisdom in keeping his disclosures outside the playroom—an issue that he struggled with for a time. I could see that he was torn about whether to talk about his experiences within our sessions or not. I held true to my agreement with him that I would not ask questions and allowed him to remain in control of this issue. He made several disclosures to his mother between sessions, and made some partial disclosures, within play, to me. Such disclosures almost inevitably led to disruptions in his capacity to stay engaged in relationship and stifled his ability to communicate symbolically through play; within therapy, he needed play more than he needed verbal dialogue. Between sessions he would occasionally make voice recordings that he wanted his mother to share. He needed to tell his story but knew on a deep level that he also needed to maintain the dramatic distance that symbolic play provides (Panksepp, 1998, p.283). The paradox is that play allows us to get closer to that which we might otherwise seek to suppress, yet need to explore and gain mastery over. At this point, the therapy could only remain safe for him to use as part of his healing if it did not turn into a space where issues were discussed on a conscious level. He needed to keep the play therapy space fully available for his symbolic and metaphorical play. He needed a separate space for disclosures.

Turning point 2: a real police person

Tony asked me to find "a real police person" so that he could tell his story. He wanted to tell what had happened to him and the other children that he had witnessed being abused. He was now moving above the consciousness dimension while still engaging in metaphorical play. He took to literally "whistle-blowing" in sessions while awaiting his appointment with a very child-centered policewoman. He explained that when the whistle blew, I would know that he really needed me. At this stage, high-intensity role play centered on giving me roles in which I was truly helpless, liable to be punished, and where my life was at risk. I gave language to my fears within the play and in keeping with the roles ascribed to me. In his more powerful roles, Tony did not hesitate to tell me that I could indeed die. I amplified my comments, highlighting my need for help and my belief that I should be safe and that it was not okay for me to be hurt. It was clear that Tony was consciously aware of the significance of some of this play and the psycho-educational components were important to him. He repeated it regularly so as to hear the message more. I am also aware that children perceive permissiveness as understanding (Rogers, 1976), so I knew that it was enough for me to speak in character rather than move into Quadrant II by engaging in a conversation about his lived world experiences.

At home, Tony's post-traumatic play was very evident. When he finally met the policewoman, he was very impressed as we met in a police station and she wore full uniform and took us both on a tour of the facility, including the cells. He was reassured that the police force could monitor CCTV cameras on the streets outside and were genuinely committed to making sure children would be kept safe. Over the following months Tony met this policewoman regularly and made full disclosures. This interaction freed him up to make leaps in his therapy process.

Emergence of true healing play

Tony now had a separate space for disclosures and thus could focus exclusively on play within our sessions. He could now regress to earlier stages in his development—stages before trauma distorted his development—and use his play to support deep healing. He gradually moved from role play (boss/slave theme moved to superhero play and then to nurturance theme), to projective play (emergency themes), and then to embodiment play. This indicated that Tony was now ready to rework his trust and boundary issues at the level of his physical identity. This was a real risk (and a shift from the ritualized play that had predominated early sessions) and was a measure of the strength of the relationship that we shared. Now he could make even more use of me as a part of his healing. For my part, I continued to make more use of myself therapeutically while in role by describing the somatic elements of my experiences and by naming the emotions that were aroused (Appendix A: 4 Self-System). I did this in a way that was designed not to interrupt the play but would provide a language that might be of use to Tony in learning to recognize and name his own physiological reactions. The path was prepared for a journey into embodied play.

A big shift at this point was the replacement of the "sorting messes" play that had focused on concrete materials (projective play) with the introduction of really messy play that allowed Tony to experience his skin as a boundary. Expansive finger, hand, and arm painting scenes emerged. There was a lot of paint and water covering a big metal board placed on a huge white plastic sheet. Squishy, messy play allowed us to pour and splash and squeeze globs of paint and spread them out so that the full mess was visible and could not be ignored. Paint dripped from our hands and arms. It spread over our big aprons, and got smeared on our faces. And all the while we both repeated (for this was now a shared language), "No matter how big the mess, we can sort it out!" And we did. Session after session saw us making a huge mess and then cleaning it up until the metal board, the plastic sheet, and we ourselves were spotless again. Other play at this stage raised themes of trickery: what is fake and what is real; what are our real names; is the baby being fed maggots or food? Tony was beginning to test reality, question his own cognitive distortions, and trust himself more. This prepared the ground for brief shifts into Quadrant I: Active Utilization (Yasenik and Gardner, 2012). Initially I incorporated psycho-educational components into the work by making general statements (as appropriate to the play scene) that would challenge distortions in his thinking and his worldview. I muttered that children are supposed to be kept safe, grownups are not meant to hurt children, that big people who hurt children sometimes say things that are not true. As we were tricked I made a linking interpretation (Yasenik and Gardner, 2012) by commenting that what happened was like what a named perpetrator had done to him—said things that were not true to confuse him.

Turning point 3: therapist to clean the mess

The next turning point came after five sessions of that really messy play when Tony concluded making the big mess and then stated: "Eileen, you don't have a cleaning-up rule." I replied that I did not, while being very aware that in each of the previous 19 sessions Tony had always insisted on tidying everything up before the end of the session. It was great to hear his next comment: "You can clean it all up so!"

Turning point 4: exploring brains and coming back to life

Finger painting now took a new turn. Instead of making a tactile mess and cleaning up, Tony began to use finger paint to make brains. He was trying to figure out how his Dad's brain was so different to his Mum's, his own, and mine. He used these images to explore his perception of the difference in all four brains. It was clear that he was now able to identify differences between his thoughts and others'. Tony had brought us directly into Quadrant II: Open Discussion and Exploration (Yasenik and Gardner, 2012). He no longer saw himself as "all bad." It was getting safer for him to begin to know himself in a different way; his capacity to differentiate (Harter, 2012) was growing.

Turning point 5: doll turning back into a boy

In a very dramatic piece of role play, Tony explored his own physical identity in relation to "turning into" a doll and having to turn back into a boy. When playing hide and seek, he wondered if he could be seen, and in the process became aware of his own physical features and drew attention to his personal traits. At this point he was beginning to show signs of integration. He delighted in sharing newly found confidence in his abilities and talked about himself as a kind person and a good friend in ways that showed he was redefining himself and recognizing his positive traits (Harter, 2012).

Turning point 6: capacity to sequence grows

Projective play also re-emerged in a new form. He explored emotions and past experiences of powerlessness in his play. This led to expressions of ambivalence and anger before his stories became more coherent, logical, and sequenced. We began to see beginnings, middles, and endings. Resolutions appeared more frequently. Play disruptions diminished and the energy level in sessions dropped.

Turning point 7: perpetrators are annihilated in play

Everything becomes calmer for a while—until the police investigation steps up a pace as he makes more explicit disclosures in relation to multiple offenders and multiple child victims. He is stronger now but intense anger comes to the surface and begins to be clearly expressed within his sessions. He draws pictures of perpetrators and begins to annihilate them by running forward and throwing wet clay at the images he has drawn on a wall-mounted blackboard while he shouts all manner of insults and expresses his feelings of pain and hatred. The throwing of many pieces of clay is accompanied by verbalization of the many reasons for his strong feelings and often includes reference to the acts perpetrated on himself and others. I am enlisted to copy his movements and his utterances and told to run faster, shout louder, and throw harder to "increase the gravity." This play is on a very conscious level. The "bad Dad" was no longer viewed as acting in response to the "naughty" behaviors of his son, as a means of trying to teach him to behave. Tony does not need the distance of symbolic play at this stage. His inappropriate feelings of guilt have diminished and his window of tolerance (Siegel, 2012) has broadened sufficiently for him to remain regulated while expressing previously repressed emotions and achieving cathartic relief. He is thinking about his feelings rather than experiencing them on an unconscious level.

Turning points 8 and 9: looking forward and a period of integration

Tony was ready to claim his own identity. At age six he asked why he shared the same surname as his Dad and decided that he no longer wanted it. He told his teacher that he was changing his name and adopted his mother's surname. He wrote his new name on all his school books. He drew a picture of himself at three stages: as a baby, now, and "old" (age seven). The future looked bright.

We began a new circuit of E-P-R, this time with a clear focus on practicing skills for the future, achieving developmental tasks, and demonstrating mastery. He invited his Mum in for part of each session and set up games that allowed him to practice being assertive, using a loud voice, saying "No! Stop!" and "Go away!" in response to being tricked, and he began to make lists with plans for the future. His embodiment play focused on demonstrating his physical prowess as he engaged in circus tricks and tackling obstacle courses. I celebrated as he returned to the earliest stages of embodiment development and moved through the three sub-stages (Prendiville, 2010). He curled up in a large bean-bag and asked to be cradled, sung to, and rocked. I was delighted by his ability to seek and accept this nurturing full body experience that is at the core of experiencing the body self (Sub-stage 1: I am/have a body) and is the root of a positive self-image and feelings of security. Play expanded to include trust falls, being carried and swung, and gradually moving out into the world as a separate person again. The next round of circus play (Sub-stage 2: What my body can do) was even more elaborate than the previous round. He now became the star of each act—the strongest person, the best juggler, the most skilled acrobat, and so on. I saw lots of physical competence play, demonstrating his awareness of what his body could do and the control he had over it. He also began to highlight positive traits that he shares with people he admires. Tony's self-confidence was growing.

The emergence of Prendiville's (2010) Sub-stage 3 (I am me, I am not you) was liberating: a brief return to finger painting (and only fingers—not whole arms this time!) to allow for cleaning up—"washing all the bad away." Play was flowing and joyful, the sessions were easy, and we enjoyed a series of very playful sessions. Games that Tony had played with intense energy and with disruptions in the past now reappeared with no evidence of being related to unresolved issues. Tony was enjoying a period of integration. The world was good.

Turning point 10: reclaiming the self and the Safe Children's Society

Tony began to recognize, within his symbolic play, his own healing. He underwent surgery to remove all the "bad glands" in his neck and his "bad heart." His teddy also needed this repair as "they did it to him too." Following this play he announced, "See how strong a man gets when he is strong." Tony showed that he was developing a clearer autobiographical self. He was now able to hold on to a here and now sense of self that acknowledged past experiences and held hope for future self as strong, competent, and confident. He expressed wishes that he had had "a better life…more like other kids" but expected that the future would be good and he would have "a nice life after all." He set up a "Safe Children's Society" with the following mission statement—"We support children"—and the following declarations:

- It's alright to be scared.
- Children have security rights.
- Children need to be safe.
- Children *have* to be safe.

As members of this Safe Children's Society we are "Making a brilliant job of our careers" and are successful in putting "a bit of goodness" into children's lives, making them very happy with no more bad dreams. Our society has managed to stop all abuse of children and contained the perpetrators! Tony announces: "Children are going to grow up to be big people and are going to make a better world."

Turning point 11: more room in my head for learning

The family court denied Tony's father application for access and refused him permission to re-enter his application. Tony greeted me with whoops of joy and shouts of "We won!!!" He announced: "Now I have more room in my head for learning." This led to a shift as cognitive competence emerged in play with a focus on academic tasks in school. Tony also began to look to the future and made himself a safety book and safety plans. This brought him into a more cognitive stage in his healing where we began to explore the various lies that he had been told by the offenders and Tony sought to understand more about the way in which he had been groomed and deliberately confused. His I-self was constructing a Me-self (Harter, 2012) that could evaluate and did not have to hold on to the introjections that had previously negatively impacted his sense of self and his worldview.

Tony set up games in which he now became the one "setting traps" for his father and we engaged in battles with him that we always won. We were equipped with "advanced powers" and tools and exercised "extreme caution." He was well and truly annihilated both in the role-play games and when making clay figures to represent him and removing body parts.

As our therapy reached the final stages it was clear that Tony had found a way to regain dignity, empowerment, and control (Norton and Norton, 2008). When I last met him for a check-in session a couple of years after his therapy had ended, Tony told me that when he was small he felt "sad and weird," he "hurt inside," and was "mixed up and weird." And now? Well, now, Tony tells me he has a "tremendous, terrifically good life."

Turning points summary

The following table illustrates the considerable movement and integration that occurred during Tony's therapy process, and possible factors, such as therapist use of self and support in weaving between quadrants, that, over time, contributed to a stronger and healthier sense of self.

Stage in process	Quadrant	Turning points	What contributed to the turning point?
Session 1: Therapeutic Touchstone	QII		• This laid the ground for development of therapeutic relationship
Initial sessions: sorting junk, boss/slave role play, building safety	QIII		• Need for confluence diminished and themes of conflict could emerge
Exploration of protection: shields, helmets, body armor	QIII	1. You can be the door	• Tony experiencing himself as in control within sessions • Play as medium

Safety established. Shift from my play role as "maid" or "slave" to "sister"	QIII, QIV, and QI Weaving process		• Repeated commentary that "even big messes can be sorted"
Tony's attempts to disclose and the impact of this on diminishing his healing play	QIV but initiated by the child	2. Whistle blowing and finding a real police person	• Tony's need to keep therapy space free for play rather than verbal processing
Using play to highlight need for help and how children should be safe	QII		• Psycho-educational component being held within play contributed to a shift in Tony's worldview
New themes: superheroes, emergencies, and nurturance	QIII, QII, and QI Weaving process—minute by minute		• Therapist making use of somatic responses aroused in role play (intended to give language to perceived somatic components of Tony's implicit memories)
Squishy messy painting	QIII		• Brings Tony back to embodiment play where healing of physical identity issues can begin
Themes of trickery	Brief shifts into QI (from QIII)	3. Therapist to clean the mess	• Testing reality, questioning cognitive distortions
Exploring brains	QIV (led by Tony)	4. Individuals think differently	• Capacity to differentiate is growing
Seeing himself	QIII	5. Doll turning back into a boy	• Awareness of own traits is heightened
Resolutions appear in stories	QIII	6. Capacity to sequence grows	• Beginnings, middles, and endings in play scripts • Therapist summarizing play sequences

cont.

Stage in process	Quadrant	Turning points	What contributed to the turning point?
Perpetrators are annihilated in play	QII (child led)	7a. Blame is assigned to perpetrators: child is no longer responsible 7b. Changes surname so no longer shares this with offender	• Physical play accompanied by verbalizations • Cathartic relief • Awareness of grooming tactics grow
Practices new roles and skills (E-P-R) Free-flowing play	QII (child led)	8. Makes plans for future 9. Identifies positive traits he shares with admired others. A period of integration	• Re-experiencing all E-P-R stages in healing play • Nurturance, competency, and assertiveness play
Reclaiming the self	QII (child led)	10. "See how strong a man gets when he is strong." Clearer autobiographical self	• Safe Children's Society—new hope for the future
Cognitive competency play	QII (child led)	11. "Now I have more room in my head for learning"	• Court decision • Understanding of the grooming process

References

Axline, V. (1947) *Play Therapy*. New York: Ballantine.
Gil, E. (2006) *Helping Abused and Traumatized Children: Integrating Directive and Nondirective Approaches*. New York: Guilford Press.
Harter, S. (2012) *The Construction of the Self: Developmental and Sociocultural Foundations* (2nd edn). New York: Guilford Press.
Jennings, S. (1999) *An Introduction to Developmental Playtherapy*. London: Jessica Kingsley Publishers.
Kestly, T.A. (2014) *The Interpersonal Neurobiology of Play: Brain-Building Interventions for Emotional Well-Being*. New York: Norton.
Norton, C. and Norton, B.E. (2008) *Reaching Children through Play Therapy: An Experiential Approach* (3rd edn). Denver, CO: White Apple Press.
Panksepp, J. (1998) *Affective Neuroscience: The Foundations of Human and Animal Emotions*. New York: Oxford University Press.

Perry, B.D. (2006) The Neurosequential Model of Therapeutics: Applying Principles of Neuroscience to Clinical Work with Traumatized and Maltreated Children. In N.B. Webb (ed.) *Working with Traumatized Youth in Child Welfare.* New York: Guilford Press. Accessed on 23/05/2018 at https://childtrauma.org/wp-content/uploads/2013/08/Perry-Bruce-neurosequentialmodel_06.pdf

Porges, S.W. (2011) *The Polyvagal Theory: Neurophysiological Foundations of Emotions, Attachment, Communication, Self Regulation.* New York: Norton.

Prendiville, E. (2010) The Play Therapy Process: Interventions with Children with Attachment Difficulties. Key Note Address. Romanian Play Therapy and Dramatherapy Association Annual International Conference, 2 October.

Prendiville, E. (2014) The Therapeutic Touchstone. In E. Prendiville and J. Howard (eds) *Play Therapy Today: Contemporary Practice for Individuals, Groups, and Parents.* London: Routledge.

Prendiville, E. (2017a) Neurobiology for Psychotherapists. In E. Prendiville and J. Howard (eds) *Creative Psychotherapy: Applying the Principles of Neurobiology to Play and Expressive Arts-Based Practice.* London: Routledge.

Prendiville, E. (2017b) Neurobiologically Informed Psychotherapy. In E. Prendiville and J. Howard (eds) *Creative Psychotherapy: Applying the Principles of Neurobiology to Play and Expressive Arts-Based Practice.* London: Routledge.

Rogers, C. (1976) *Client Centred Therapy.* London: Constable.

Schaefer, C.E. and Drewes, A. (2014) *The Therapeutic Powers of Play: 20 Core Agents of Change* (2nd edn). New Jersey: Wiley.

Siegel, D. (1999) *The Developing Mind: Toward a Neurobiology of Interpersonal Experience.* New York: Guilford Press.

Siegel, D. (2012) *The Developing Mind: How Relationships and the Brain Interact to Shape Who We Are* (2nd edn). New York: Guilford Press.

Terr, L. (1983) Play Therapy and Psychic Trauma: A Preliminary Report. In C.E. Schaefer and K.J. O'Connor (eds) *Handbook of Play Therapy.* New York: John Wiley & Sons.

Yasenik, L. and Gardner, K. (2012) *Play Therapy Dimensions Model: A Decision-Making Guide for Integrative Play Therapists.* London: Jessica Kingsley Publishers.

5

TURNING POINTS IN TREATING COMPLEX TRAUMA IN CARLOS, A FOSTER CARE CHILD

—— ATHENA A. DREWES ——

Case introduction

Carlos, an African-American boy, has been a fostered child on and off since age four. His birth and early childhood were within the normal range of development and attachment. However, as his early years progressed, his mother was not able to care for him due to her drug use, domestic violence, and fear of her own potential physical abuse of him when she was angry. When Carlos (a compilation of several cases and non-identifying name for purposes of anonymity) was four years of age, his mother called the Department of Social Services (DSS) and asked for help due to her feeling overwhelmed and on the verge of physical abuse. Feeling that she was doing the right thing, since she had no family or other resources to assist her, she was hoping that the DSS would offer her in-home services. Instead, the DSS placed Carlos in foster care. Over the next year, his mother did well in attending programs and seeking help with her drug use. During that time she attended family play therapy sessions with myself and her son, working on better communication, limit setting, and parenting. Because of her progress and therapist advocacy of reunification of the family (as well as Carlos's desire and verbal pleas to return to his mother's care), Carlos was returned to his mother at age six. Unfortunately, after six months his mother became involved in a rocky relationship with a man who was dealing drugs and was physically aggressive toward her and threatening to Carlos. There was domestic violence involved and the police were periodically called to the home. During one of the last times the police were involved, the mother became verbally and physically aggressive toward them in trying to prevent Carlos from being taken from her. Carlos witnessed the police rough-handling his mother and experienced having the police put him in the police car to be out of harm's way. All of which was traumatic for him. At that point, at age eight, he was again removed from his mother's care and placed into foster care, with the same agency as before, where he has since remained. He stayed in his initial foster home for six months, but due to defiant behavior and verbal and at times physical aggression, the foster mother had Carlos removed. He was placed in two other homes over a span of a year and a half, both of which failed to manage his behaviors, until he arrived at his current and final foster home.

While his mother worked hard to break the cycle of being involved with men who were abusive and dealt drugs, she repeatedly found herself back in these abusive circumstances. Subsequently, the DSS filed the court for termination of her parental rights, while they also worked with her to voluntarily surrender but be able to have some contact. By surrendering her parental rights, it would shorten court involvement, and would allow her son to be adopted into a "forever home" with a family that could give him the stability and nurturance he needed. Rather than have absolutely no contact or information about her son, Carlos's mother voluntarily signed over her rights, with the agreement that she would receive photos and an update of how he was doing at least twice a year. Carlos was in a foster home that indicated that they would adopt him, and this was the convincing factor for his mother to sign over her rights.

When Carlos was ten years old, his foster father suddenly got ill and went into hospital for surgery. Due to complications of the surgery, and possible hospital negligence, he died unexpectedly within a few days, leaving Carlos bereft of a positive male figure. Carlos and his foster father were very close. The foster father was a strong, positive role model. He would speak with Carlos about how he should act, treat women, and be as an African-American male, and gave him space to talk about his childhood and loss of his mother. As Carlos had grown up without any male figures in his life, and without knowing anything about his biological father, the foster father soon became a strong male role model and father figure in his life. Upon his death, the foster mother, who was not as nurturing as the foster father and often was verbally punitive, became depressed and lacked motivation to interact with Carlos. In spite of working full-time, she was unable to give Carlos more than the minimal basic care, often sleeping a lot after coming home from work, leaving Carlos on his own, or having her grown sons watch him after school and discipline him. The foster mother was often verbally harsh, and sometimes physical, toward Carlos, who was having a difficult time dealing with his feelings of grief, anger, and sadness over having lost first his biological mother and then his pre-adoptive foster father. As a result Carlos became verbally and physically aggressive in his behaviors at home with the foster mother and her grandchildren and also in school: pushing peers, throwing over tables and chairs, and threatening his teacher when upset. Carlos's anger would explode outwards, like a volcanic eruption, with no warning. He would scowl, tighten his fists, and then strike out or yell and curse over what often seemed like the smallest issue or incident. Carlos had little insight into what was making him feel so full of rage, nor how best to control it. In addition, he gained a lot of weight as a side-effect of the psychiatric medications he was taking to lessen his aggressive and angry behaviors and depression. As a result, he was heavier and taller than other children his age, which led to adults thinking he was older and thereby expecting more mature behavior from him (and becoming intolerant of even some age-appropriate behaviors). As a result, Carlos evidenced depression, low self-esteem, impulsivity, and poor judgment and problem-solving skills. Carlos was constantly seeking food because he was hungry and to help self-soothe and was being restricted by his foster mother from taking additional food. Consequently, he was always feeling hungry, unnourished, and irritable.

Carlos was constantly at risk of removal from his small-sized special education class and put on restriction from riding on the school bus due to his physical aggression toward peers. He was often anxious and worried as he feared removal from his current foster home because of repeated threats voiced by his foster mother and upsetting comments from her adult children about how he did not belong in their family. The foster mother's fear was that she would not be able to ever adopt him, especially as a single parent, and be able to manage his behaviors if they became even more physical in nature, especially given his large physical size.

This chapter presents his journey, ages 8 to 11, with a total of 95 sessions utilizing play therapy, with play as therapy and play in therapy from a prescriptive integrative approach. It was a circuitous journey through complex trauma with underlying grief, loss, feelings of abandonment, bullying, and family systemic issues, expressed through aggression and emotional dysregulation with several significant turning points. As a result Carlos is now a boy with self-esteem, self-regulation, and coping strategies along with more satisfying ways of being. While Carlos continues in therapy and in foster care until he is 18 years of age, he has accepted that his current foster mother will not adopt him. He is now able to think about the future and reunification with his mother, and adequately manages his behaviors, with agency staff support, to the point of no longer needing a special education class and is back in his regular school district classrooms. Through weekly child-led play therapy and directive play-based approaches integrated into play therapy, Carlos was able to gain insight into and safely release the anger he felt, as well as learn better ways to self-soothe and deal with his sudden negative emotions and consequent disruptive anger. He could then start to find pleasure in his accomplishments and age-appropriate abilities.

Theoretical orientation

Prescriptive integrative therapy (Drewes, 2011) has gained prominence since the 1990s. This approach was previously called eclecticism, but integration or integrative has become the preferred term—the blending together of theory, technique, and common factors in one interactive and coordinated means of treatment (Norcross, 1987).

Basic concepts, goals, and techniques

- *Technical eclecticism*—This prescriptive approach looks at the best treatment for the individual person, at this time, for this symptom/problem. Treatment is guided by research of what has worked best for others in the past with similar problems and having similar characteristics.

- *Theoretical integration*—This takes the best elements of two or more approaches to therapy and blends them with the expectation that the result will be more than the sum of the two separate therapies. The emphasis is on integrating the underlying theories along with integration of therapy techniques. Consequently, this result leads to a new direction for both practice and research.

- *Common factors*—This approach ascertains the underlying core ingredients that the different therapies share in common. The goal is to come up with the simplest and most effective treatment based on those commonalities. Grencavage and Norcross (1990) came up with 89 different commonalities in 50 research publications. Schaefer (1999) and Schaefer and Drewes (2014) ascertained that there were at least 20 core agents of change involved in play therapy that made treatment successful: self-expression and gradual exposure; access to the unconscious; metaphorical insight; narrative creation; abreaction; stress inoculation; counter-conditioning; catharsis; distraction; physical health; sublimation; attachment and relationship enhancement; moral judgment; power/control; competence; self-control; creative problem-solving, divergent thinking, and coping ability; improvement in cognition and literacy; and reality testing and behavioral rehearsal.

- *Assimilative integration*—The clinician is required to have a strong grounding in one theoretical system but a willingness to selectively incorporate or assimilate practices and views from other systems. This approach combines the advantages of a single coherent theoretical system with the flexibility of a broader range of technical interventions from multiple systems. Rather than throw away the one theoretical approach learned, there is a reworking of the approach resulting in gradually incorporating parts and methods from other approaches and molding it into a new form (Norcross, 2005). For example, the assimilative integrative approach that I utilize within therapy sessions would look like this for a particular session:

- After meeting the client, there would be a series of strictly non-directive sessions for assessment, rapport, and therapeutic alliance building, and establishing emotional safety with the therapist and room.

- Five-minute check in—how the past week was, any calls from parent/school, homework tried from the last session; unfinished issues related to the past session; changes in future sessions due to vacation or holiday—transparency and congruence by the therapist.

- 15 minutes: directive technique around behavioral issues, treatment plan items, affect regulation, feelings identification, developing coping skills.

- 20 minutes' non-directive, child-led play.

- Five minutes' clean up with deep breathing and mindfulness techniques.

Prescriptive-integrative play therapy allows you to individualize and tailor-make each session for each client. It is not a one size fits all approach, as research has shown that no *one* treatment approach or theory is able to work across all diagnoses. It is a combination of types of interventions—supportive, directive, and exploratory. The different forms of interventions utilized (such as child-led and more cognitive-behavioral play-based techniques) are complementary and *not* contradictory. However, an integrative approach does require the play therapist to be flexible and playful in their treatment approach and versed in both forms of treatment. The play therapist needs to learn how to blend these approaches and styles of working, especially when working with complex trauma. The integrative approaches can be utilized within the session and/or across sessions.

First, the therapist needs to start with an empathic connection in order to forge the therapeutic relationship. This can be through initial sessions utilizing strictly a non-directive, child-led approach and then moving into a more directive, play-based approach as indicated. These initial sessions allow the therapist to see the world through the child's eyes and heart, and assess the child's developmental and emotional levels, systems dynamics, dependency/independence of the child, emotional regulation and feelings identification abilities, as well as play skills and themes.

The therapist should also have a solid grounding in at least one theoretical approach from which to use as a lens in looking at the treatment issues and thinking of the treatment planning and dynamics. The ability to theorize in several ways of working and theoretical understanding allows you to individualize and tailor-make each session for each client. Integrative play therapy does not have a linear model of psychopathology and dysfunction. Rather it views psychopathology and dysfunction as multi-causational, with equal weight given to various aspects of personal functioning, seen as blended and unified: cognitive, dynamic, interpersonal, behavioral. Treatment does not jump from one protocol to another, but rather uses a wider array of tools to work with. Stein and Kendall (2004) recommend a three-pronged integrated approach to trauma and specifically child sexual abuse: cognitive/behavioral interventions for problematic behaviors; building new skills; and psychodynamic interventions to help integrate traumatic memories and emotions, along with buried parts of self. The integrative play therapist also needs to pay close attention to systemic issues, particularly family interactions, and sequences of action and reaction, in order to root out any that maintain and reinforce symptoms.

As psychological disorders for children and teens are frequently multi-layered, complex, and multi-determined, a multi-faceted treatment approach is required. Often there are overlapping symptoms and diagnoses, such as anxiety and attentional problems, along with phobias and behavioral issues that underlie complex trauma (domestic violence, community violence, sexual and physical abuse, attachment issues, foster care, all combined). Having to deal with such multi-faceted diagnoses forces the therapist to wear multiple hats and become skillful in changing from one therapeutic stance to another in order to meet the needs of the child and people in the child's life. For example, the therapy may start with a child-centered approach to build empathic relationship and safety within the settings, then deal with evocative, conflictual issues in play that require setting limits, reflection, and understanding play themes and issues, then move toward needing to engage the parent or school system or classroom teacher with psycho-education, and finally move toward directive work addressing affect regulation and alternative coping strategies for optimal behavioral functioning.

Treatment of trauma requires non-verbal strategies that utilize symbolic language, creativity, and pretend play (Gil, 2006). Treatment needs to include a neuro-sequential model of working with the amygdala through expressive arts, rhythmic, patterned movement, and soothing activities (Perry and Hambrick, 2008; van der Kolk, 2005). This requires a flexible approach that can utilize both non-directive and directive approaches.

Case study conceptualization

Having been trained originally in psychodynamic play therapy, it is my initial approach and theoretical framework and lens with which to conceptualize the treatment and sessions. Consequently, I always utilize a child-led approach during the initial stages, as well as during sessions, in order to create the therapeutic alliance, feelings of safety by the child within the therapeutic holding space and with the therapist, and rapport building through a more passive, reflective, stance (Quadrant III). Over the years, I found that "one size does not fit all" therapy situations, especially when working with complex trauma, sexual abuse, and attachment issues. Consequently, I became prescriptive and integrative in incorporating the theoretical framework and treatment approaches of cognitive behavioral, attachment, and systems lenses into my play therapy treatment approaches within and across therapy sessions. I needed to work prescriptively in finding the best treatment approach for this particular child's issues and symptoms at this time.

I move back and forth between utilizing a child-led, non-directive approach (Quadrant III) and inserting directive, play-based techniques within the sessions (Quadrant IV). The amount of time would vary being spent in either direction within a session or even across sessions depending on many multi-faceted aspects of the individual child: developmental and cognitive level; emotional level and issues; symptoms and treatment issues; level of self-regulation and attachment; ability to play and family; and school systems and dynamics.

Using the Play Therapy Dimensions Model, my initial approach would be that of working in Quadrant III: Non-intrusive Responding. Consequently, during these child-led sessions I view myself as operating simultaneously on three levels of awareness and interaction as the therapist: the observer, the detective, and the player (as led by the child). I am first observing the child's play in many quadrants and across dimensions: for example, is the child's play age appropriate? What are the child's strengths? What are areas of deficit? Can the child tolerate frustration? How immersed is the child in the play and can the play be sustained over time? Where are the breaks in the play perhaps due to anxiety or flooding of affect? Is the child independent or dependent in their play process and relationship to the therapist? At the same time (or moving up and down this continuum), I am internally, mentally, creating hypotheses based on what I am observing and what I may know about the child's history, presenting problems, and treatment plan: for instance, who could this figure represent? Why did the play break off at this moment? Why did they ask me whether I am married and have children at this point in the session and treatment process? Could this scenario be an enactment of their life experience that is known or not known? Finally, I am engaged in the child's play to the extent that they want my involvement. I am formulating my own prescriptive approach to what might be the result of the observations: sitting quietly and reflecting the play (Quadrant III: Non-intrusive Responding) or actively joining in as per the direction of the child's internal script (using theatrical asides to ask "What should I say next?" or "What should I do?") or direction (Quadrant II: Open Discussion and Exploration and Quadrant IV: Co-facilitation), or whether I need to help in the play process which has become stuck and stagnant. The child has their own internal script, as they are the author, director, producer, and audience wrapped up into one as their play unfolds. Even if a week or more has passed, the child has the unique ability to internally hold onto their story and scene such that once they re-enter the room they can pick up immediately where they left off as though no time has passed at all! As the "player," I am still following the child's lead, but I am trying to put the pieces together as to what this might mean and how best to reply, respond, and reflect (verbal use of self). Do I speculate about the play ("I wonder what will happen next" or "I wonder if helpers might be able to come in to offer aid")? Do I help to expand the play or just stay with the play and reflect internally upon the intuitive responses felt within me (emotional use of self) and even physiological feelings (anxious feelings, intrusive thoughts or emotions)? I am in tune, on both an intuitive and physiological level, with how the play scenario and activity is going, and can I make sense of it and follow along on the child's journey or is it more of a rollercoaster ride with abrupt shifts, changes, and seemingly contradictory actions or feelings ("Hmmm, first you were doing this, now you are doing that, and then you decided to do this. I am feeling so confused"; or "It feels like no matter what I try my side is always getting defeated. I feel so hopeless and helpless")?

At the start of each session, I am very transparent and congruent in letting the child know what I know (Quadrant II: Open Discussion and Exploration) and in working together on what should be the treatment goals. I do not keep secrets from them, nor try to trick the child with questions that would feel manipulative, such as "How was your week?" when I already have gotten a call from the parent stating the child was suspended from school for aggression. This only leads to the child responding, "Oh it was a great week," and my having to contradict them or indirectly imply they are lying. Rather I am upfront, treating the child with dignity and self-worth, stating that their mother called, told me some information, and that we can use our time and safe space to talk about it or play it out. This time also allows for revisiting the past session, addressing unfinished comments, questions, or issues raised by the child, thereby allowing space for any other conversation that might be needed. I am also very transparent and congruent throughout the session (Appendix A: 2.2 Emotional Self) as well, sharing if I am not feeling well or if I am feeling distracted or uncomfortable with a request to act or play a certain way (such as pretending I am hurting, stabbing, or abusing the child).

After this point, I might become much more directive, working on play-based techniques to address various components of the treatment plan, such as affect regulation, feelings identification, relaxation and mindfulness skill building, problem-solving skills, role playing and social skill building, working on a trauma narrative, and so on (Quadrant IV: Co-facilitation). Children with poor self-regulation and inability to self-soothe due to trauma (e.g. sexual, physical, and verbal abuse, complex trauma), may require flexibility on the part of the therapist as to the number of sessions needed to allow for the utilization of a neuro-sequential model (Perry and Hambrick, 2008) of utilizing play therapy materials to help soothe the amygdala (Goodyear-Brown, 2010; Perry and Hambrick, 2008). Having items such as a jump rope, beanbags, clay, goop, nerf ball, small soft balls, rhythm instruments, and yoga movements or stretches can help in relieving tension and angry feelings, and releasing early traumatic memories. Without this initial course of grounding and soothing, the child cannot enter into play or even engage in the treatment process. Once better regulated, the therapist can then move into using the next 15 minutes for more directive work.

After the directive time, the child/teen then has the remainder of the session (about 20 minutes in a 45-minute session) to choose what they want to play with, including the sandtray, use of board games, drawing, expressive arts, and so on. Then as we near the end of the session, time is spent cleaning up (usually by the therapist as I do not make this a mandatory component, as it can usually end up in a power struggle or resistance by the child, which can delay the ending of the session). During the clean up, the child is taught to practice and use mindfulness deep breathing exercises to help in relaxing them as they transition out of the therapy room and to utilize the technique during the week when they feel it is needed.

I let the child know this is the outline of the session, especially with regard to the directive work. During the directive work we are getting into many of the emotionally laden issues that brought them into therapy. Because children would prefer not to go where memories are emotionally charged and painful, they are likely to avoid the topic altogether if possible, even through their play. This is what brought me to become an integrative play therapist, because the sexually abused children I worked with in a residential treatment facility often did not bring out their abuse issues during non-directive play. If they avoided the topic, even in play, and you did not bring it up, it was fine with them. And if you chose not to talk about it, or work on it, then they speculated that perhaps you could not handle their rage, fury, and volcanic eruptions or were afraid to deal with them. And so, a dance ensued, of waiting for the important issues to emerge (by the therapist) and seeing how long therapy could go on without bringing them out (by the child). But by having a time-limited section to the treatment where such emotionally charged issues could be addressed safely, the child was able to tolerate the work needing to be done. Once the directive period of time ended, I would be sure to let the child know we are finished. I would then give the child the choice as to whether or not they wished to continue with the activity, or move on to the child-led time. Depending on the age of the child, some would continue with the directive play-based tasks they were working on, while the majority would choose to move on to the child-led time in order to leave behind the emotionally charged activities.

Therapy process: turning points and emergence of self
Engagement phase of treatment: sessions 1–10 (age eight)

> *The engagement phase was spent predominantly in Quadrants II and III building a therapeutic relationship and felt safety in the therapy room and with the therapist. The turning points (Quadrant IV) evolved through anger expression, attachment play, and attachment building.*

Carlos inevitably would enter the room with his head down, a scowl on his face, and at times pulling the hood of his sweatshirt over his head. He would lumber in, stomping his feet, sighing heavily, and sit down at the table. Carlos would then put his head down on the table and not look at me nor acknowledge my presence (Quadrant III). If I even greeted him with a simple "good to see you" or "hello," Carlos was quick to anger and would tell me to stop talking and ask, "Why do I even need to come here?"—reflecting his resistance to working on the issues at hand.

During this initial five minutes I would reflect his anger and reluctance to be here, but offer the safety of the space and therapeutic relationship to help him (Quadrant III, Quadrant II). There would be periods of silence between us, and gentle exploration in my talking to him (Quadrant II). I would then share whatever information I had gotten from his foster mother about events that may have transpired over the past week, leaving it to Carlos to talk about this or not (Quadrant II). We would remain in silence depending on whether Carlos would escalate his anger because I was talking to him or he was able to tolerate hearing what I had to say. If he clearly stated he didn't want the therapist to speak directly to him, I would take a monkey puppet from nearby, who I referred to as Freddy (Appendix A: 3.1 Physical Self). This monkey puppet did not talk out loud (as that was his persona), but rather would whisper in my ear anything he wanted said, so that I was his spokesperson! In turn, I would talk out loud to the puppet telling him my thoughts about Carlos and what was happening, reflecting empathically what was being expressed by Carlos (Quadrant III), underlying feelings that might be going on (Quadrant II), and how sad I was that I was not able to connect with him. While Carlos would not acknowledge that he was listening to this discourse between me and the puppet, it was apparent that he took in Freddy's validating comments about not wanting to talk, feeling upset and angry, and not cared about, evidenced through the relaxation of his body, shifting his position to sitting up and not slumping, and eventually taking off his hood. But he still would not look at me. Carlos would then say he was hungry, not having eaten lunch or not gotten a snack on the way to therapy. There would be a discussion as to whether he wanted to ask his foster mother for money to go next door for a snack or have something I always kept for him (Quadrant II). Carlos was often afraid to ask his foster mother, fearing she would reject him and his request, and in fact at times the foster mother was annoyed with him for his attitude toward her in the car or home, and would initially withhold giving him snack money.

In session Carlos could then tolerate using a nerf ball or beanbag to throw against the wall to let out his anger physically and even verbally (Quadrant IV). I would encourage him to say out loud what he was angry about or who he was angry with and what he would like to say to them. Often it was about his foster mother, who had punished him for something he did or said at home or school, and that the punishment felt excessive (restriction from going to play with friends for a week, or going to bed early, which meant no supper). Carlos was then encouraged to say how he would have liked to respond, or a listing of positive things about himself (Quadrant IV). At that point, he was ready to try some deep breathing or mindfulness technique to lower his emotional level and feel better centered. Carlos then used the remaining time to explore the room and utilize whatever he wanted until the end of our session.

Sometimes he would ask to play a card game (War or Gin Rummy or Uno) or board game (usually Sorry!) but he always needed to win. During this time, Carlos would often start to spontaneously share events that might have happened that day or previously in school or at home that were contributing to his anger and try to figure out what was bothering him (consciousness dimension). We then utilized problem-solving skills and coping strategies to help deal with understanding and moderating his behaviors. Each session Carlos would also choose to play hide and seek, turning out the lights and giving me a flashlight (torch) to shine in trying to find him, or the flashlight himself in order to be found (Quadrant III). During hide and seek, I would prolong finding him. I would look under every possible location—tables, chairs, desk, sandtray, and so on—and state, "No, he's not here under here; nope, not under here at all," and with strong affect state, "Oh where oh where could Carlos be? I miss him. I hope I can find him soon" (Quadrant IV). Carlos enjoyed this play, helping to re-establish object constancy and create feelings of being wanted and missed. As I verbalized more and more "I can't even hear him; how will I find him?" he would either shine the flashlight as a signal of his location or make a noise so that I could then finally find him (Quadrant IV). He would ask me to repeat this play again and again, playing hide and seek, over and over, at least three times in each session, resulting in Carlos smiling and laughing, with toddler-like glee, whenever he was found.

We would then end the session with cleaning up and again use a deep breathing or mindfulness technique (directive dimension) to help transition out of the session. He would also utilize them over the week whenever he began to feel angry or upset (and let me know at the next session how it worked or didn't work for him).

Middle phase of treatment: sessions 20–40 (age nine to ten)

During the middle phase, play was mostly in Quadrant IV, with Carlos becoming more fully immersed and co-facilitative. Although themes were often repetitive about loss, abandonment, and hopelessness, Carlos began to become aware of his unconscious communications. Turning points occurred with conscious awareness and feeling validated by the therapist, resulting in a significant decline in physical and verbal abuse toward his foster mother and others in school.

As these initial child-led sessions progressed, Carlos began to feel more comfortable in utilizing the play materials and the sandtray to express his feelings. He was able to enter the session without having his sweatshirt hood over his head or sitting initially in silence. Rather, Carlos began to settle in to eat his snack and would chat about his day and week during the initial five minutes of the session. We would then work for about 15 minutes using various play-based techniques (Quadrant IV: Co-facilitation) to help create coping strategies based on whatever issues he brought up, role play verbal responses he could utilize with peers or his foster mother, or work on feelings identification using the experiences he'd recently had.

Once we finished the directive tasks, Carlos would go to the sandtray. Rather than make an actual "picture in the sand" of his day, he preferred, much like a younger child, to play with the miniatures in the sand. Carlos would draw a line in the sand and divide the sandtray into two. He had one side and I was given the other. He would then choose several skeleton and skeleton-like items for his "team" and would allow me to select some for my side. He then moved to select flying dragons, various aggressive animals (usually lions, tigers, alligators), a few people (man, woman, ninja), marbles and globes, cannon, and a wizard. In turn he would direct me to select similar items so we had the same categories. Occasionally, he would take one of the items I had chosen for his side, diminishing the number of items I could have. The battle was then set. Carlos would establish the rules, which often were only for his "team" and could not be used by me. He would arbitrarily set up a force field that was impenetrable by my team, but my force field was permeable, or his marbles and globes were bombs that wiped out my aggressive animals but his would come alive again after the bombs exploded. My role became more fully immersed and co-facilitative of the play (Quadrant IV). Carlos was able to tolerate me gently shifting the play scenario to allow my "team" to gain advantage or copy Carlos's ever-changing, arbitrary rules and exceptions. He would allow me to "make a move," only to find another exception and then obliterate my army, which he would not allow to come alive again, effectively ending the game and session. Each play scenario would end with all of my "characters" being dead, buried, or overpowered. There was no way to win or outsmart Carlos's army. After repeated re-enactments of this play week after week, I was aware of feelings of not looking forward to the sessions with Carlos because of leaving the play feeling hopeless and helpless in whatever action was taken or tried (Appendix A: 4.1 Embodiment). At this point, I began to make soft interpretations regarding the play, and utilized the Emotional Self to convey Carlos's underlying unconscious communications (Quadrant IV: Co-facilitation and Quadrant I: Active Utilization) that I was feeling (Appendix A: 2.2 Emotional Self). It was as though Carlos's metacommunications were setting up a parallel process within me, understanding on an experiential level what he was going through (Appendix A: 4.1 Embodiment). Carlos was taking me down to the depth of despair, confusion, anger, sadness, and loss that he was feeling. Indeed, he was experiencing feeling very hopeless and helpless in his current life situation. The loss of his foster father, emotional distance of the foster mother, and physical loss of his bio-mother made it hard for him to feel that his world was stable and that there was nothing, he perceived, that he could do to stop it from constantly changing for the worse. This was a significant turning point for Carlos. As we moved through the unconsciousness dimension more into the consciousness dimension through Carlos's awareness of his feelings, experiences, and visual, symbolic representations in his sandplay, along with Carlos being able to truly "hear" on a deep emotional level my validation of his feelings and experiences, his negative behaviors began to change. He was no longer being verbally abusive in school or toward his foster mother. He began to want to get his homework completed and get good grades, basking in the glow of verbal praise and reward for academic achievement. Carlos began to bring homework into the session to complete before choosing to play, so that he got it out of the way. Carlos's teacher started to comment on his increased energy and interest in learning and his high grades were an immediate reflection of this change. Carlos began to more fully embrace his developmental level and sense of achievement and mastery.

Ending phase of treatment: sessions 60–95 (age 10 to 11)

During the ending phase, Carlos's play moved into Quadrant II and moved much more from the unconsciousness to the consciousness dimensions. He dealt with the death of his foster father and was able to face his fears and angry feelings. By the end of therapy, Carlos was able to move into Physical Use of Self (Appendix A) and more age-appropriate co-facilitative play. Significant turning points were when Carlos was able to deal with the loss of his foster father and feelings of abandonment that subsequently resulted in his ability to utilize self-soothing and calming strategies, lessening angry outbursts, and increased joy and positive affect in his daily life and personal interactions.

Through this period the format of the sessions remained approximately the same. Carlos would come in with much better eye contact and emotional investment in the session. The range and depth of his emotions and ability to verbalize and express them markedly increased. During the first five minutes Carlos would initiate discussion about events that he could have handled better. We were productively able to utilize the next 15 minutes in directive play-based techniques utilizing cognitive behavioral therapy (CBT) concepts. Carlos was willing to work on ways to better manage his emotions, and not get so easily angered and explosive; he was more aware of physical correlates to feelings as trigger points with which to then utilize an assortment of coping strategies; and we would rehearse the coping strategies, relaxation methods, and role-play verbalizations he could use when being bullied or feeling angry. During the child-led time, Carlos began to shift his play in the sandtray. There was a noticeable difference in the play scenarios. The "teams" were no longer so adversarial. While the scenarios started out the same, with the selection of miniatures and setting up battle sides in the sandtray, the play process and ultimate outcome was shifting. Carlos would introduce cooperative ways the two sides could team up and help each other; miniatures came back alive on both sides after dying; rules were similar for both sides rather than unfairly dictated by and only used by his side; and the end result of total annihilation was slowly lessening until ultimately it stopped. The ending became more friendly and hopeful; other helpers entered into the scene to help keep peace; friendships formed and cooperation was displayed. Carlos continued to use the same categories of miniatures, but his emphasis started to shift to exploring the issue of loss and death. Carlos would have the male figure die in battle and be buried. He would use the skeletons to sit on top of where the male figure was buried and add marbles as though they were tombstones (moving along the unconsciousness to consciousness dimension). The therapist would at first non-intrusively reflect (Quadrant III) the action and associated feelings. But with repeated enactments over many sessions, it was apparent that Carlos was dealing with the death of his foster father and associated questions and feelings. The therapist moved into Quadrant I: Active Utilization, offering soft interpretations, but also reflective comments about death ("That person can no longer breathe, eat, feel, see, or touch now that he is dead"; "In the real world once dead, he cannot come back to life again"; "One minute he was alive, feeling well, and the next he was suddenly dead"; "Sometimes people think they might have made someone they love die just by their negative behaviors or thoughts"). These reflections led to another significant turning point for Carlos. He was then able to be more direct (consciousness dimension) in verbalizing his feelings and thoughts about his foster father dying so suddenly, expressing his long-held fear that he had somehow contributed to his death by being so negative in his behaviors and actions; worrying that his foster mother would die and leave him abandoned; and trying to understand his biomother's choice to terminate parental rights and leave him. Carlos was able to express his anger and rage that his foster father died just when he might get adopted, how much he missed their time together talking and doing things together, and that there was no other male in his life that he could do these things with. He also was able to explore his rage and underlying sadness and confusion that he felt about his mother signing over her parental rights. This awareness allowed us to be more directive in addressing his fears and feelings (Quadrant II: Open Discussion and Exploration) both during our 15-minute directive time "slot" but also during the child-led play. Carlos was more receptive to talking about the concept of death in general and specifically about the death of his foster father. The use of bibliotherapy about death and being freed for adoption; having the foster mother join part of the sessions to talk about how she was taking care of her health and planned to be around a long time for him, and her commitment for him to remain living in her home; and planning to take Carlos to see the grave of the foster father to get closure—all helped to deepen the turning point around Carlos's losses. We also were able to use physical interventions (Appendix A: 3.1 Physical Self) in helping Carlos vent his anger and rage around loss, death, and feeling abandoned, by safely throwing the beanbag or clay at the wall; using rhythm sticks to bang and pound while offering space for regulation; and playing catch in throwing balls back and forth while talking about emotionally laden feelings and memories. During these physical activities, I was able to move more into Physical Use of Self (Appendix A), as well as in Quadrant IV: Co-facilitation, in directing the activities as well as following Carlos's lead. Sessions continued to end with relaxation and mindfulness techniques to help transition out of the sessions and to practice utilizing them in the home and school during the week.

Toward the end of these sessions (sessions 75–95), Carlos chose to utilize board games more and more, rather than the sandtray or any other materials, ultimately no longer using the sandtray. Initially he would tease and taunt me while playing a board game, to the point of almost becoming a bully, whenever he won and I lost ("You are a loser"; "I am better than you are"; "You can't beat me"). I would often reply instead in role modeling ways (Appendix A: 1.3 Restating Content, Non-intrusive Responding/Co-facilitation), such as "Congratulations. Good job!"; "I didn't win this time, maybe I will next time"; and "I am not so good at Uno, but I am better at chess." A turning point was noticed as Carlos began to start incorporating my words and comments into his way of responding to his win or loss. This change within the therapy time was noticed outside in the school setting and at home. Reports from his teacher and foster mother indicated that Carlos was becoming much less of a bully and turning into a friend and even a "big brother" to other peers who were being bullied. Significant change was noted in his ability to stop himself when he started to feel angry, take some deep breaths, and decide to walk away from the situation (or use other coping strategies) rather than throw a desk or become physical toward a peer. Academically, Carlos was now getting on the Honor Roll, which meant his grades were quite high with no behavioral issues in class. During this time Carlos's demeanor in the therapy sessions was much more relaxed and calmer, with frequent laughter and smiling noted.

Final remarks

This chapter presents a prescriptive integrative play therapy approach that weaves through non-directive and directive dimensions in the journey of Carlos from ages 8 to 11. It covers a total of 95 sessions, journeyed through complex trauma with underlying grief, loss, feelings of abandonment, bullying, and family systemic issues, expressed through aggression and emotional dysregulation with several significant turning points. As a result, Carlos is now a boy with positive self-esteem, self-regulation, and coping strategies along with more satisfying ways of being.

Turning points summary

Stage in process	Quadrant	Turning points	What contributed to the turning point?
Engagement phase	QII and III	Building of a therapeutic relationship and felt safety	• Therapist's consistency in response, reflection, play of hide and seek

cont.

Stage in process	Quadrant	Turning points	What contributed to the turning point?
Engagement phase	QIV	Anger expression, attachment play, and attachment building with therapist	• Directive play using feelings identification, anger release, reflection by the therapist, and establishing object constancy with Carlos
Middle phase	QIV	More fully immersed and co-facilitative in play; repetitive themes of loss, abandonment, hopelessness. Significant decrease in verbal and physical aggression toward foster mother and in school settings	• Unconscious becoming conscious through play and therapist reflection and soft interpretations
Ending phase	QIII	Movement from unconsciousness to consciousness in dealing with death of foster father and facing Carlos's fears and angry feelings. Physical Use of Self and co-facilitative play at age-appropriate level. Carlos was able to express and deal with the death of his foster father and feelings of abandonment	• Directive play activities to help foster feelings expression, therapist reflection, use of sandtray

Ending phase	QI	Active Utilization and soft interpretations about what death was, and fantasies children have about it and causing the death	• Soft interpretations by therapist, use of sandtray to evoke issues around death, burial, loss	
Ending phase	QII	Open discussion during the beginning of session about his previous play themes, links from his daily life to time he spent with foster father	• Directive discussion and invitational exploration by therapist about Carlos's life with his foster father vs. now. • Physical interventions of throwing clay, venting his anger in healthy and helpful ways, practicing directive play-based calming activities (deep breathing, bubbles, playing catch)	

References

Drewes, A.A. (2011) Integrating Play Therapy Theory into Practice. In A.A. Drewes, S.C. Bratton and C.E. Schaefer (eds) *Integrative Play Therapy*. Hoboken, NJ: Wiley.

Gil, E. (2006) *Helping Abused and Traumatized Children: Integrating Directive and Nondirective Approaches*. New York: Guilford Press.

Goodyear-Brown, P. (2010) *Play Therapy with Traumatized Children: A Prescriptive Approach*. Hoboken, NJ: Wiley.

Grencavage, L.M. and Norcross, J.C. (1990) Where are the commonalities among the therapeutic common factors? *Professional Psychology: Research and Practice 21*, 5, 372–378.

Norcross, J.C. (1987) *Casebook of Eclectic Psychotherapy*. New York: Brunner/Mazel.

Norcross, J.C. (2005) A Primer on Psychotherapy Integration. In J.C. Norcross and M.R. Goldfried (eds) *Handbook of Psychotherapy Integration* (2nd edn). Hoboken, NJ: Wiley.

Perry, B.D. and Hambrick, E.P. (2008) The neurosequential model of therapeutics. *Reclaiming Children and Youth 17*, 3, 38–43. Accessed on 23/05/2018 at http://childtrauma.org/wp-content/uploads/2013/08/NMT_Article_08.pdf

Schaefer, C.E. (1999) Curative factors in play therapy. *The Journal for the Professional Counselor 14*, 1, 7–16.

Schaefer, C.E. and Drewes, A.A. (2014) *The Therapeutic Powers of Play: 20 Core Agents of Change*. Hoboken, NJ: Wiley.

Stein, P.T. and Kendall, J. (2004) *Psychological Trauma and the Developing Brain: Neurologically Based Interventions for Troubled Children*. New York: Haworth Press.

van der Kolk, B. (2005) Developmental trauma disorder: Towards a rational diagnosis for children with complex trauma histories. *Psychiatric Annals 35*, 5, 401–408.

6

SHAME CAN GET STUCK IN YOUR THROAT

The Rise of Consciousness for Five-Year-Old Freddy

──── PARIS GOODYEAR-BROWN ────

Case Introduction

Freddy is a four-year-old male who was sexually abused by a male teacher in a faith-based environment. His parents became aware that something was amiss when they walked in on Freddy engaged in inappropriate sexual behavior with his younger brother. The therapeutic work described below all occurred during the first session, as Freddy moved in between different ways of relating to me, exploring and using the space, and moving towards and away from his trauma narrative in ways that were sometimes "told" somatically, sometimes shown through post-traumatic play, and sometimes verbalized overtly. Freddy saw me for around 20 sessions of individual and family work and several parent coaching sessions following this initial joining session. Together we were able to leach the emotional toxicity from his experience and he was able to resume his childhood in hope and health.

Theoretical orientation

The integrative approach allows room for a variety of ways of working (within the broader field of play therapy) to be thoughtfully and intentionally applied within a single therapeutic process, both in response to the client's moment-to-moment demonstrated need and in the larger context of the child's development of self over the continuum of therapy. This approach acknowledges that children and families have many needs on their healing journey and that we may narrow our ability to perceive those needs clearly the moment that we constrict our field of vision to seeing through only one lens. The "need" is communicated through play, words, idiosyncratic behaviors, or symptoms manifested at different junctures in the play therapy process. As the needs of the child are ever-evolving, evidence-informed treatment goals are crafted and understood to be potentially necessary, but are flexibly endorsed over a child's recovery process. The attuned therapist respects the dance with the child, following "the developmental need of the moment."

The Flexibly Sequential Play Therapy (FSPT) model, grounded in attachment theory and developed by myself for trauma work with children and families, allows clinicians to follow the child's demonstrated or expressed need, articulate this need in the form of a "here and now" goal for therapeutic work, and draw from both non-directive and directive approaches, or ways of relating, to facilitate that goal being met (Goodyear-Brown, 2010). FSPT offers clinicians a framework for placing the treatment needs of traumatized children within a general sequence that is evidence informed and developmentally sensitive, while allowing for clinical finesse and a respect for the nuance expressed in the therapeutic relationship to guide the moment-to-moment interactions (see Figure 6.1).

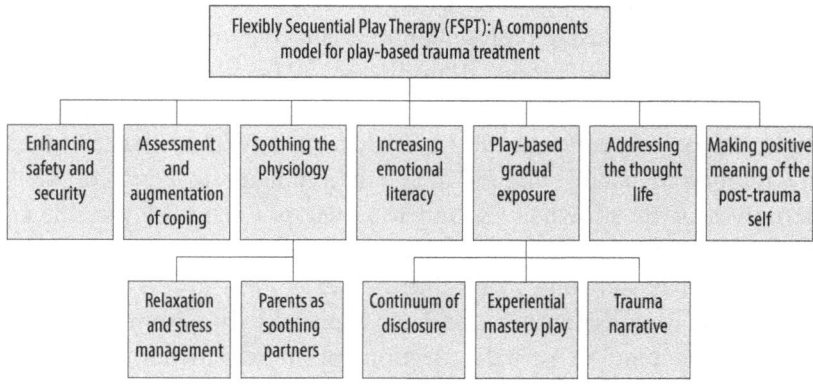

Figure 6.1 Components of FSPT

FSPT recognizes the need for the child to work with content metaphorically, symbolically, linguistically, and non-linguistically, giving permission for all forms of approach to trauma content stored in the body, brain, attachment relationships, and worldview. FSPT values an understanding of bottom-up brain development (Gaskill and Perry, 2012; MacLean, 1990; Perry, 2009; Perry and Hambrick, 2008) and the profound interruptions and implications that traumagenic experiences can have for the child's developing ability to self-soothe, to harness executive functioning systems to make sense of trauma, and to simply feel safe in the world. As Freddy's case unfolds, you will see times in which the immediate need in session is to soothe the physiology through co-regulation, other times where the expressed need is to somatically "tell" the story, other times where he needs open discussion, and still others where Freddy circles back to enhancing safety and security (the first goal within the model) late in treatment. Consciousness is raised as reflections on the play projection are given, the "showing" of sensory perceptions of the trauma are tracked, and Freddy makes cognitive shifts towards integration. The exponential growth in our understanding of brain development and interpersonal neurobiology (Cozolino, 2014; Schore, 2003; Siegel, 2006, 2012) has given us new language to describe the dance towards and away from trauma content that is often seen over a course of play therapy. A focus on the attachment relationship between therapist and client as a vehicle for enhancing regulation and creating a coherent story is the bedrock of the FSPT model. Superseding even the arc of treatment is the importance of understanding the needs of the child at any given moment. The invaluable representation of attachment needs offered by the Circle of Security Project (Powell *et al.*, 2014) acts as a scaffold on which I perch while making my moment-to-moment assessments of how to proceed therapeutically. I work from a premise that children are hungry to make sense of their environments, to craft coherent narratives of their own lives, and to develop a sense of the self as both good and competent. Coherence, however, seems to come in layers and may sometimes look like the Texas Two-Step. A client may have a rise in consciousness, perhaps expressed through a profound evolution in play, in verbal reflection, or in somatic or emotional integration of previously overwhelming trauma content, followed almost immediately by regression in behavior or developmental return to somatic or symbolic processing. As thoughts, feelings, and behaviors are all connected and all experienced in relation to the somatic self (Damasio, 1999), a new cognitive shift or rise in consciousness related to an integration of trauma content may be followed swiftly by what looks like decompensation or disorganization but is actually the disequilibrium (D'Mello and Graesser, 2012; D'Mello *et al.*, 2014) that precedes new levels of somatic comfort with emerging emotions or thoughts engendered by the step towards integration. In this way trauma recovery for children can mirror other developmental processes with children in which periods of equilibrium and disequilibrium need to be respected as necessary components of an iterative process. In practice, the therapist can feel a bit like the heavy silver ball in a pinball machine, ricocheting back and forth between levels of awareness, sometimes even getting all the way down to the somatic heart of the trauma and being catapulted to higher levels of consciousness or to planes of play that provide more safety for a child after the child has offered a nugget of their internal experience. At all times, our job is to remain attuned to the child as they lead the dance. As FSPT practitioners grow in their ability to "dance" with the child, the pinball effect becomes more comfortable, certainly more expected, and even enjoyable.

Case study conceptualization

When Freddy came to treatment, he had just disclosed his abuse to his parents, was engaging in sexually reactive behavior, was exhibiting unusual aggression, was manifesting symptoms of separation anxiety, and was moving from periods of intense activity to periods of intense withdrawal from family interactions and previously pleasurable activities. He was having difficulty finding his internal balance, swinging wildly from hyper-arousal to hypo-arousal (Ogden, Minton and Pain, 2006). Therapeutic work with Freddy was grounded in an understanding that he had endured injuries to the developing sense of self at the hands of a trusted adult. We move forward with the hypothesis that the interpersonal nature of the sexual violations he endured may have led to potentially global interruptions of his development (van der Kolk, 2014). In other words, he may have delays or differences in his social, cognitive, or emotional development, and is likely to have had neurophysiological experiences during his abuse that would have led to distorted extremes in his vagal responses (Porges, 2011) and potential dysregulation of his autonomic nervous system (Corrigan, Fisher and Nutt, 2011). All of this has negatively impacted the development of his self-regulation abilities. Children who have been traumatized have often lost contact with their ability to acknowledge and process the somatic information that their bodies send them. In Freddy's case, he developed an effective strategy for disconnecting his mind from his body during moments of abuse. While this served him well in coping with extreme distress during unavoidable situations, he lost valuable developmental time in processing both proprioceptive and vestibular input in relation to the external world. What did this mean practically speaking for Freddy? He did not relate to his environment in a nuanced manner, often bringing more physical force than was necessary to a situation. Indeed, some of the work of therapy included games that allowed him to experiment with "Not enough, just enough, and too much." Part of his work was learning to feel the physiological cues that his body was giving him and respond in ways that were safe both for himself and for those around him. His processing, even within this first session, moved with surprising alacrity back and forth between quadrants. At times he engaged in energized post-traumatic play (Gil, 2011, 2017; Goodyear-Brown, 2010, in press).

Therapy process: turning points and emergence of self

Freddy's rise and fall of consciousness felt a little like an intense piece of classical music, with moments of intense energy, moments of collapse, moments of clarity in verbal articulation, moments of chaotic play, and invitations to Quadrants I, II, III, and IV (Yasenik and Gardner, 2012) all in the midst of one session. The following is a moment-to-moment unfolding of Freddy's content and my responses. You will see that I weave in and out of quadrants as his need is expressed and perceived.

FSPT practitioners always begin treatment in Quadrant III: Non-intrusive Responding, to give power to the child, and facilitate introduction to the play space, the play materials, and the relationship with the therapist. We amplify the child's voice and describe the play activity as it happens. It is also understood that, some time within the first session, the therapist will offer a developmentally sensitive explanation for what they know about the traumatic experience(s) that preceded the child's entrance into therapy, making a quick foray into Quadrant II: Open Discussion and Exploration. This information is shared matter-of-factly and includes language giving permission for the child to talk/play/draw and so on about the scary thing that happened in the playroom and equal permission not to. The therapist is trained to make an immediate return to Quadrant III following their explanation, unless the child's need drives the therapeutic choice in a different direction. Meanwhile, how the client responds to this initial telling (responding verbally or in play to the content, ignoring the content or the therapist altogether, returning to the previous play pattern, having a sudden burst or cessation of kinetic activity) informs the therapist about the client's current window of tolerance for conscious awareness of trauma content and their preferred methods for coping.

Freddy's parents had been on one of those outings that adults with children rarely get to have: a date. They had left Freddy in the very competent care of his grandparents. He and his little brother had spent countless hours with cousins running freely through the acres of the grandparents' farm. On this particular day, the parents got out of their car, called for the children, and then followed the giggles to a giant magnolia that the brothers liked to pretend was a desert island. Dad crouched down low, as he had many times before, and slipped under the umbrella of the lower leaves. All he saw was the blur of children jumping up and pulling their clothing back into place. Sensitive to the potential of embarrassing Freddy, he waited until he had Freddy alone later to ask him about what he had seen. Within moments, Freddy broke down crying and said that he was playing "the privacy game." As the parents explored further, Freddy, now five years old, explained that "Mr. B" had played the privacy game with him at church class when he was three. Freddy's parents reported that Freddy looked relieved, as if a big weight had been lifted. Over the next 24 hours, Freddy began to share details of the privacy game, such as "he bit my butt" and "he took me to the potty and hurt my bottom." The parents also reported that, at one point, he made a "weird" facial expression in which his mouth repeatedly opened wide and he made a clicking sound in the back of his throat. It was at this point that the parents reached out for help. They reached out to me first and I explained to them the sometimes frustrating process for abuse reporting and investigation. The parents, armed with the understanding that they needed to have a forensic interview before beginning therapy, said they would be back in touch after that process was complete. True to their word, I heard from them a few weeks later and, after coordinating with the forensic team, it was agreed that therapy could begin.

Attachment theory is a foundational scaffold for the FSPT model, and understanding that a child's development of self, the "I," is born and nurtured in thousands of reciprocal interactions with the "You" (the other) informs our hypothesis that Freddy may have a distorted or delayed sense of self following the injury to trust with this supposedly safe adult. Further, the distorted sense of self is likely to show up in the play therapy room. As it shows up, it will need to be held and reflected in order to create an environment for transformation. However, interpersonal trauma will often shut down the exploratory system for children, and activate the attachment system in a way that looks like developmental regression and can scare parents, who fear the child is irrevocably damaged. Parents themselves will need a great deal of support throughout the child's therapy process. In Freddy's case, parents are both secure attachment figures, who had historically provided a secure base from which he could explore. The telling of the secret had raised a question for Freddy about whether or not his parents were still a secure base for him, whether they still "liked" him, and how safe they were as containers for the hard stuff. To this end, there were several sessions with just the parents, in order to create a therapeutic team for

Freddy, unpack the importance of their responses throughout this time, and to provide support and coaching for how to hold Freddy's story without inserting their own anxieties or content. I also offered practical, play-based strategies for demonstrating their continued delight in him on a daily basis, assigning nurturing dyadic activities for the parents to do with Freddy in the morning and at bedtime (Booth and Jernberg, 2009). As my play sessions with Freddy began, we still interspersed parent sessions every few weeks. In addition, there were family talk and play sessions, in which we established sexual behavior rules in the house, playfully reinforced each individual's rights and boundaries within the family (Goodyear-Brown, 2013), and coached the family in cooperative methods for resolving conflict.

Freddy came in for his first play therapy session and was shown around the building. At Nurture House we have a fully equipped playroom, a fully equipped sandtray room, an art studio, and a snug playloft upstairs. Children are often taken on a tour of all the rooms as part of their initial orientation to the space. When we got to the sandtray room, Freddy exclaimed, "This room is cool. Can we play in here?" I said yes and moved to shut one of the doors (the room has three). Freddy went and shut the other two, communicating either a desire for privacy and/or indicating that he felt comfortable to be alone with me. It helps to remember that this child had "good enough" attachment figures who had been meeting needs and delighting in him consistently since he was born and who had worked hard to respond appropriately since his disclosures. The speed with which he built the first fibers of trust with me is in part attributed to the power of these borrowed attachments.

Freddy moved immediately over to the Jurassic sand, ran his fingers through it, and commented on its softness. I tracked his exploration and reflected his awareness of how soft the sand felt to him. Freddy then moved to the white sparkly sand and commented on its sparkles. He similarly explored the room for the first ten minutes of the session. It became clear that Freddy was a sensory seeker, kinesthetically connecting with the space in order to learn about it and make himself comfortable. My work was exclusively in Quadrant III: Non-intrusive Responding during this part of the session.

Turning points 1 and 2: can you hold it?; can you hear it?

After exploring the first two types of sand and several miniatures, Freddy thrust his hands into the sandtray filled with kinetic sand. Freddy remarked, "Oooh, this sand feels like kaka." Freddy slid his eyes to the left, referencing me, while squeezing the sand in his fists. He seemed to have understood at this point that my job was to hear his voice and reflect his language and play choices. Understanding this, he "upped the ante" by giving me a word to reflect that may be slightly "taboo."

Paris: Ah, the squishy sand feels like kaka to you!

He seemed delighted at my reflection of the word "kaka" (I was wondering if perhaps other grownups had shut down his use of this word in other environments?). Knowing that this child's current distress was related to his recent disclosures of sexual abuse, my internal question at this point was: "How do I show him I am a strong enough container for whatever yucky material he might need to show me?" I tend toward higher degrees of self-immersion in my work and often work from the premise that traumatized children may need more active alignment from the therapist in order to feel safe in the space than children who present with other clinical concerns, but always begin with non-intrusive responding and allow them to invite me into this more active alignment. Freddy didn't take very long to do so. He looked me in the eye, with some degree of challenge, and demanded, "Feel it! It feels like kaka." Here he invited me into a deeper level of immersion by requesting the interaction of my physical self. I made eye contact with him, imitated his thrusting of hands into the sand with my own, and while squeezing sand in both my hands agreed, "It does feel like kaka." Then I matter-of-factly state, "Although this stuff isn't warm like kaka usually is right after we've pooped." This is an expansion, a communication that I can hold even more than he has given me, and represents a "quick scoot" into Quadrant IV: Co-facilitation. It also appeared to lead to the first turning point in the therapy process. Freddy giggled with delight and stepped closer to me. I perceived this physical shift as a non-verbal cue of his growing comfort with me and an acceptance of this level of responding. He asked for the sand I was holding, packed his sand into a ball with mine, and left it sitting in the middle of the kinetic sand. I moved back to Quadrant III and reflected that he decided to leave "the big ball of kaka right there." Freddy said, "Yep," walked over to the sandtray shelves, and began looking at my collection of dragons.

I remained in Quadrant III, reflecting that he was "checking those out." Freddy picked up a two-headed dragon. On this figure a very long neck supports each of the two heads. He brought the dragon over to the Jurassic sand and began shoving sand into one of the dragon's mouths. This play brought a new level of intensity to his focus and energy, so I remained quiet, providing honoring silence for what he was communicating somatically. After a couple of minutes of vigorous sand shoveling, he began making unconscious grunting sounds (sexual in nature) while he continued pushing the sand down the dragon's throat. I was quiet for a moment, silently witnessing his unspoken communication.

> Paris: You're putting that stuff in there.

Freddy nodded, but began shoving the sand even more aggressively into the dragon's mouth while making a disgusted face himself and having the dragon's body writhe around in the sandtray. My sense was that he wanted a different use of self, a more intense level of immersion from me, so I spoke again with more concern (emotion) infused in my tone and said, "He has to take more and more, so much that he's choking!"

Turning points 3 and 4: deeper immersion; the vulnerable gets a voice

Freddy stopped play for a moment, looked at me with somber eyes, and said, "He has to eat it, but he doesn't like it."

> Paris: He has to swallow it (infusing voice with sadness and resignation), even though he doesn't want to (emphatic and slightly angry on behalf of the dragon).

The nuance of responses and the use of self extends into our choice of which communications to amplify. My choice is often to amplify the affective component of the self-object's (child's) communication through the play (Quadrant I, using reflective interpretations).

Freddy went back to shoveling sand, and said (with sadness in his voice this time), "Yep, he has to." The tenor of his play shifted from intense, almost angry, energy to a slower, quieter cadence.

Freddy: It tastes bad.

Paris: It tastes yucky.

Freddy: *Real yucky!*

Freddy kept filling the dragon's mouth and began making choking noises once again.

Paris: He sounds like he's in trouble.

Freddy: He's choking! It's disgusting!

Paris: It's so disgusting. He wants it to stop. The dragon says, "Stop! Please stop! I'm choking!"

Here I moved into Quadrant IV, taking on the voice of the dragon to give voice to the feelings that the client may have had during the trauma.

Freddy smiled and became more energized, speaking to the dragon and saying, "Shut up! Just swallow it!"

Paris (as the dragon, making gagging sounds): Please! I don't want to swallow it. I can't breathe! Somebody help me!

I stayed in Quadrant IV with a high level of immersion, giving voice to the potential panic and overwhelm that Freddy may have felt at the time of the trauma, and to begin testing the "soft hypothesis" (Yasenik and Gardner, 2012) that Freddy's worldview may include the belief that there is no help available to him.

Freddy nodded at me and whispered, "You keep choking." He left the two-headed dragon in the tray with its mouth full, while I continued to gag and ask for help. He began choosing scary creatures and putting them in the tray and I offered verbalizations, in character, such as "I only see bad guys…is no one coming to help? No one is coming to help me. I am all alone," and eventually, "I am scared."

Freddy: These are the bad guys.

I reverted from Quadrant IV back into Quadrant III: Non-intrusive Responding: "You put lots of bad guys near the dragon."

Freddy found an especially tall, scary figure and remarked, "He's a really scary guy!" I agreed that he was really scary.

Turning point 5: you can hold it!; asking the therapist to help

Freddy said, "Here, you hold him," and thrust him in my direction. Here Freddy again invited me to move deeper into the play, this time as a resource. I reflected his choice to have me hold him—"You want me to hold him right here"—and amplified Freddy's power in play by looking at the figure and speaking to the potential perpetrator symbol, saying, "Alright, scary guy—you've got to stay right here because Freddy says so." Freddy smiled and returned to arranging figures in the sand. (When I spoke to the scary guy, I began to enter the play metaphor as an ally to the child, moving again into Quadrant IV. My goal was to amplify Freddy's sense of power and control in this environment, testing the soft hypothesis that he was hungry for a greater experience of mastery.)

Turning point 6: you can hold me too; trusting for protection

While holding the bad guy, I returned to Quadrant III, giving my full focus to Freddy's continued construction of his sand world with several more minutes of non-intrusive responding. Eventually, Freddy chose a broken mummy from the sandtray collection. The mummy was missing a leg that was broken off several years ago, and only a string held on the mummy's helmet, so that the pock-marked face of the figure underneath the mummy wrapping was visible.

> Freddy: He's hurt.
>
> Paris (infusing concern in my voice): Oh, this one is hurt.

Freddy took the scary guy out of my hands and dropped him in the tray next to the dragon. He then put the broken mummy into my hands, saying, "You hold *him* now."

> Paris: You gave the hurt guy to me to hold.
>
> Freddy: Yeah, you keep him safe from the bad guys.

Working on the hypothesis that this was a self-object and that the client was asking for a more overt enhancement of safety between us, and perhaps testing for protection, I risked moving into more overt safety building work by offering myself as a resource, while mitigating the risk by communicating this safety within the play metaphor.

In making these choices, I moved into Quadrant IV again (Co-facilitation, unconscious/directive).

> Paris (speaking gently and with great nurture, directly to the mummy figure cupped in my hands): I've gotchya! You are safe with me.

Freddy made a face, as if suddenly struck by an idea, and exclaimed, "We need a jail!"

> Paris: You decided. We need a jail.

Freddy looked around and asked, "Do you have a jail?" I gestured to where we keep the jails in the sandtray room while being sure to keep the mummy protected. He chose a medium-sized wooden jail and put it in the sand. Then he picked up the "really bad guy" that he had dropped near the dragon in the sandtray and puts him inside the jail.

> Paris (speaking to the bad guy): You've got to stay in there. Freddy decided.

Freddy smiled at me and said, "Yeah, *I* decided."

Freddy and I sat there for a long moment, looking at the tray, feeling what it felt like for the bad guy to be contained, and then Freddy sighed.

Turning points 7 and 8: becoming a team and acknowledging the problem

He had been standing right near my chair, inches from my knees, while we looked at the sandtray together. When he sighed, and while our joint attention was riveted on the sandtray, he leaned over ever so slightly until his hip was leaning against my knee. I mirrored his sigh while keeping my eyes focused on the tray. He picked up the two-headed dragon again and shook the sand out of its mouth. I wasn't sure what he needed from me at the moment, so I returned to Quadrant III, reflecting his actions: "You got that stuff out of his mouth."

> Freddy (with a sense of sadness): Yeah.

> Paris (speaking to the dragon—moving back to Quadrant IV): Oh dragon, you seem sad.

> Freddy (as the dragon, in a gravelly voice): Yeah.

> Paris: I wonder if sometimes it still feels bad even after the stuff is gone.

This was an interpretive offering and moved me into Quadrant I, offering a rise of consciousness, with the goal of normalization around the potential sense of shame or dirtiness that Freddy may carry even though he was no longer being hurt.

> Freddy (in the voice of the dragon): I'm still dirty.
>
> Paris (speaking to the dragon): You still feel dirty.
>
> Freddy (in the voice of the dragon): I want to be clean. Can you help me?

Turning point 9: offering a resource in metaphor

> Paris: Hmmm, you want to be clean again… (I introduce a helping symbol here, working in Quadrant IV.) You know, I have had other dragons who feel dirty long after they are safe. I keep a very special tree that can help dragons who feel dirty. (I get a luminescent tree with glowing green leaves and iridescent fruit down from the top shelf.) This tree has magical leaves and grows magical fruit. Some have said that if you eat the fruit, it makes you clean again. (The phrase "some have said" leaves room for the child to embrace the metaphoric healing or reject it without pressure.)
>
> Freddy (delighted and in the voice of the dragon): Yay! I will eat the fruit… (pretends to eat it). Yummy! It's cleaning me in my belly.

After this play communication, I followed Freddy back to Quadrant III and engaged in non-intrusive responding while he continued play. Freddy brought the dragon back to the tree several times in play because he got "hungry for more cleaning."

Eventually Freddy stepped back from the tray and said: "I'm done." He began putting the figures from the sandtray back on the shelves.

Turning point 10: it is not too big to name

I shifted gears at this point in the session, making a foray into Quadrant II: Open Discussion and Exploration. Initial rapport had been built, play themes involving safety building, dirtying, cleansing, and containment had all been witnessed and explored, I had hopefully established myself as a safe enough and big enough container for him, and he had completed a cycle of play. One of my core tenets when working with children who have been sexually abused is that I want them to know that I already know, at least in part, what has happened to them. I said, "Mommy and daddy told me about what happened with Mr. B."

Freddy looked at me from the other side of the sandtray and said, "He made me play the privacy game." I met his eyes with mine and explained that I see lots of children who have been made to play privacy games and that he could show me and tell me anything he needed to or not, that nothing he told or showed me would change the way I feel about him, and that my job was to help. Here, I made a decision to bring the treatment issue into conscious awareness— not forcing the child to talk about it, but opening a pathway for conscious, perhaps verbal, processing. Not every client journeys a road of detailed verbal processing of their sexual abuse, but offering the involvement of language early in treatment allows for the child to utilize any and all of the developmental portals for communication that feel most empowering for him or her. Early in my work with this population I found that children may choose not to approach difficult content in the playroom for all kinds of reasons, but I don't ever want one of those reasons to be a question about whether or not I already know what has happened or because the child has a confused need to protect or shield me from the scary content. Part of how we show that we are "bigger, stronger, wiser, kind" (a mantra from the Circle of Security project) is to demonstrate that we are willing to speak of the unspeakable. I once heard Esther Deblinger, one of the creators of Trauma Focused-Cognitive Behavior Therapy (TF-CBT), speak about a young lady who came into her care after having been with a support-oriented therapist in the community. When she met the child she asked how much she and her previous therapist had talked about the sexual abuse. The child said, "We didn't talk about it." Dr. Deblinger wondered out loud about that, and the little girl sighed and said, "She wasn't ready yet." In my work, I want children to understand that they can begin any level of processing related to their abuse as soon as we begin a relationship and I will dance with them towards and away from the trauma content in whatever titrations of safety and content are needed for them to move forward. I want them to know that I *am* ready when and if they are. In some cases, the statements I make near the beginning of therapy about what I know go without verbal reaction and sometimes without any reaction at all. In this case, however, Freddy used lots of words.

He surprised me by leaving his self-imposed clean-up process to come and sit across from me. He said, "It was scary and it really, really happened." He looked up with his big blue eyes, asking with his eyes if I believed him, and said, "I was *scared*," with a great emphasis placed on the word scared.

Turning point 11: amplifying his voice

I wanted to amplify his voice, as he had chosen this way of communicating. I got out a piece of paper and a marker and said, "This part of your story is really important to you, so I will write it down." I began to write as I slowly repeated, "It really, really happened and I was scared." I put the same tonal emphasis on the word scared and wrote it in all capitals… Freddy leaned in and asked which word was "scared." I pointed to the word and he reached out with his small hand to touch the word. He said, "You made it big because I was big scared!" Freddy then said, "He was creepy…and the game…well, he sneaked of it when I was in the three-year-old class." I repeated his verbalizations, slowing them down as I wrote them down. Freddy appeared comforted and validated by the writing and leaned into me as I wrote.

Freddy then said: "Write my name on the other side." I wrote his name in giant capital letters on the backside of the paper. Freddy picked up the paper, turned it over and back over a couple of times, and then said, "My name is even bigger than the SCARED!" I reflected his words to him. He asked to go show mom and dad (who were waiting in the lobby) the paper and this is how we ended the session.

Freddy had moved quickly into testing my ability to become a container for the ugly stuff. In essence, the kaka play was really a way of asking, excuse the vulgarity in advance, "Can you handle the shit?" He then engaged in testing for protection, offering somatically encoded post-traumatic play, and enlisting me as an ally in re-establishing safety, but through the use of the symbols and the play metaphors themselves. In this first session, Freddy gave me a self-object to care for. In subsequent sessions, the mummy showed up again and again, sometimes being hurt by the bad guys, sometimes being protected from them, and often having to go to the hospital to be re-wrapped. Often after Freddy had revealed a new dynamic of his abuse, either through post-traumatic play or through drawing, storytelling, or verbalization, he would reintroduce the mummy and invite me to care for it in some way. Over the course of the next few individual play sessions, Freddy's play continued to include dichotomous themes of safety/harm, aggression/immobilization, and protection/containment. My role moved between use of self as a container—giving reflections, descriptions, and accurately tracking the play, while in Quadrant III—to entering the roles assigned to me in play in a co-facilitative manner (Quadrant IV). This required a high degree of self-immersion, as I would verbalize and enact the thoughts and feelings related to helplessness (just having to take the mistreatment given to me) when I was put in the role of the victim, while also becoming larger (Norton and Norton, 1997) in my role as rescuer in the play when he assigned me roles that required this response.

Freddy moved from having mighty battles in the sandtray between good guys and bad guys to making us the physical good guys and bad guys. In this way, he asked for, indeed demanded, full embodiment (Levine and Klein, 2006; Rothschild, 2000) of the extremes in dysregulation that he had experienced as a result of the abuse. During this same period of time, there were several talk-oriented sessions that involved his parents and were related to establishing safety rules in the house and helping Freddy experience supported experiences of delight with his parents. Over a period of ten sessions or so, Freddy became much more regulated both at home and in session. His aggression decreased tremendously, but this left Freddy with a new problem. It seems that Freddy had identified aggression with strength. As he moved from the play metaphors of good guys and bad guys to choosing a figure to be "Mr. B" and imagining all the ways that he would hurt Mr. B if he ever saw him again, Freddy felt strong and in control, and when the aggression left, simply put, Freddy felt weak. It almost felt, as his play partner, that aggression abandoned him and left him with a developmentally regressed version of the self. The weakness mixed with shame for Freddy, as it was in his weaker three-year-old self that he had been forced to swallow semen and made to feel powerless and dirty. It was the shame, as much as the semen, which had gotten stuck in his throat. Freddy's growing edge became wrestling with the question of: how does one have strength without aggression? For several sessions, Freddy asked to go directly to the "nook," which is a small space in the loft of Nurture House that is filled with pillows and lots of natural light. It is the perfect spot for a nap, and Freddy would get comfortable on the papasan cushion, ask to be tucked in, and then "go to sleep." There was tremendous trust in the relationship at this point and I would always begin in Quadrant III, reflecting his decision to nap. Freddy quickly invited me into a co-facilitation (Quadrant IV) role and I had specific tasks, such as rocking him, tucking him in, watching out for bad guys, and waking him when it was time to go. I felt that Freddy could benefit from in vivo moments of delight that met him at this regressed point in development. His play behavior during this time mirrored that of a three-year-old and I wondered if he wasn't hopeful to have corrective emotional experiences and a communication of his preciousness even during the time when he was being hurt. I began incorporating Theraplay® games into the time we spent together in the nook. I played the pillow stacking game with him, challenging him to balance more pillows. Freddy squealed with delight as he realized he could stack three at a time. After several rounds of this, he jumped up and demanded, "More strong games!!" Freddy had found a way to feel strong in his body while still feeling connected to others. Soon after this session, Freddy asked me to use the washable markers to make a lion's face on him. I delighted in his brown nose and counted each whisker after I had drawn them on his cheeks. He beamed and asked if mom could see. We did one better, having mom and dad come participate in the next couple of sessions, delighting in him at a younger developmental level. After Freddy's play had developed into that of a five-year-old's again, eye movement desensitization and processing (EMDR) was integrated into the play and mom told the story of the scary things that happened while he worked in the sand. Freddy began playing soccer and became one of the best players on his team, using the power in his physical body to help his team. Freddy was kind with his siblings, connected to his parents, and competent in social, academic, and family situations. One day, towards the end of treatment, Freddy came into the playroom and picked up the two-headed dragon again. I paid close attention, getting ready for another round of co-facilitation if necessary. Freddy filled the dragon's mouth with sand once, poured it out, and said,

"He doesn't have to swallow it anymore." It seemed that the shame of his sexual abuse was no longer stuck in his throat.

Turning points summary

Stage in process	Quadrant	Turning points	What contributed to the turning point?
Session 1	QIII: Non-intrusive Responding		• Freddy was empowered to lead in the session • Freddy understood that he could set the pace and that I would reflect or "hold" his content
Session 1	Weaving between QIII and QII, more physical immersion of self	Turning point 1 "Feel it! Feel the kaka!"	• As Freddy led and I reflected, Freddy was emboldened to test me for containment capacities and to invite me more physically to participate in the play
Session 1	Weaving between QIII and QIV: Co-facilitation, more therapist immersion	Turning point 2 Dragon choking on the sand, sexual grunting	• My expansion of "kaka" to "poop" communicated an ability to hold yucky things, and Freddy immediately rewarded the holding by showing somatic experiencing of the trauma in play
Session 1	QI	Turning point 3 "He has to eat it but he doesn't want to!"	• I had just highlighted the helpless position of the dragon in play, saying, "He's got to take more and more"
Session 1	QIV, deeper level of immersion	Turning point 4 "Shut up and swallow it!"	• I deepened the level of immersion, becoming the voice of the dragon, soft hypothesis testing, and Freddy responded by taking the voice of the perpetrator
Session 1	QIV	Turning point 5 Gave me the bad guy to hold	• I augmented safety through containment of the perpetrator in the play metaphor when invited
Session 1	QIV	Turning point 6 Gave me the mummy to hold	• I augmented safety by speaking nurturing protection to the self-object in the play metaphor when invited

cont.

Stage in process	Quadrant	Turning points	What contributed to the turning point?
Session 1	QIII	Turning point 7 Getting the "stuff" out	• Reflecting awareness of his choice to get rid of the stuff
Session 1	QI	Turning point 8 Voicing of the problem that dragon was still dirty/asking for help in play	• Offering/wondering in the play metaphor if dragon still feels bad
Session 1	QIV	Turning point 9 "It's cleaning me in my belly"	• I functioned as a co-facilitator in the play metaphor, offering a resource for possible use
Session 1	QII	Turning point 10 "It really, really happened"	• Instead of returning to play or ignoring the words, Freddy offered verbal details, seemed hungry to do so; I recorded them, validating and amplifying his voice
Session 1	QIII	Turning point 11 "My name is bigger than the SCARED!"	• I returned to reflection, validating the potential that he might be able to be bigger than his fear

References

Booth, P.B. and Jernberg, A.M. (2009) *Theraplay: Helping Parents and Children Build Better Relationships through Attachment-Based Play*. San Francisco, CA: John Wiley & Sons.

Corrigan, F.M., Fisher, J.J., and Nutt, D.J. (2011) Autonomic dysregulation and the Window of Tolerance model of the effects of complex emotional trauma. *Journal of Psychopharmacology 25*, 1, 17–25.

Cozolino, L. (2014) *The Neuroscience of Human Relationships: Attachment and the Developing Social Brain* (Norton series on interpersonal neurobiology). New York: W.W. Norton and Company.

Damasio, A. (1999) *The Feeling of What Happens: Body and Emotion in the Making of Consciousness*. New York: Harcourt, Inc.

D'Mello, S. and Graesser, A. (2012) Dynamics of affective states during complex learning. *Learning and Instruction 22*, 2, 145–157.

D'Mello, S., Lehman, B., Pekrun, R., and Graesser, A. (2014) Confusion can be beneficial for learning. *Learning and Instruction 29*, 153–170.

Gaskill, R. and Perry, B. (2012) Child Sexual Abuse, Traumatic Experiences, and Their Impact on the Developing Brain. In P. Goodyear-Brown (ed.) *Handbook of Child Sexual Abuse: Identification, Assessment, and Treatment.* Hoboken, NJ: Wiley Publishing.

Gil, E. (2011) *Helping Abused and Traumatized Children: Integrating Directive and Nondirective Approaches.* New York: Guilford Press.

Gil, E. (2017) *Posttraumatic Play in Children: What Clinicians Need to Know.* New York: Guilford Press.

Goodyear-Brown, P. (2010) *Play Therapy with Traumatized Children: A Prescriptive Approach.* Hoboken, NJ: Wiley Publishing.

Goodyear-Brown, P. (2013) *Tackling Touchy Subjects.* Publisher: Author.

Levine, P.A. and Kline, M. (2006) *Trauma through a Child's Eyes.* Berkeley, CA: North Atlantic Books.

MacLean, P.D. (1990) *The Triune Brain in Evolution (Role in Paleocerebral Functions).* New York: Plenum Press.

Norton, B.E. and Norton, C.C. (1997) *Reaching Children through Play Therapy: An Experiential Approach.* Denver: The Publishing Cooperative.

Ogden, P., Minton, K., and Pain, C. (2006) *Trauma and the Body: A Sensorimotor Approach to Psychotherapy.* New York: W.W. Norton and Company.

Perry, B.D. (2009) Examining child maltreatment through a neurodevelopmental lens: Clinical applications of the neurosequential model of therapeutics. *Journal of Loss and Trauma 14,* 4, 240–255.

Perry, B.D. and Hambrick, E.P. (2008) The neurosequential model of therapeutics. *Reclaiming Children and Youth 17,* 3, 38–43. Accessed on 23/05/2018 at http://childtrauma.org/wp-content/uploads/2013/08/NMT_Article_08.pdf

Porges, S. (2011) *The Polyvagal Theory: Neurophysiological Foundations of Emotions, Attachment, and Communication.* New York: W.W. Norton and Company.

Powell, B., Cooper, G., Hoffman, K., and Marvin, B. (2014) *The Circle of Security Intervention: Enhancing Attachment in Early Parent-Child Relationships.* New York: Guilford Press.

Rothschild, B. (2000) *The Body Remembers: The Psychophysiology of Trauma and Trauma Treatment.* New York: W.W. Norton and Company.

Schore, A. (2003) *Affect Dysregulation and Disorders of the Self.* New York: W.W. Norton and Company.

Siegel, D.J. (2006) An interpersonal neurobiology approach to psychotherapy. *Psychiatric Annals 36,* 4.

Siegel, D.J. (2012) *Pocket Guide to Interpersonal Neurobiology: An Integrative Handbook of the Mind.* New York: W.W. Norton and Company.

van der Kolk, B. (2014) *The Body Keeps the Score: Brain, Mind, and Body in the Healing of Trauma.* New York: Penguin Books.

Yasenik, L. and Gardner, K. (2012) *Play Therapy Dimensions Model: A Decision-Making Guide for Integrative Play Therapists.* London: Jessica Kingsley Publishers.

7

CORRIE AND THE T-REX

Courage Reclaimed

LINDA E. HOMEYER

Case introduction

Corrie was just over three years old when she came to play therapy. Corrie was average size for her age with brilliant blue eyes and short, flyaway blonde hair. She was part of an intact family, with an infant brother. Her mother and father were both working professionals, and when they worked, Corrie was cared for by her grandfather who also resided in the home. All was well until Corrie was 18 months old when, upon the death of her grandfather, she was placed in daycare. She soon began demonstrating oppositional behavior problems: distress when taken to daycare, saying there was a "bad lady." At home, Corrie began crying when diapered and experiencing sleeping problems, being awakened by nightmares and night terrors. When a parent came to her aid at night she would bite, hit, and could not be calmed; after about 45 minutes of being asleep, she would also "claw" at her face, cheeks, and vagina. Corrie's parents reported possible sexual abuse at the daycare but the investigation was inconclusive. The decision was made to again care for Corrie at home.

After another year of the problem behaviors continuing, Corrie was brought for play therapy. Presenting concerns at the time of initiating play therapy included continued problems with sleeping ("extremely traumatic nightmares" and night terrors); fear of certain people and places (she could not tolerate being driven past her previous daycare); and hypervigilance (easily startled). She also began to experience seizure-like episodes. These episodes involved her collapsing suddenly to the floor and resulted in injuries such as bloody lips, facial cuts, and bruises. A pediatric neurologist consultation (which occurred after several weeks of play therapy) resulted in these being labeled "trauma seizures" and Corrie was prescribed medication for bedtime for sleeping support. The parents believed all her problem behaviors were based in the sexual abuse they believe she experienced at daycare.

Theoretical orientation

Adlerian play therapy (AdPT) was developed by Terry Kottman (2003) and is based on Individual Psychology developed by Alfred Adler (Ansbacher and Ansbacher, 1956; Kottman and Ashby, 2015). Adlerian therapy views people as holistic, creative, goal directed, and socially embedded. People are seen as having social interest: needing to belong and to be connected with others. People develop a system of beliefs/misbeliefs, private logic, and lifestyles, all of which contribute to their purposeful behavior and meeting life tasks (Kottman and Ashby, 2015).

An Adlerian play therapist facilitates the:

> exploration of the child's (a) beliefs about self, others, and the world; (b) methods for attaining a sense of belonging in the child's family; and (c) the behaviors that stem from the child "acting as if" his or her beliefs about himself/herself, others, and the world are true. (Kottman, 2009, p.2)

These "acting as if" behaviors were articulated by Dreikurs and Soltz (1964) as four goals of misbehavior: attention, power, revenge, and inadequacy. These are based in the child's need to find a way to belong and count in the family and the world (school, peers, etc.). The use of "Crucial Cs" (Lew and Bettner, 1996, 2000) is a strength-based view of the child's development of the sense of self. The Crucial Cs are: feeling Connected to others and having a felt sense of community, feeling Capable of taking care of oneself, believing that they Count and are valued by others, and demonstrating Courage (Kottman and Ashby, 2015; Lew and Bettner, 2000). The Crucial Cs are also useful in helping caretakers and other adults in the child's life to work with the child from a positive, prosocial perspective rather than the problem-focused view.

Adlerian therapy is a stage or phase theory. Although these are fluid over the course of intervention, they do provide a framework for the play therapist to understand and identify progress. The four phases (adapted from Kottman, 2009, p.6) are:

1. establishing an egalitarian relationship between the play therapist and the child, indicating that each is equal in understanding the therapeutic issues and power within the relationship

2. exploring the child's lifestyle, which includes the goals of misbehaviors and prioritizing the Crucial Cs

3. helping the child gain insight into their lifestyle/goal of misbehavior (often referred to generally as the working phase)

4. reorienting and reeducating the child.

Each phase varies in length depending on the complexities of the issues, child, and family. This includes the presenting issues, family atmosphere, and psychological birth order. Adlerian play therapists seek to help the child understand how to belong and count in constructive, positive ways. This includes correcting misbeliefs, which in turn changes private logic and resolves goals of misbehavior. Because we see children as socially embedded, working with the family and school (if applicable) is important. Again, this varies with the need of the particular child and family unit.

With young children, like Corrie, AdPT appears non-directive, recognizing the developmental appropriateness of the child-led interaction. As Yasenik and Gardner (2004) state, the AdPT therapist "may initially work with the child non-directively, and over time more directively" (p.35). Indeed, as this case will show, this is how I work with Corrie. The AdPT therapist provides the verbal tracking and joining in the play to assist the child to be able to feel and think about self in a healthier, more constructive manner. And when appropriate, to challenge the misbeliefs which are driving an unproductive private logic.

As part of the overall case formulation, other areas impacting child development need to be considered to have a fully inclusive view of the whole child. Is the child securely attached to the caretaker(s)? If not, what is the attachment style, and how able are the caretakers to work on developing a stronger attachment? Just as Adlerian play therapists seek to understand the caretaker's lifestyle/personality priority, it is also important to understand their adult attachment style. Securely attached parents more frequently use their lifestyles in constructive ways. With the stress of a child needing play therapy and other impacting life experiences, this stressor (whatever the cause) frequently results in the adults living out the destructive side of their lifestyle.

Additionally, being aware of any traumatic life experiences is critical, including any possible trauma experienced by the caregivers in their family or community. This could be interpersonal trauma, natural disasters, or community/state/national tragedies. Because Adlerian counselors see individuals as socially embedded, any and all life events impact the person's beliefs/misbeliefs, private logic, lifestyle, and ability to successfully complete life tasks. For example, one child I saw in AdPT had a history of living with his family in a foreign country when he was three years old. His mother reported never feeling safe there. The child sensed that "not-being-safe" from his mother and internalized that belief. When he then needed surgery, in a hospital where no one spoke English, his private logic continued to form: he was not safe and his parents could not keep him safe. When I saw him at age eight, he was reacting to the Gulf War in the Middle East and believed missiles could strike his house, just like the houses he watched on the televised news. His private logic was firmly established: "I must take care of myself. Others cannot keep me safe. The world is a scary, unsafe place; therefore, I must take care of myself, taking and wielding power wherever and however I can."

Finally, an awareness of the neurobiological impacts of the case assist in understanding what has occurred and how to help the child and caregivers. The neuropsychological perspective weaves throughout, including attachment, trauma, and ability to regulate (Badenoch, 2008; Perry and Szalavitz, 2006/2017; Siegel, 2012; van der Kolk, 2014). Understanding the brain's reaction to threat, the "window of tolerance" (Ogden and Fisher, 2015; Ogden and Minton, 2000) and polyvagal theory (Porges, 2011) are key concepts to understand and apply when working with the children and their families.

Case study conceptualization

Pulling together all of these aspects of AdPT and other developmental issues, I conceptualized Corrie in the following way:

1. Private logic: "I am very small, weak, and inadequate. Others are too big, too strong, and hurt me. The world is a painful, scary, unsafe place; therefore, I don't have the courage to cope and I must show how weak I am."

2. General development: Corrie appeared to be on track developmentally.

3. Attachment: Corrie had a strong, healthy secure attachment to her parents. Both parents appeared to be securely attached as well. Corrie's mother experienced some complicated grief reactions following her father's death (Corrie's grandfather).

4. Neuropsychological: Corrie's trauma seizures were an expression of her hypo-arousal reaction of collapse/faint. The pseudo-seizure is the result of the nervous system becoming overwhelmed and having no other adaptive coping mechanism. Doctors call these stress-related reactions psychogenic non-epileptic seizures (PNES).

5. Other assessments:

    – *Child Behavior Checklist* (Achenbach and Rescorla, 2000): completed by Corrie's mother, Corrie scored in the clinical range in Sleep Problems and the borderline clinical range in Somatic, Internalizing, and Externalizing subscales.

    – *Child Sexual Behavior Inventory* (Friedrich, 1997): Corrie scored in the clinically significant range in all subscales: Total Score, Sexual Abuse Sensitive Items, and Developmentally Related Sexual Behavior.

    – *Changes in Behavior Checklist*: an informal list of behavioral changes of children who have experienced sexual abuse, developed by myself, identified several behaviors of concern.

6. Trauma: with all of these assessments and the information from parents, Corrie had been traumatized by witnessing the death of her grandfather and the subsequent sexual abuse.

Based on this, we worked from the belief that Corrie had experienced sexual molestation at the daycare, even without a conclusive official investigation nor available knowledge as to what exactly had happened.

Therapy process: turning points and emergence of self

Reference to Yasenik and Gardner's Degree of Immersion: Therapist Use of Self Scale (Appendix A) and the quadrants of their Play Therapy Dimensions Model will both be used throughout the case study. For the reader's information, it is noted here, however, that I did not use Quadrant II: Open Discussion and Exploration, nor 1.1 Here and Now Discussion, nor 1.4 Interpretations. Most AdPT therapists are likely to use these and I made the purposeful decision not to do so. Corrie's age and her ability to effectively use symbolic and metaphoric play did not require their use.

Corrie began her sequence of 19 play therapy sessions with play typically used to establish the egalitarian relationship. From the beginning in the initial session she invited me to join in her exploratory play. This indicated Corrie's level of social interest and served as an indicator of her ability to connect: positive indicators for change. She played about mommies sleeping with the kids to keep them safe and she sang her own made-up songs about happy families. She also shared there was a monster in the house (hypothetically indicating the need for the mom to sleep with the kids) and displayed hypervigilant responses (e.g. to my squeaky chair).

Throughout these two initial sessions I stayed in Quadrant III: Non-intrusive Responding (Yasenik and Gardner, 2004) and used Immersion levels 1.2 Reflecting and Tracking Statements and 1.3 Restating Content (Appendix A). This provided Corrie with the ability to lead the play, pace her own level of safety, and establish her egalitarian relationship with me.

Turning point 1: being protecting parents

In the third session, Corrie expressed her developing sense of comfort and safety by playing out a shift during the session. Corrie began by continuing her nurturing, feeding play identifying herself for the first time as my "Mommy" and referring to me as "Honey." She cooked food for Daddy and me and cared for a crying baby. (This was reflective of the daily routine at home, although her mother informed me that no one in their family is called Honey. This appears to be a special name assigned to me when in this role.) Corrie then shifted in the same session to select guns and swords for herself, as Mommy, and for me as her Daddy. I resonated with her new sense of self, now playing the parents who protect: acting "as if" she could be strong and protect. Corrie was testing her misbelief that she had no courage. This was her segue into AdPT Phase 2: Exploring lifestyle and beliefs/misbeliefs. She had chosen to begin to challenge the misbeliefs of her being weak and grownups as unable to keep her safe. The high level of engagement and drive in protective play in the roles of her mother and father, and Corrie's insertion that we are fighting against the "bad and dangerous," resulted in her having difficulty ending and leaving the session.

With Corrie beginning to use role playing, we moved into Quadrant I: Active Utilization (Yasenik and Gardner, 2004). Corrie was using her own metaphors, yet using the role play of her parents (who she believed could not/did not protect her) and verbally labeling the "bad" and "dangerous" had a consciousness level to it. I entered her play and expanded it, but did not use interpretation (1.4 Verbal Use of Self-Interpretations). Rather, I used Immersion levels 3.1 Physical Self at a moderate level of following her direction and 4.1 Embodiment, being aware of my own self-system in a moderate way. I still continued to weave in the previously used 1.2 and 1.3 (Appendix A).

Corrie's mother requested a parent consultation. The sleeping difficulties were increasing to more nights a week. Her mother reported that, after about an hour of being asleep, Corrie begins crying, verbalizing "don't hurt me" and such. Corrie cannot tolerate nap time at her new daycare so her mother picks her up early every day. We discuss that as Corrie begins to move into the working stage, and becomes more consciously aware of her issues, she will display distressing behavior. I discuss the concept of the "window of tolerance" (Ogden and Fisher, 2015;

Ogden and Minton, 2000) and Corrie's movement back and forth within and breaching the boundaries of tolerance. We discuss how the behavior may well become more difficult as Corrie works through the distress and her neurobiological systems learn to tolerate the perceived fear. As Corrie works through her fears in AdPT and develops a sense of self as courageous, capable, and competent, she will learn to regulate and stay within the window of tolerance.

Turning point 2: death and danger

Corrie's play continued to expand as she expressed the tension between needing protection (play in which kids are capable of successfully fighting off alligators and snakes) and a heightened awareness of danger (the "bad lady" entered the dollhouse play; the Mommy and Honey died). The fifth session was a marked change of presentation and play which became the second turning point. Corrie was clearly dysregulated from the moment she began the session. Her intensity level was high throughout the session including very active play such as pulling toys off shelves. She also needed more limits to be set. When she finally settled into a longer play sequence with the giraffe family, her symbolic play provided the opportunity to focus and abreact. The giraffe children were going too close to "dangerous," too close "to the fire." The parent giraffes tried to protect them, admonishing the children, "Don't go to danger (fire)... You'll get hurt. Maybe dead" (said the mommy giraffe to the child giraffe); but alas, some of the kids went too close and died. Attuned to Corrie, I sensed how important this play was: danger, danger, death, death! (Even while writing this, I am aware my heartbeat is speeding up; I lean back from the computer and breathe deeply to regulate, pausing for a moment, honoring both our connection and work in that session.) I was in Immersion level 2.1 Emotionality. Even though I was not role playing in this play sequence and it was being completely child-led, I felt emotions on many levels. I matched Corrie's intensity of the danger and inability to protect: pace, tone, my facial expressions, and prosody (as indicated by Appendix A). Throughout this session, I continued in Quadrant III: Non-intrusive Responding (Yasenik and Gardner, 2004) letting Corrie lead and continued being in Immersion levels, using 1.2 Reflecting and Tracking Statements and 1.3 Restating Content (Appendix A). The turning point in this session was key to the play that followed.

I spoke with her mother immediately after this session. While having a great deal of experience with children who have been sexually abused, Corrie's danger vs. protection play was expected, but fire was new. Our strong resonance during the play spoke of the importance of the fire—it was more than danger; it was death. When exploring the fire play with her mother, her mother's eyes welled up with tears, and she said, "They told me she wouldn't remember." She went on to talk about the day that she, her husband, and her father fought a large brush fire near their home. The grandfather had a heart attack, fell on the ground, hitting his head on a rock. Corrie, only 18 months old, observed all of this, although she was quickly moved away. It was the death of the grandfather, Corrie's caretaker when her parents worked, that resulted in her beginning to go to daycare. Corrie's parents had initially interpreted her oppositional behavior regarding daycare as simply the transition in her care and the absence of her grandfather. Later they both felt guilty forcing her to go when it was likely that sexual abuse was occurring. It was clear Corrie and I were in AdPT Phase 3, obtaining insight on her lifestyle and mistaken beliefs: Her world was an unsafe place where people died and she got hurt. She had to figure it out.

Turning point 3: grandfather is dead

After the fire and death play, Corrie played several sessions around the themes of competency, security, and self-empowerment. While still using toys for this play, Corrie shifted to including me more and more in role playing. Embracing the deeper level of safety and connection in the playroom, the third turning point soon occurred and Corrie had sufficient courage to face the death of her grandfather/caretaker. As she had me play the dead grandfather by lying on the floor, she repeatedly "doctored" me, but session after session she failed. Corrie valiantly attempted to "save me." She wrapped my head with a long ace-bandage and gave me shots and other medical care. But she could not save me. My previous experience with children who had me die in the playroom was that they told me to come back to life at the end of the session. Not Corrie: I was dead, really dead. Of course, as a play therapist I was able to be a talking dead person. I reflected how important it was for her to try to help me, how she tried everything she could to help me, that I was "so sick" and she was "so brave." I was challenging her misbelief that, somehow, someone could have saved her grandfather.

These three sessions were primarily in Quadrant I: Active Utilization, my playing the role of the grandfather (by her direction, not mine), using some expanding reflections about how much she wanted me (grandfather) so much and she (the doctor) tried so hard (Yasenik and Gardner, 2004). Using Immersion levels 1.2 Reflecting and Tracking Statements and 1.3 Restating Content continued as I joined her in the struggle of understanding death (Appendix A).

Turning point 4: sleeping with a T-rex

Finally finished with the processing and accepting of her grandfather's death, and able to tolerate the finality of it, the next turning point occurred. Beginning in the ninth session, Corrie made a bed on the floor (using a large towel and a pillow) and instructed me to lie down. She covered me with a baby blanket and on top of the blanket added snakes, alligators, giant spiders, and many of the other creepy crawly, aggressive-type toys. Finally, I was given a T-rex dinosaur to hold as if it were a teddy bear. Wishing me a "good night," she went to the kitchen to cook dinner for Daddy. As I lay there, covered with danger, I wondered if the T-rex is symbolic of how much protection I need, or is it the increased level of danger? We played this over and over for several sessions. Occasionally, she fed me before bedtime, or had me die after being bitten by a snake, but then revived so I could go to sleep again with the danger. In subsequent sessions Corrie gradually reduced the number of scary toys that went to bed with me. T-rex stayed. She consistently called me Honey and she was the Mommy. She might talk with Daddy or with "Grammy" on the phone while cooking. One session she killed all the "dangerous" (hearkening back to session five's play with the giraffe family). She instructed me to say "I'm scared; Mommy, I'm scared" on and off throughout these sessions, which are entirely spent with me in bed on the floor.

I was fully in Quadrant IV: Co-facilitation. In this egalitarian relationship I fully trusted her as a co-therapist. I was in the play at her invitation. She knew what direction this play must take, much more fully than I: egalitarianism at its best. I began expanding my responses, reflecting the depth of fear she had, being so alone in her terror. I stayed in her fantasy and symbolism (Yasenik and Gardner, 2004, p.38). I was using several Immersion levels: 2.1 Emotionality, as I inserted emotion into her scenario; 2.2 Emotional Self, as I had the felt sense of her fear and terror (snakes and T-rex's will do that to you!); 3.1 Physical Self, as I lay on the floor session after session, being her Honey—there is no high physical-energy disbursement, but I was "all-in"; and 4.1 Embodiment, in tune with my own internal experience (Appendix A).

Meanwhile, in addition to individual play therapy, I was teaching her mother filial therapy, one-on-one. Mother and Corrie were now having special playtimes at home. We were working on their family atmosphere, where Corrie and her mother were able to be more strongly connected: where Corrie could experience the "being-capable" of another, her mother. With the mother's growing understanding of Corrie's Crucial C needs and the neuropsychological perspective, Mother was less fearful and more empowered as well. This allowed Mother to shift back into the constructive side of her lifestyle. Mother reported Corrie was having fewer nightmares. Corrie was generally happier, more verbal in many ways, including her ability to label her feelings, and was easier to "deal with." Corrie had begun attending another daycare a few days a week and could now fall asleep at naptime without any incidents.

Turning point 5: the kiss on the cheek

The play slowly changed. We still played me/Honey going to bed, her being the Mommy and cooking dinner for Daddy. But there was less energy about not being safe and more play about being strong and powerful during the scary night time. I no longer was covered with scary things; but I did have the T-rex. I had decided it was my protector. And then Corrie added a camping lantern and turned on the light. As this play changed, I began making more empowering statements, like "I feel so safe tonight" and "I don't think I'll have any nightmares tonight." We were in the final Adlerian stage of reorientation and re-education. Through her play she was informing me that night time was no longer scary. I reinforced that, with my words within our play, she could hear my words regarding being safe and nightmare free. It was safe. She was experiencing safety at night at home as evidenced by her sleeping through the nights, and within the session by adding the nightlight (camping light) to our in-session "home play" and I was reinforcing it all with my words. Her left and right brain, explicit and implicit beliefs and memories, were working together for her now balanced sense of safety. Her behavior was now well within the margins of window of tolerance and reflected in her ability to stay regulated. On what turned out to be our final bedtime play, Corrie replicated putting me to bed, complete with the T-rex and camping lantern. Before she left to go to the kitchen to cook dinner for Daddy, she leaned down, kissed me on the cheek, and patted me on the back, saying "I love you Honey, have a nice sleep!" Her nighttime fears were over; she was safe and she sang while fixing dinner.

This was the longest thematic, intense play theme across sessions (seven sessions), continuing in Quadrant IV: Co-facilitation (Yasenik and Gardner, 2004), as in the previous segment of play. I was staying in the moment with her and reflecting to her through macro-communication my understanding of her play, identifying Immersion levels: 2.1 Emotionality; 2.2 Emotional Self; 3.1 Physical Self; and 4.1 Embodiment (Appendix A).

Turning point 6: happy faces and butterflies

The final four sessions had no more nighttime play. A parent consultation with her father after session 16 revealed that Corrie continued to be sleeping well, daycare was fine, and there had not been a "seizure" in weeks. We decide to terminate, but taper off, with the last three sessions to be every other week.

AdPT had come full circle. I was back in Quadrant III: Non-intrusive Responding (Yasenik and Gardner, 2004). I was enjoying the being-with Corrie as we begin to disengage (Appendix A).

In session 17, Corrie brought me a gift of a happy drawing she had done in school. In session, she made an art and crafts picture of smiley faces and butterflies. At her direction we played flutes and danced. In our final session, she dressed both of us up in pearls, feather boas, and crowns. She announced she was Honey and I was Mommy, and I was to send her happily off to school. Yes, she was Honey, and I had known it all along. I was honored to have role played her distress, and pain, and loss. I was equally as delighted to transition into the courageous, creative, and delightful girl she was. Joined and connected, we both worked our way through the mire and out the other side.

Turning points summary

The following table organizes the case narrative of Corrie into a concise overview.

Stage in process	Quadrant	Turning points	What contributed to the turning point?
Sessions 1–2: AdPT Phase 1: Establishing an egalitarian relationship	QIII: Non-intrusive Responding		• Developing safety and a connected relationship in which the play and healing can occur
Sessions 3–4: AdPT Phase 2: Exploring child's lifestyle and mistaken beliefs	QI: Active Utilization	Turning point 1 Shifting from nurturing to protective play	• With safety established Corrie can role play parents who can protect
Session 5: AdPT Phase 2: Exploring child's lifestyle and mistaken beliefs	QIII: Non-intrusive Responding	Turning point 2 Giraffe family: danger and death	• Using toys to play out the dangers of fire, where parents cannot protect and death occurs
Sessions 6–8: AdPT Phase 3: Helping Corrie gain insight into lifestyle	QI: Active Utilization	Turning point 3 Dead grandfather play	• Grandfather cannot be healed, cannot return to life • Mastery and acceptance
Sessions 9–15: AdPT Phase 4: Reorientation and re-education	QIV: Co-facilitation	Turning point 4 Scary night time with T-rex	• From intense symbolism of night terrors to the resolution of fear
Sessions 16–19: Termination	QIII: Non-intrusive Responding	Turning point 5 The kiss on the cheek	• Re-emergence of creative and courageous self
Session 17: Termination	QIII: Non-intrusive Responding	Turning point 6 Happy faces and butterflies	• Child directly self-references as the character "Honey"

References

Achenbach, T.M. and Rescorla, L.A. (2000) *Manual for the ASEBA Preschool Forms and Profiles*. Burlington, VT: University of Vermont Department of Psychiatry.

Ansbacher, H. and Ansbacher, R. (eds) (1956) *The Individual Psychology of Alfred Adler*. New York: Basic Books.

Badenoch, B. (2008) *Being a Brain Wise Therapist*. New York: Norton.

Dreikurs, R. and Soltz, V. (1964) *Children: The Challenge*. New York: Hawthorn/Dutton.

Friedrich, W. (1997) *Child Sexual Behavior Inventory*. Lutz, FL: Psychological Assessment Resources.

Kottman, T. (2003) *Partners in Play: An Adlerian Approach to Play Therapy* (2nd edn). Alexandria, VA: American Counseling Association.

Kottman, T. (2009) Treatment Manual for Adlerian Play Therapy. Unpublished manuscript.

Kottman, T. and Ashby, J. (2015) Adlerian Play Therapy. In D. Crenshaw and A. Stewart (eds) *Play Therapy: A Comprehensive Guide to Theory and Practice*. New York: Guilford Press.

Lew, A. and Bettner, B.L. (1996) *Responsibility in the Classroom*. Newton Center, MA: Connexions.

Lew, A. and Bettner, B.L. (2000) *A Parent's Guide to Motivating Children*. Newton Center, MA: Connexions.

Ogden, P. and Fisher, J. (2015) *Sensorimotor Psychotherapy: Interventions for Trauma and Attachment*. New York: Norton & Company.

Ogden, P. and Minton, K. (2000) Sensorimotor psychotherapy: One method for processing traumatic memory. *Traumatology* 6, 3, 149–173. doi: 10.1177/153476560000600302

Perry, B. and Szalavitz, M. (2006/2017) *The Boy Who Was Raised as a Dog*. New York: Basic Books.

Porges, S. (2011) *The Polyvagal Theory: Neurobiological Foundations of Emotions, Attachment, Communication, and Self-Regulation*. New York: Norton & Company.

Siegel, D. (2012) *The Whole-Brain Child*. New York: Random House.

van der Kolk, B. (2014) *The Body Keeps the Score: Brain, Mind, and Body in the Healing of Trauma*. New York: Penguin Books.

Yasenik, L. and Gardner, K. (2004) *Play Therapy Dimensions Model: A Decision-Making Guide for Therapists*. Calgary, AB: Rocky Mountain Play Therapy Institute.

8

ACKNOWLEDGING THE UNEXPRESSED BENEATH TRAUMA

An Encounter of Subjectivities through Play Therapy

CAROLINA S. ARAYA, MAGDALENA S. OYANEDEL, AND FRANCISCA JENSCHKE SMITH

Translation and proofreading
by Soledad Sánchez D.

Case introduction

This chapter describes the case of a four-year-old boy, Benjamin,[1] who was a victim of sexual abuse. Specifically, it illustrates a few turning points along the play therapy process, which contributed to the child's path toward healing. These turning points took place during the first eight months of therapy when the sexual abuse had not yet been disclosed. They were moments in which the child and therapist embarked on a shared journey that would ultimately result in the unveiling of the abuse.

The child was initially referred to psychotherapy because of the multiple and severe symptoms he presented, such as irritability, nightmares, enuresis, encopresis, and compulsive masturbation. His parents expressed their concern that Benjamin might have been mistreated at the preschool he attended.

---

1   The name of the child and some of his personal data have been changed to protect his identity.

Once therapy began, Benjamin's play turned from that characterised by topics of defensiveness, into play themes that included threats, impotence, angst, and chaos. In the meantime, as successive play therapy sessions were analysed in group supervision meetings, and due to the severe exacerbation of pre-existing symptoms, the hypothesis of recent sexual victimisation began to take form.

The use of therapist's self, and particularly the use of therapist's subjectivity, was crucial to elucidate the underlying trauma. The construction of a safe relational space was the primary therapeutic goal during this initial period. The safe space was intended to facilitate Benjamin's disclosure of the abusive experience, as well as to protect him. At the same time, it was intended to establish the grounding necessary for the therapeutic encounter and elaboration process.

As therapists, we know that the disclosure of sexual abuse in a context of current transgression is extremely difficult. The child's psychic survival is at stake: the sense of coherence of his self depends on the activation of powerful defence mechanisms. Even at the cost of impoverishing his personality, those devices allow him to cope with a reality that threatens to disintegrate his self.

So, how could this young boy talk during sessions about things he needed to deny to survive? Which elements should we consider while establishing the therapeutic framework or setting, and which ones were most relevant for selecting appropriate interventions? Different theoretical approaches answer these questions in unique and sometimes disparate ways. At Metáfora (Chile), we use an integrative intervention framework. However, the theoretical ideas from Intersubjective and Relational Psychoanalysis have offered us useful concepts to reach a deeper understanding of play therapy processes, particularly with traumatised children. This theoretical approach differs in several aspects from classic psychoanalysis. While the classic approach recommends the use of neutrality and abstinence, the relational psychoanalytic approach highlights the therapist's subjectivity as the clinical tool. Importantly, the relational psychoanalyst acknowledges the inevitability of reciprocal influence between therapist and patient and recognises the co-construction of a mutual interactive domain as the core of the therapeutic process. In other words, for Intersubjective and Relational Psychoanalysis, both subjectivities (from the patient and therapist) are considered as critical components of the therapeutic process.

In the following section, we describe some of the main contributions to current streams of psychoanalytic thinking which can enrich the practice of play therapy. Conveying an in-depth account of the most important ideas of this approach is certainly beyond the scope of this chapter. Instead, we describe four concepts that were our "lighthouses" during the analysis of Benjamin's treatment: intersubjectivity, relational trauma, object-presenting, and affective regulation.

Theoretical orientation

To establish a common ground, we will briefly describe the historical development and assumptions of this conceptual framework.

In 1983, Greenberg and Mitchell were the first authors who synthesised ideas of diverse and even antagonistic schools of thinking under this contemporary perspective. They included original ideas and contributions from Ferenczi, Winnicott, Sullivan, and Kohut (Jordan, 2009; Orange, 2013). In the following decades, this approach expanded extensively.

Strictly speaking, this is not a unified framework. Intersubjective and Relational Psychoanalysis are different theoretical trends that share certain premises. Both approaches were developed in New York during the last decades of the twentieth century.

Although we recognise the differences between both theoretical trends, with regard to the case presented and analysed in this chapter, we will underline their commonalities.

First, they share an epistemological perspective strongly influenced by phenomenology (Husserl, 1954/1970) and dialogical hermeneutics (Gadamer, 1977/1999). Accordingly, they admit the impossibility of separating the person who knows from that which is to be known. In a way, the cognoscente and the object of their knowledge intertwine. As a corollary, both approaches claim that the mind is not an individual entity driven mostly by biological impulses. Rather, it is the result of an intersubjective matrix in which one's subjectivity is embedded, developed, and sustained (Jordan, 2009; Orange, 2013). The broader system created by the mutual interplay between both the analyst's and the patient's worlds become the core of psychoanalytic research. These authors propose the abandonment of the focus on the isolated mind (Stolorow and Atwood, 1992/2004).

This epistemological point of view is critical of Freudian metapsychology and introduces conceptual and methodological changes to the psychotherapeutic process. Regarding the conceptualisation of the clinical relationship, patient and therapist are acknowledged as mutually influencing subjects. Hence, the technique allows for therapist's self-disclosure. However, this use of the therapist's self is not indiscriminate; even though the relationship is reciprocally influential, it is, at the same time, asymmetrical. This notion implies that the therapist has an ethical responsibility towards their patient and must preserve both the patient's healing process and their general wellbeing. The therapist must be aware of the power involved in the therapeutic relationship (Aron, 1996/2002; Beebe and Lachmann, 2003).

Intersubjective and Relational Psychoanalysis have developed broadly in the field of adult psychotherapy. However, their contribution to child psychotherapy, particularly play therapy, has been less elaborated. Through the analysis of turning points identified in this case, we hope this chapter advances this discussion and supports practitioner understanding and applications of this approach.

1. Intersubjectivity

The acknowledgement of the intersubjective nature of the therapist-patient relationship established by this model redefines our understanding of the psychotherapeutic process. Such a process will be defined as "an encounter of two subjectivities", that is, as an experience that relies on the reciprocal influence between the interacting minds of both participants.

Stolorow and Atwood (1992/2004) claim that the therapist should become an expert investigating how their internal world's organisation modalities "interact" with the patient's, the implication being that the therapist is not a specialist in "what happens" to the patient any more.

The change psychotherapy pursues will no longer be an intrapsychic process—it will not be an insight propitiated by the analyst's interpretation. On the contrary, therapeutic change will begin with a change in the interpersonal field created by both therapist and patient. As a result, patterns of relationships transform, and new styles of communication are co-created in an interactive way. As Beebe and Lachmann (2003) pointed out, "expectancies that regulate intimate relating can be reorganized in the implicit domain without necessarily reaching conscious awareness. Therapeutic action can occur in the implicit mode without ever being translated into words" (p.391).

2. Relational trauma

Ferenczi (1933/1949) pointed out the relational origin of trauma. He proposed that an incident experienced as a threat of severe damage to physical or psychological integrity could originate trauma. Indeed, it becomes a trauma when the environment (the others) does not acknowledge nor validate the emotion that accompanies the event. The trauma, in that case, is always present, here and now. It is manifested through the body, the sensorial perceptions, and, of course, during the child's play. The lack of caregiver's validating empathy eventually damages the child's sense of truthfulness of their experiences. The child's ability to tolerate intense emotions is harmed, and the dissociative mechanisms become the last resource to preserve the integrity of self.

The traumatic experiences, plus the defence mechanisms deployed, have the power to obliterate nuclear aspects of psychic growth, disturbing the development of identity and autobiographical memory processes (Schore, 2010, 2011; van der Kolk, 2003). The dissociation becomes a stable mode of functioning that impoverishes the spectrum in which the life could be lived (Bromberg, 2009).

3. Play and object-presenting

Winnicott (1971/1999) described three functions that a "good enough" environment must provide to the child. Two of them refer to emotional behaviour and certain disposition from the mother (or primary caregiver) toward the baby: the holding and handling of the infant's physical and emotional needs. The third function is particularly important to us because it makes possible the development of play. Winnicott called it "object-presenting".

According to Winnicott, the good enough mother is the one who actively adapts to the infant's needs and can anticipate and satisfy them at the precise moment the baby expects this to occur. In doing so, the mother presents to her baby the appropriate object, in proper dosages that fulfil the baby's need, and simultaneously creates a "potential space". In other words, the well-fit coupling between mother and baby will allow the child to have an encounter with the reality in a creative form: the infant will have the omnipotent illusion of having created the object he/she needed.

The process of illusion will progressively give way to disillusionment. As the child matures and develops new resources and strengths, the good enough mother should "fail" more often in the satisfaction of their needs. To promote the child's awareness of their uniqueness, this lack of coupling must be sensitive, gradual, and appropriate. They will recognise themselves as an "other" separate from the mother. The increasing tension will be resolved creatively, through the emergence and use of transitional objects.

Applying Winnicott's ideas to our clinical practice, we subscribe that to promote therapeutic change in the patient the therapist should emulate the "good enough" mother's disposition. Having that goal in mind, and to allow the child to meet the therapeutic space creatively, the therapist's interventions have to be carefully and sensitively paced. They must be respectful of the timing of responses, sensitive to the child's needs, and aware of their use of self to avoid imposing their interpretation of needs or actions on the child. Further, we think that every time we, as the therapists, offer to the child or merely display miniatures, puppets, or expressive materials in the play therapy room we are carrying out the function described by Winnicott as object-presenting. Using toys or creative activities, such as clay and painting, the child can express their feelings and think in a way that was not previously available for them. The play therapist, as an adult sensitive to children's needs, brings the world closer to the child in a way that corresponds to their needs. Thus, the therapist allows the child to explore their world without fear and through play.

4. Affective regulation

There is sound scientific evidence showing that early and repeated experiences of co-regulation influence the development of children's ability to modify their mood and regulate the intensity of their emotional expression. According to Schore (2002), the infant refines their self-regulatory system, learning to regulate their emotional states through the interaction with significant others. Thus, the mother modifies her baby's inner state from outside.

This early interactive mechanism of emotional regulation has a long-term impact on development: it becomes an organising principle of the self. In the future, the individual will manage their affective experiences based on the internalised model (Beebe and Lachmann, 2002; Fosha, 2001).

Along with its function of the structuring of early psychic life, the mechanism of affective co-regulation also enables clinical interventions that promote therapeutic change. As Beebe and Lachmann (2002) have noted, the dyadic processes of interaction in psychotherapy can reorganise the primal principles of self.

Case study conceptualization

The turning points depicted here happened during the initial phase of Benjamin's therapeutic process. The first interventions took place in the compelling context of having to unveil the abuser's identity to protect the child. For that, the therapist worked simultaneously with the parents, the school staff, and the justice system, with clinical supervision as a continuous framework.

During this initial phase, it was not the time to introduce novelty in play. The therapist stayed mostly in Quadrant III: Non-intrusive Responding (Yasenik and Gardner, 2012), respecting the child's process and timing, and favouring the construction of a therapeutic bond. The verbal use of the therapist's self varied from low to moderate levels. She worked mainly at the level of the child's metaphorical play, using mostly reflective statements about content. Over time, the therapist gradually introduced reflective statements about emotions, as her growing emotional attunement with Benjamin allowed for a greater adaptation to his affective experiences during play. Due to the traumatic context, there was a frequent discrepancy between the emotions expressed in play and the ones expressed by his behaviour. Then, the focus on the therapist's subjectivity was more relevant. Further along the process, the therapist would generate interventions in the dimension of directiveness, approaching a co-facilitation role to integrate her perceptions gradually and in a playful way.

At first, Benjamin's playmates were a princess who was always threatened by a witch, and a protective lion that saved her every time. The therapist kept herself in a non-intrusive role, occasionally alternating with brief verbal statements, characteristic of Quadrant I: Active Utilization. Those verbal statements attempted to explore more profound contents and advance higher levels of consciousness. Notably, Benjamin systematically rejected this kind of intervention, evidenced by interruptions in his play. This put the therapist under much pressure since the symptomatology was still present and the hypothesis of current abuse seemed increasingly plausible. At this point, his play narrated a story of protection; Benjamin seemed calm. The therapist nonetheless was experiencing feelings of anxiety, fear, and impotence while she watched the play unfold.

The understanding of the supervision team was that Benjamin's play expressed how he hoped things would have been, but beneath that—dissociated, not explicitly or consciously aware—lay what he could not show or fully articulate and talk about. The therapist was "feeling that which Benjamin could not tolerate". Her challenge would be to advance towards a level in which she could favour the child's process and his protection.

Therapy process: turning points and emergence of self
Turning point 1: the monkey is the victim

Even before the first turning point, the themes evident in Benjamin's play had varied. He had moved from themes that were defensive to ones in which there was a constant atmosphere of threat. For example, earthquakes began, and the play expressed destruction, disaster, and disorder. The therapist's emotional involvement in the sessions had increased significantly, and she frequently used reflective statements about emotions. Benjamin's response to this kind of intervention was positive.

The therapist was emotionally immersed in the play to the degree that she could feel the threat of imminent destruction and the intensity of the impact. However, Benjamin did not integrate any characters that suffer the consequences in his play. That realm of experience was dissociated: omitted from the play. He embodied the power of destruction (as an earthquake) and seemed proud when the therapist was able to account for its magnitude. The therapist perceived and was affected by the intensity of the impact. She felt anguish and impotent.

In the context of an intersubjective matrix, the therapist was the one who experienced those feelings Benjamin could not tolerate. In her emotional self, she appraised the magnitude of the damage that had taken place and, in turn, needed to do something to support Benjamin to identify the dissociated affect. She worked to find a way to give expression to these feelings in a manner that Benjamin could approximate and tolerate.

At some point the intensity of Benjamin's play diminished, the earthquake had already taken place, and he ended his play. The therapist extended another invitation, watching closely to see if Benjamin accepted it, before attempting a new movement. She included a parrot, a puppet that in a previous session had offered a gateway. In that session, Benjamin had picked it and had suggested that the parrot knew what was bothering him.

> Therapist: What about the parrot? Where is it? (By that time the parrot had become a travel companion; Benjamin used it in every session.)
>
> (Benjamin activates himself, goes to the puppets' corner, and brings it.)
>
> Therapist (to Benjamin, looking doubtful): Does the parrot have friends?
>
> Benjamin: Yes, it does. A very dangerous lion (he growls).

Once more, Benjamin has chosen a character that represents aggression, just as earthquakes do. Hence, the therapist decides to advance in the dimension of directiveness but staying in the symbolic realm (Quadrant IV: Co-facilitation) by bringing in a new character. She introduces a character that could embody these experiences.

> (The therapist brings a monkey puppet into the play scene and places it close to the parrot in total silence. Then she makes the monkey tremble on the floor with its head hidden between its hands. She looks at Benjamin, who has not seen the new character yet. When their eyes meet, the therapist looks at the monkey and looks back at Benjamin with a puzzled expression.)
>
> Benjamin: What's going on with it?
>
> Therapist: I'm not sure...it looks like it's scared...

(Benjamin looks at the monkey and nods. Then he picks animals and starts attacking the monkey repeatedly.)

Therapist (voice-off, to Benjamin): How does the monkey feel?

Benjamin (voice-off, to the therapist): They are hurting him a lot, and the monkey is in pain.

Therapist (increasing the shaking of the monkey): Does anybody see what is happening to the monkey? Can it tell someone?

Benjamin: But look! See what's going on! (He begins to incarcerate the bad guys.) The monkey is afraid that they might escape. Look, look! They are escaping now!

The therapist thought Benjamin could not imagine that others would be able to acknowledge his victimisation and protect him. She decides to make one more movement. She picks the parrot and gives voice to it as a character that sees what is happening to the monkey. Benjamin includes it in the plot and even adds that they "were very good friends". A new gateway is opened in the play.

Therapist (as a parrot): Little monkey, you are so afraid!

Benjamin: Tell the parrot to watch! (He starts closing the gaps through which the "bad guys" were escaping.) And tell it to tell the monkey. Look, look! Don't worry; they are going to close the holes now!

The turning point here occurs with the addition of the new character (the monkey), which embodies the experience of harm (dissociated in the previous play), and the expansion of the parrot's role, which is now aware of the monkey's experiences. The therapist respects the symbolic space that Benjamin feels safer while favouring a deeper exploration of the issue of victimisation. The "monkey" is a victim, and the "parrot" knows what is happening to him. This allows Benjamin to have a new emotional experience regarding helplessness and harm, in the context of a validating and holding relationship.

In this scenario, the puppet (monkey) is the one who holds and feels those feelings Benjamin does not tolerate. By asking Benjamin to describe the nuances of the monkey's experience, the therapist respects the child's timing, enters the emotional scene defined by him, and expands it. The puppet is the one who suffers. The therapist expresses this in the tone of her voice and the way she handles the puppet. The addition of the monkey's character as a victim allows both Benjamin and his therapist to place this emotional experience of harm and helplessness "in the open space"—in the shared symbolic realm.

Suddenly, the words of Ferenczi resonate: the relational trauma occurs due to lack of recognition of others. The trauma freezes. Only when another (the therapist) recognises the emotion initially associated with the traumatic event does the event become an experience that can be symbolised or elaborated in therapy. This step is the cornerstone of trauma elaboration.

The parrot, on the other hand, embodied the possibility of awareness and validation of such experiences, thus initiating a new range of experiences for Benjamin, in which acknowledgement and help are possible. The monkey (handled by the therapist)—and through it, the child—learns how it feels being accompanied while facing pain, being contained and comforted. That sequence of play enables Benjamin to gradually begin to feel and think about his story in a different way.

The projection of feelings, especially those that were dissociated, onto the puppets, their embodiment in play, and the possibility of experiencing them (playing them) with the therapist will be the main ingredients of the elaboration task that Benjamin and his therapist are now undertaking. Bringing the dissociated feelings into the relational domain not only promotes the surfacing of implicit clinical issues but it also gives an opportunity to hold the accompanying emotional activation and turn it into a new experience of affective co-regulation.

Turning point 2: just one boy knew what the lion was doing

In the previous meetings, Benjamin played with the miniatures on the floor. As previously discussed, Benjamin often chose a lion and a princess. He described the lion as the most kind and protective figure. In this session, Benjamin includes something different. Another side of the lion emerges: it is also the worst guy, though it still has admirable traits.

> Benjamin: Look! It was mean to the birds! (He smashes them with his foot.) The birds try to run away from him, but it catches them and puts them in the cage. It was mean to the trees (Benjamin grabs them and throws them away), mean to everyone, everybody. But look! It

was good to the birds, good to the trees, look! It even planted one of them!

The therapist identifies the change in the play's narrative, but she feels confused. She watches herself reflecting both features of the lion, though she feels trapped as if she could not adopt an integrated position facing the lion. However, she sustains the tension and does not force the child to choose between the dissociated aspects of the character. The lion can be both simultaneously.

In working cases of sexual abuse, we know that offenders have a role that allows them to exert power over their victims, and they frequently maintain a relationship of emotional dependence. The person who hurts the child is at the same time someone they love. Thus, the description of this lion indicates progress in Benjamin's play, though it also poses the challenge of integration. The way in which the therapist gets involved in his play allows Benjamin to amplify his awareness and deepen the view of himself, and the feelings regarding the experiences of transgression. Sheltered in the safe space of play, he can say there is only one boy who knows what is happening.

> Benjamin: Look! It was good even to the bridges, and it always cared no one would fall, and he also loved the kids very much. He did not want them to die, and he did this to them. (Benjamin stops for a moment and then makes the gesture of licking the boy's face.) He caressed them that way. Lions don't have hands as we do.

In this segment of play, Benjamin shows no significant emotional involvement. In describing how good the lion was, his speech has an emotional tone that conveys kindness and tenderness, feelings that are not connected to those he shows when he talks about how mean the lion also is. Benjamin can stay in the "serenity" provided by dissociation and contemplate the "good" part of the lion; he does not appear to be impacted by the "mean" part of the same character. The therapist's experience of the same scene is different. She perceives the dissonance arising from the dichotomy between both aspects and begins to feel restless due to the vulnerability implicit in the inability to integrate the good and the mean parts. Registering her own subjectivity and moved by the lack of an affective response that accounts for the transgression of limits that is implicit in the act of licking the boy's face, the therapist looks for appropriate intervention. She experiences herself in the position of the boy being licked by the lion. The therapist feels disgusted and frightened. Then, she tries to acknowledge and validate those unexpressed feelings by asking him a question:

> Therapist: And how do the boys feel about the lion licking them?
>
> Benjamin: They think it's mean!

This intervention is successful and allows Benjamin to begin to bring the experience of transgression to the play scene. The therapist repeats the story aloud and decides to make an additional intervention.

> Therapist: What can they do to stop the lion from doing this?
>
> Benjamin: Just one boy knew what the lion was doing. He is a silly and ugly boy. (Benjamin includes the miniature of an alien to represent the silly boy.) And the lion did this to him. (At that point Benjamin stops, hesitating.) Since this is play, I can do this. (He takes the miniature and licks its whole head.) It licked him all over his head.

The tension in the play scene increases; the therapist's intervention helped Benjamin begin to consider or think about the ordeals he, in fact, has experienced. Benjamin becomes physically restless, and the therapist decides to increase the degree of consciousness by making a brief interpretive/reflective comment and a supportive statement, characteristic of Quadrant I: Active Utilization.

> Therapist: Benjamin, I know you have also been through some things you don't like, with people that are good and bad at the same time. We will work together so these things don't happen again. (Benjamin does not respond verbally, but says he wants to play.)
>
> Benjamin: Can we play with the monkey, the cages, and the lion too? Oh, yes, this one is the only one who knew the lion had done mean things.
>
> (The therapist takes the monkey. Benjamin assembles the cages, puts the mean characters inside, and, taking off the puppet parrot, starts hitting them.)
>
> Benjamin: The bad ones all run when they see the parrot because they are afraid of it.

Therapist (voice-off, to Benjamin): This time it's different for the monkey. This time there is someone who notices the bad guys that hurt him, someone who protects him.

Benjamin: That's true! Now I'm going to tell you a story, and then you tell it to the parrot, okay? There was a bad guy who pretended to be good, but he actually robbed money and children.

The child is now incorporating nuances of the characters in his play. They are not simply good or mean as in the previous scenes, but ambivalence appears, as some characters might be simultaneously good and bad. We think that the ability of the therapist to reflect this back to the child and connect him with his own experience (Quadrant I: Active Utilization) promotes a turning point in Benjamin's process. After this, Benjamin begins to express his experience, at the symbolic level, in a more structured and clear way, with a deeper and richer manifestation of clinical themes.

Additionally, there is a turn in the ending of the stories, as bad guys are identified and punished. We believe this might be associated with changes in Benjamin's self-image. Due to the transformation that is taking place in the identity of the characters, one could hypothesise that a change is beginning to take place in Benjamin's image of his I-Self (Harter, 2012), which for the first time has an active role in the fight against those who use threats.

Turning point 3: the parrot's phone

In this session, Benjamin did not begin to play spontaneously. He asked for his therapist's guidance. She decided to move towards Quadrant IV: Co-facilitation by entering the play in role and proposing they build a telephone for the parrot. Benjamin looked excited. When the phone was finished, Benjamin took the parrot, placed himself under the table, and started calling. The therapist answered and verified she could hear all right. The parrot (Benjamin) narrated various events regarding situations Benjamin had experienced at school. Then he came out of his hiding place and commented on how well one can hear on this phone. The therapist encouraged Benjamin to try hearing a secret by wondering: Can one hear the secrets as clearly as other things?

In that episode, we can see how the therapist adapted to the scene but also introduced the theme of the secret. Considering what has taken place in the previous sessions, she thinks Benjamin has gained in strength and might be more willing to reveal his traumatic experiences. At the same time, the symptomatology had increased, especially the masturbatory behaviour, the encopresis, and the affective dysregulation. The intensity of these symptoms seemed to indicate that sexual abuse was a current experience. Accordingly, the therapist felt compelled to open the discussion with the child, once more. The certainty of the present victimisation suffered by Benjamin was creating great anguish for the therapist. Perhaps the advances achieved in the therapeutic process might allow for a different answer from Benjamin this time.

Benjamin: Let's try! (He goes under the table.)

Benjamin (as the parrot): Hello, hello?

Therapist: Hello parrot. Can you hear well? What would you like to tell me?

Benjamin (as the parrot): What secret do you want to talk about?

Therapist: Do you want to tell a secret?

Benjamin (as the parrot): Yes.

The therapist was aware the intervention had been successful, for Benjamin had accepted the invitation to talk about a secret. However, she noted that Benjamin was speaking softer and perceived his insecurity. Since in previous attempts Benjamin had rejected interventions oriented to consciousness or had interrupted his play, she was insecure herself. The therapist decided to explore the secret's theme, careful not to pressure the child.

Therapist: For how long have you been keeping that secret?

Benjamin (as the parrot): For 1000 years.

Therapist: And how does it feel to keep a secret for 1000 years?

Benjamin: Fine.

Therapist: How does Benjamin feel about that secret?

Benjamin (as the parrot): Mmmm... Not so good.

The child accepted the therapist's movement toward a higher level of consciousness. As we already knew he felt terrible for keeping the secret, the goal was to connect his play to his experience. The therapist also wished to understand if he had been able to talk to somebody, but Benjamin (as the parrot) could no longer answer, and the play stopped. At that point, Benjamin said he wanted to poo.

Benjamin: Right now, I want to poo.

Therapist: Sometimes worries make us want to poo.

The therapist could feel Benjamin's anguish. She felt that the traumatic experience expressed by the play was evident and perceived the child's tension. Moving to Quadrant II, the therapist held Benjamin's hands:

Therapist: Benjamin, do you remember when we met? I told you I knew you were going through some painful stuff, and I also knew it was very hard to talk about that.

Benjamin: Yes.

Therapist (pausing, noting that the child is receptive to the intervention): Have you been able to talk to someone about what you are going through?

Benjamin: No.

Therapist: I know that person is good but does things that make you feel bad. Do you think you can tell someone who that person is?

(Benjamin changes the subject.)

Therapist (taking his hands again): I know children who have lived the same things you have.

Benjamin: What happened to them?

Therapist: A grownup hurt them.

Benjamin: Just like it happened to me?

Therapist: That's right. I learned from them that it is very hard to talk about what is going on, but when they managed to do it, we did things to prevent it from ever happening again.

The therapist felt that both she and Benjamin had given a reality status (for the first time) to the assaults Benjamin endured. She knew Benjamin could not talk directly about the sexual abuse he suffered, but in this session, they had acknowledged the existence of a painful secret related to the adult who assaulted him.

The session ended after the therapist handed Benjamin a talisman to which children tell their secret when they still cannot say it out loud. He approached the talisman and said his secret silently. Then, Benjamin decided to put the talisman in the monkey's house (a place he knew, and where other children had left their talismans previously). When leaving the therapy room, he came back, took some masking tape, and stuck some pieces on the monkey's house. He said: "So, his house resists."

This was a turning point in the therapeutic process. After this session Benjamin revealed the identity of his abuser to his mother. The therapist's movement towards a higher level of consciousness (Quadrants IV and II) was well received by Benjamin and made it possible for him to put into words what had previously been unnameable—and probably unthinkable—until now. The encounter with a therapist who adapted to his timing and defences, who provided a space in play to elaborate his traumatic experiences, coupled with the work with his parents, gave Benjamin a context that offered the safety and validation he needed for letting go of his secret.

Turning point 4: the bad guys' school

After Benjamin's revelation, there were some recanting episodes. Dealing with the reality of his experience was sometimes unbearable for him and his family as well. As the elaboration process progressed, Benjamin's need to rescue positive traits of his abuser—with whom he had a very significant affective bond—was more apparent.

In this session, the therapist began in the role of Non-intrusive Responding (Quadrant III) to explore the play themes that Benjamin brought forward spontaneously. Once the abuse was revealed, that seemed the best way to approach and observe the evolution of Benjamin's play.

Benjamin built a school where there was a dragon that misbehaved (it hit others, made a mess everywhere, and did "things" to other people's private parts). During play, it was indicated that the dragon should learn to behave. Two characters oversaw keeping guard on its behaviour. If the dragon did terrible things, they locked it up at school "until it learns". Then, they released it to see if it had learned. In the beginning, it appeared it had, but then it always backslid. "It looks like it will never ever learn. It's been almost a year of this", Benjamin said. He checked again, and this time the dragon behaved fine. Benjamin congratulated and rewarded it, and allowed it to go outside. But it hit out again, and Benjamin locked it up once more.

Benjamin played with characters that were both good and bad on various occasions; he emphasised that they do good and bad things. The therapist thought this seemed to be important to him and hypothesised that Benjamin needed to integrate an experience that could be very confusing and contradictory. The therapist decided to support the movement to a higher level of consciousness, and this became another turning point.

> Therapist: It's amazing how this dragon learns some things. Do you think W[2] does good things too?
>
> Benjamin: W does many good things, and look at the good things the dragon does (he points at the play): he caresses but with his horns.
>
> (Then Benjamin looks at his therapist and implicitly tries to obtain her disapproval of W's behaviour. The therapist confirms his objection and aligns with him.)
>
> Benjamin: So, go learning at school!
>
> Therapist (taking what Benjamin has put in his play, and making another statement to support consciousness again): W should also learn to caress appropriately.
>
> Benjamin: He caresses in a very nice way, but also in a bad one.
>
> (The therapist then makes a reflective statement, reaffirming what Benjamin just said.)
>
> (Benjamin resumes his play and adds a character that sets rules for the dragon. In a whisper, he tells the following rules to the therapist and asks her to tell them to the dragon.)
>
> Therapist (addressing the dragon and naming the rules): 1) no hitting; 2) no messing up; 3) no touching other people's private parts.

---

2   W is the name of the abuser.

(Benjamin also speaks to the dragon, trying to check if it learned the rules. He specifically asks the dragon about each rule, and he answers as the dragon. The only rule the dragon has not learned is the one about not touching private parts.)

The therapist's intervention made it easier for Benjamin to integrate his experience into his play in a concrete and quite literal manner. Affection and abuse could coexist in play in a way that Benjamin was able to tolerate. The dragon could do good things for which it was recognised, but if it did not comply with the rules, there would be consequences.

Tension had been decreasing in the therapeutic work with Benjamin. His selection of play modalities was flexible and diverse, and the therapist could accompany him in different ways: tracking his play, joining it, and even making invitations for various kinds of play activities. There was less defensiveness now. Benjamin integrated themes of harm and punishment, ambivalent feelings, and the need for the bad guy to learn to behave. Since he had been able to reveal his experience, it was now possible for the therapist to support Benjamin in moving toward higher levels of consciousness. The elaboration of the traumatic experience was at the centre of the work. In this phase, the therapist used reflective statements more frequently. These comments helped deepen his experience, acknowledged and validated his feelings, and identified and strengthened his resources. There were definite rules of behaviour in his play; those who did not comply with them were penalised, and there was acknowledgement and protection for the victims.

Turning point 5: the builder

In this session, Benjamin was playing with the miniatures and wanted to build something with cages. He took a long time to assemble his work and looked very satisfied and proud of what he made, stating, "It is a huge school." He added, "You will be surprised at all the patients we are going to have." He brought over a bunch of "bad guys" who did not behave. Benjamin and his therapist were the ones in charge of detecting and trapping those that did not follow the rules. It was hard work because Benjamin was conceding increased powers to the bad guys. In consequence, the therapist decided to take a more active role in the play.

> Therapist (giving voice to school staff, looking at Benjamin): What a big school! Are you the builder of this school Mr.?
>
> Benjamin (smiling, changing the tone of his voice and his posture): That's right. I'm the builder.
>
> Therapist: Mr Builder, since you are very big, and you see everything, please let us know if you see anyone who doesn't comply with the rules.
>
> Benjamin: Okay, I will tell you. (He begins catching the bad guys in a very calm and efficient manner. He says he can see those who misbehave. He looks very proud of himself in that role.)
>
> Benjamin (adding in that precise moment): But now the meanest guy is out, and no one, no one can catch it. The police officer and the security guards try to, but they fail. The dragon hits everybody in the world, it is harmful, and it destroys the school.
>
> (The therapist looks at Benjamin; she could feel how close the re-entry of feelings of destruction and inevitability are again in the play. As a result, she needed to open up the possibility that Benjamin, through the metaphor of play, could exert control or power by activating a different strategy this time.)
>
> Therapist (looking at Benjamin with a worried face): What can be done in that world?
>
> Benjamin: Nothing.
>
> (The therapist sustained her gaze toward Benjamin, which perhaps created an opening for a new answer from Benjamin.)
>
> Benjamin (responding with great confidence): But I am bigger (referring to some of the toys), and I can grab it.

In retrospect, this was another turning point in the therapy process. The therapist facilitated an opportunity for Benjamin to embody, in first person, the role of builder of the big school. The goal of introducing this idea was not only that Benjamin could gradually increase his power role in the context of his play, but also that he would experience the feeling of safety and protection. He accepted this play insertion and identified with this position. This turning point offered Benjamin a new perspective, promoted the expression of feelings of power and control, and gave him the opportunity to identify and become in touch with personal resources.

> Therapist (as a police officer, talking to a bad guy): We know you are mean and powerful, and there is nothing we can do, but there's something you ignore. The builder is much bigger, powerful, and braver than you are, and he can catch you. (At this point, Benjamin easily catches the bad guy.) He is not afraid, and it is not difficult to leave you at school.
>
> Therapist (as a foreman): Now you will have to learn; since you are the meanest of all, clearly you aren't brave, and you won't tell us what you've done, but it doesn't matter because the builder is taller.
>
> Benjamin (interrupting the therapist): I'm taller than you, I see everything you do, and I've told them everything you do.

In this play segment, Benjamin was playing in first person, in an influential role, but needed to share his experience with the therapist and to receive her explicit confirmation.

The turning point was implicit in the act of impersonating the builder. This role provided Benjamin with a safe place in his play and made it is impossible to doubt his perceptions. Indeed, he was taller than the other characters (he enjoyed telling them this repeatedly), and from that position, he could clearly see what they did. Nothing could cast doubts on his ability.

> Therapist: Yes, we know exactly what you have done, so you will stay here until you manage to learn everything all over again. Now we know it's you, and you won't be able to do any more harm. We're sorry for you, but the builder sees everything.
>
> Benjamin: *And I tell everyone.*

The last statement speaks to Benjamin's empowerment. The strengthening of his self-esteem was evident, as was a positive self-perception. Furthermore, there was a fundamental change in the narrative about the self, the Me-Self, and the I-Self (Harter, 2012), which had been compromised by the abusive experience.

Final remarks

The clinical case described in this chapter illustrates our therapeutic approach in the context of relational trauma. The unveiling of sexual abuse, and, after this, beginning the process of elaborating the experience, was made possible through the encounter of the child and his therapist's subjectivities.

We think there were at least three elements that sustained Benjamin's psychological growth in this therapy phase. First, the ability of the therapist to act as a "good enough" caregiver who could adapt to the child's needs while at the same time encouraging him to approach those very emotions and experiences he actively avoided. In practice, this meant staying with the child long enough in the metaphorical space (Quadrants III and IV). Certainly, moving towards higher levels of consciousness (Quadrants I and II) was initially difficult, but then it became a great tool. The balanced and flexible interaction between these factors was at the core of the turning points we identified in Benjamin's therapeutic process.

Second, the tool provided by the analysis of the intersubjective matrix was a critical component of the healing process. Although this "interpersonal device" lay at the foundation of the whole therapeutic process, it was through the puppets' play that the intersubjective dance becomes increasingly noticeable. Therapist and child were playing and expressing feelings, ideas, and experiences. The matrix guided the play's script. The therapist's degree of immersion was higher and involved more activation of her physical self, her emotional self, and her self-system. She was constantly monitoring her subjectivity, along with the emotional atmosphere in the sessions and Benjamin's reactions to her behaviour.

The importance of placing the child-therapist relationship at the centre of the therapeutic work was confirmed throughout the whole process. The sensitivity of the therapist to recognise and adapt herself to Benjamin's timing and functioning style, the respect for his ways of understanding and expressing himself, the use of creativity, and the ability to tolerate and contain very intense experiences and emotions were significant resources. However, the cornerstone was the human encounter of feelings and ideas. This encounter between therapist and child manifests itself in play—they both shared and encountered that emotional experience multiple times.

Third, aligned with the notion of intersubjectivity, Winnicott's ideas (1971/1999) regarding the role of the environment in the presentation of the object were highly relevant to the underlying processes. When we, as therapists, add novelty to play we must be able to present this reality in a way that allows the child to encounter it creatively. The child must feel that they meet something and create it at the same time (Winnicott's notion of illusion). Although strictly speaking we know the therapist and child co-create the experience, none of them defines the story by themselves.

To conclude, both the therapist and the child witnessed what was being played, felt, and elaborated in play and their relationship. The content was not only projected on to the miniatures or the artistic expression but was resonating in the relationship, thus opening new opportunities for affective co-regulation. To the extent that the therapist sustained the emotional experience and helped the child process it, the recognition of harm at the relational level was feasible. Now the unexpressed was a shared and acknowledged experience. At that moment moving forward became possible.

Turning points summary

Stage in process	Quadrant	Turning points	What contributed to the turning point?
Initial sessions: There is an atmosphere of threat, destruction, disaster, and disorder in play; working for the establishment of the relationship and a shared language in play	QIV: Co-facilitation	The monkey is the victim	• The dissociation of the emotion connected to the traumatic experience is making itself apparent in Benjamin's play • The therapist experiences those feelings, and she brings them to the shared play scenario • That happens through the inclusion of a new puppet: the monkey. The character embodies the damage experience and expands the parrot's role: now he knows how the monkey feels

cont.

Stage in process	Quadrant	Turning points	What contributed to the turning point?
Confounding sessions: Dissonance between clinical themes and child's affective involvement	QI: Active Utilization	Just one boy knew what the lion was doing	• When the therapist can see the dissociated and contradictory aspects of a character, she feels confused • The therapist feels concern in front of the boy's lack of coherent affective response, while he was dealing with the evil character. She felt compelled to intervene in the play's plot, putting her ambivalence and confusion at the service of the process • Both the therapist and the patient recognise that characters and people might be good and bad at the same time. And facing that ambivalence, it is legitimate to feel rejection sometimes and fondness, at other times. That is especially true when the person who hurt you is somebody emotionally close
Play is more organised; the boy has gained in strength	QIV: Co-facilitation, QII: Open Discussion and Exploration	The parrot's phone	• The achievement of integration between isolated events and emotions, all along the play therapy sessions, have allowed the arising of a stronger sense of self in Benjamin. So, when the traumatic memories re-appear in the play narratives, the therapist decides to move forward to a higher level of directiveness in her interventions. She uses strategies from Quadrants II and IV to connect the boy's play with the traumatic experiences • The acknowledgement of emotions felt during the assaults suffered facilitates the disclosure to his mother of the sexual abuse endured

The boy has revealed the abuse. He runs the play and is dealing with his feelings towards the abuser	QI: Active Utilization	The bad guys' school	• Acknowledgement and validation of the possibility of having ambivalent and contradictory feelings towards the same person • Benjamin includes new characters and plots in his play. He opens new possibilities: the bad guys have the chance of learning how to be good. This allows for a more hopeful and benevolent perspective regarding people who behave in hurtful ways. At the same time, the boy establishes clearer limits between acceptable and unacceptable behaviour. The movement towards Quadrant I promoted by the therapist facilitates the validation of the wide range of feelings the boy experienced in his relation with W
The play is more organised: Benjamin is more empowered. He has created a school for bad guys to learn to behave	QIV: Co-facilitation	The builder	• Benjamin includes a new character in his play. He chooses to impersonate the character. That allows him to discover a new position. Now it is impossible to doubt about his perceptions. "I see everything, and I've told them everything you do" • He feels proud of himself. The disclosure is not just a threatening situation any more

References

Aron, L. (1996/2002) *A Meeting of Minds: Mutuality in Psychoanalysis* (Volume 4, Relational Perspectives Book Series). Hillsdale, NJ: The Analytic Press.

Beebe, B. and Lachmann, F. (2002) Organizing principles of interaction from infant research and the lifespan prediction of attachment: Application to adult treatment. *Journal of Infant, Child, and Adolescent Psychotherapy 2*, 4, 61–89. https://doi.org/10.1080/15289168.2002.10486420

Beebe, B. and Lachmann, F. (2003) The relational turn in psychoanalysis: A dyadic systems view from infant research. *Contemporary Psychoanalysis 39*, 3, 379–409. https://doi.org/10.1080/00107530.2003.10747213

Bromberg, P. (2009) Reduciendo el Tsunami. Regulación afectiva, disociación y la sombra de la inundación. *Clínica e Investigación Relacional 3*, 1, 93–110.

Ferenczi, S. (1933/1949) Confusion of tongues between the adult and the child (The language of tenderness and of passion). *International Journal of Psycho-Analysis 30*, 225–230.

Fosha, D. (2001) The dyadic regulation of affect. *Journal of Clinical Psychology 57*, 2, 227–242.

Gadamer, H.G. (1977/1999) *Verdad y Método I*. Octava edición. Salamanca: Editorial Sígueme.

Greenberg, J.R. and Mitchell, S.A. (1983) *Object Relations in Psychoanalytic Theory*. Cambridge, MA: Harvard University Press.

Harter, S. (2012) *The Construction of the Self: Developmental and Sociocultural Foundations* (2nd edn). New York: The Guilford Press.

Husserl, E. (1954/1970) *The Crisis of European Sciences and Transcendental Phenomenology*. First printing. Evanston: Northwestern University Press.

Jordan, J.F. (2009) Una introducción al psicoanálisis intersubjetivo y relacional. *Revista Chilena de Psicoanálisis 26*, 1, 6–12.

Orange, D.M. (2013) *El desconocido que sufre. Hermenéutica para la práctica clínica cotidiana*. Santiago, Chile: Editorial Cuatro Vientos.

Schore, A.N. (2002) Advances in neuropsychoanalysis, attachment theory, and trauma research: Implications for self psychology. *Psychoanalytic Inquiry 22*, 3, 433–484. https://doi.org/10.1080/07351692209348996

Schore, A.N. (2010) El trauma relacional y el cerebro derecho en desarrollo: Interfaz entre psicología. *Gaceta de Psiquiatría Universitaria 6*, 3, 296–308.

Schore, A.N. (2011) The right brain implicit self lies at the core of psychoanalysis. *Psychoanalytic Dialogues 21*, 1, 75–100. https://doi.org/10.1080/10481885.2011.545329

Stolorow, R. and Atwood, G. (1992/2004) *Los Contextos del Ser. Las Bases Intersubjetivas de la vida Psíquica*. Barcelona: Editorial Herder.

van der Kolk, B.A. (2003) The Developmental Impact of Childhood Trauma. In L.J. Kirmayer, R. Lemelson and M. Barad (eds) *Understanding Trauma: Integrating Biological, Clinical, and Cultural Perspectives*. Cambridge: Cambridge University Press.

Winnicott, D.W. (1971/1999) *Playing and Reality*. London: Routledge.

Yasenik, L. and Gardner, K. (2012) *Play Therapy Dimensions Model: A Decision-Making Guide for Integrative Play Therapists*. London: Jessica Kingsley Publishers.

9

THE THERAPEUTIC DANCE

The Role of Affective Synchrony in Guiding Therapists When to Lead and When to Follow in Psychotherapy with Traumatized Children

—— KATHERINE OLEJNICZAK ——

Case introduction

I vividly recall the first time Shyanne introduced herself to me. "You be the worm," she said, as she gazed at me intensely with her dark, moist, "puppy dog" eyes. Yet these "puppy dog" eyes were not of innocence or naivety. Rather, they conveyed the wisdom of deep self-knowing—of having tested the safety of our emerging relationship—and with imploring vulnerability she was communicating, "Here I am…I trust you…I need you to help me…I want you to help me."

In fact, I had actually first met Shyanne eight weeks earlier and we had been having weekly therapy sessions since then. I had come to learn a lot about her and her trauma history, and the impacts of this now manifesting in her life. Most importantly though, I had learned that Shyanne still held a flickering light of hope for connection with others, despite her protective defenses against this which had kept her safe in her world where she could not trust adults to do this for her.

Shyanne was seven years old when she was first referred for trauma therapy. She attended a total of 42 therapy sessions with me over a period of two years, with an integrative play therapy approach being the primary therapeutic intervention, within a trauma therapy framework.

This chapter explores the integration of principles from trauma therapy, neuroscience of psychotherapy, and the Play Therapy Dimensions Model (PTDM; Yasenik and Gardner, 2012), in guiding clinical practice with traumatized children like Shyanne.

Theoretical orientation
The Play Therapy Dimensions Model—Revised (PTDM-R)

Central to my work with children is the critical consideration of what the child's therapeutic need is and what is in their best interests. Hence, my practice is grounded in child development and attachment theories, and underpinned by neuroscience, privileging the child's need for developmentally appropriate and neurobiologically sensitive interventions. Thus, play therapy has become my primary therapeutic modality, utilizing an integrative play therapy approach and the PTDM (Yasenik and Gardner, 2012) in guiding my clinical decision-making.

Integrative play therapy offers flexibility in responding to children's individual needs, particularly traumatized children (Drewes, Bratton and Schaeffer, 2011; Gil, 2006, 2012), with the maxim being to "follow the child's need" rather than "follow the child's lead" (Goodyear-Brown, 2010). That is, in taking the philosophical stance of therapeutic practice based on the child's needs, the child communicates whether they need the therapist to follow their lead (i.e. being non-directive), or to facilitate part of the therapeutic process with greater "immersion" (i.e. being more directive).

Olejniczak (2013) proposed an enhancement to the PTDM, referring to this new model as the Play Therapy Dimensions Model—Revised (PTDM-R). The PTDM-R adds several new neurobiological domains as central to mediating clinical decision-making along both directiveness and consciousness dimensions. Of focus here is the Regulation and window of tolerance (WOT) domain (Figure 9.1).

Olejniczak (2013) asserted that the child moderating factors proposed by Yasenik and Gardner (2012) in conceptualizing the child's presentation during the play therapy process are largely a function of the child's regulatory capacity at any point in time. When a child becomes dysregulated and moves outside their WOT, their functioning becomes compromised across a range of developmental and functional domains (Cook *et al.*, 2005). These impacts are subsequently observed in the play therapy process as regressions in the child's functioning on the child moderating factors: play, communication, and relational skills, development, emotional expression, self-regulation ability, attachment organization, worldview, defense mechanisms, and resilience.

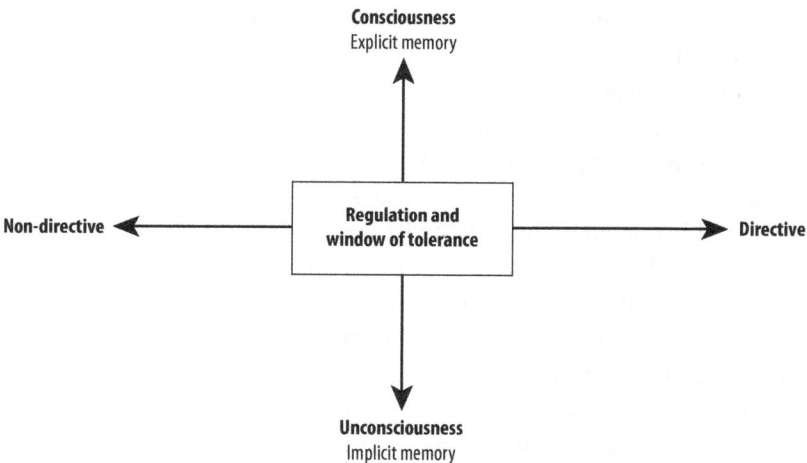

Figure 9.1 Play Therapy Dimensions Model—Revised (PTDM-R; Olejniczak, 2013)

Thus, the therapist developing an intimate understanding of the child's regulatory profile through the WOT enables moment-to-moment assessment of the child's functional abilities associated with her arousal state and capacity for movement through the PTDM quadrants within, and between, sessions.

The WOT conceptualizes the arousal system as a "zone within which various intensities of emotional and physiological arousal can be processed without disrupting the functioning of the system" (Siegel, 1999, p.253). When our autonomic and affective functioning is regulated, we are operating within our WOT and our bodies communicate to us that we are in a state of physiological safety—we feel safe (Porges, 2011). We are functioning in our most optimal state (Hill, 2015; Ogden, Minton and Pain, 2006), being at our most flexible and adaptable, effectively responding to the changing circumstances of our internal experiences and the world around us (Siegel, 1999). We are able to access our social engagement system to effectively relate with others (Porges, 2011), and we have capacity to act on our innate biological drive of curiosity, to explore and play (Perry, Hogan and Marlin, 2000). Our cognitive functioning allows us to undertake complex functions such as thinking and reasoning, and we are at our most creative (Perry, 2006). Our brain and body have been able to effectively integrate the sensory, affective, and cognitive aspects of our experience (Hill, 2015), and we are able to make meaning with a coherent narrative and integrated self-system (Schore, 2003; Tronick and Beeghly, 2011).

However, when we become distressed, arousal moves outside our WOT, evoking a dysregulated survival response of mobilization/hyper-arousal or immobilization/hypo-arousal. Our bodies become primed to respond to threat—we do not feel safe. We are operating outside our WOT, with our attention oriented towards perceptions of threat. We become less able to integrate incoming sensory information, storing only fragments of the experience to avoid it in future. We are less adaptive to changes in our internal and external worlds, and our cognitive function, and capacities to socially engage, be curious, explore, and play become compromised. Experiences often remain fragmented, impacting our ability to make meaning of them, with chronic states impacting on development of an integrated experience of self (Hill, 2015).

An important element of play therapy intervention with traumatized children is recognizing the child's states of mobilization/immobilization, managing their physiology to within an appropriate WOT. This minimizes the duration and impact of their dysregulated states that may further maintain their trauma symptomology (Goodyear-Brown, 2010; Ogden et al., 2006; Perry, 2006). As therapy progresses, trauma intervention focuses on working with a child's regulation and affect at the edges of their WOT (Cozolino, 2010; Ogden et al., 2006). This helps to broaden their WOT by supporting them to "re-experience dysregulating affects in affectively tolerable doses in the context of a safe environment, so that overwhelming traumatic feelings can be regulated and integrated into the patient's emotional life" (Schore, 2009, p.130).

Affective synchrony and affect regulation in psychotherapy

The dysregulated arousal response in children is, in the first instance, modulated by the child's caregiver. Through the attuned caregiver in the intersubjective space of the caregiver-child dyadic relationship, the child develops affect regulation (Tronick, 2007) and, ultimately, a healthy emergence of self (Schore, 2003). The synchronist dance between caregiver and child affective states during these attuned interactions are like a dance, with the caregiver moving together with the child's rises and falls of the body, co-creating a shared, psychobiologically attuned experience (Ham and Tronick, 2009).

As in secure attachment, affective synchrony is essential in play therapy; it is the foundation for safety and trust in the therapeutic relationship. The attuned therapist is psychobiologically in sync with the child's affective and physiological states and responding to these, co-creating an intersubjective space within which the child experiences a felt sense of "being with" (Dalai Lama Center, 2011) and of empathy and acceptance (Golding and Hughes, 2012). This enables the therapist's use of self to "co-create play contexts that can form an attachment, a bond of emotional communication and interactive regulation" (Schore, 2017, p.129).

Inherent in the play therapy process with traumatized children are the misattunements, ruptures, and repair characteristic of any relationship (Tronick, 2007), particularly as the child re-enacts attachment trauma within her relationship with the therapist. It is in this space of interactive repair that therapeutic change can occur, with the child being held in a synchronistic dance that provides the co-regulatory milieu within which they can safely experience a range of positive and negative affect, broaden their WOT, and develop new ways of responding to these new relational experiences with self and other (Schore, 2017).

Using the WOT to guide decision-making through the PTDM quadrants facilitates the therapist's attunement with the child's titration to their traumatic material at the edges of their WOT—without an escalation in their physiological arousal beyond that which they can tolerate. Within the context of relational safety, the therapist is able to engage in the roles as both partner in their dance and as a titration agent (Goodyear-Brown, 2010), providing attuned and contingent responses. However, for the child who moves outside of their WOT during this process and who has poor self-regulation capacity, the therapist is able to utilize a more directive approach to co-regulate the child back to within their WOT. This relationally rich reparative context offers the child interactive repair, providing co-regulation of their internal state, thereby developing increased self-regulation capacities.

The relational context of play therapy, structured in a sensitive manner to children's needs, can reconfigure a child's neurobiological balance and promote more adaptive responses. The flexibility of the dimensions of the PTDM allows for the synchronistic dance to occur between the child and therapist, as the therapist ultimately supports the child to process and integrate their trauma experiences within an appropriate WOT. Furthermore, the inclusion of the Regulation and WOT domain to the PTDM-R offers therapists a model of practice congruent with the trauma paradigm and therapeutic framework. It articulates the processes through which to support the child to function within their WOT, expanding this by working at its regulatory boundaries, and thus supporting the weaving process of unconscious implicit memories to be integrated into conscious explicit memory.

Case study conceptualization

Shyanne was seven years old when she was referred for trauma therapy by child protective services. She was of Australian Aboriginal culture, although her family did not identify strongly with their aboriginality. She was living in her third foster care placement after being removed from her mother (Karli) eight months earlier due to protective concerns. Shyanne had experienced family violence (including in-utero), parental mental health issues and drug misuse, neglect, and abandonment. She had also been physically abused in her initial foster care placement.

Shyanne's trauma symptomology included hyper-arousal, anxiety, trauma intrusion, dissociation, and sleeping and memory difficulties. Her relational template was one through which she experienced adults as being unpredictable, unreliable, neglectful, and physically and emotionally abusive. Her adaptive response was to rely on herself to meet her own needs.

Despite these challenges, Shyanne's primary resource was her desire for connection and relationship. In addition, her current foster care placement was consistent, nurturing, and reparative, although under stress and vulnerable to breakdown due to challenges associated with Shyanne's escalating trauma-related behaviors.

Therapy process: turning points and emergence of self

Shyanne's therapy process and key turning points are presented here, looking specifically through the context of the 3-phase trauma therapy framework (Cloitre *et al.*, 2012; Ford and Courtis, 2013; Goodyear-Brown, 2010). Each phase has specific therapeutic goals:

1. safety and stabilization—promote relational safety; soothe the physiology and support the child to operate within an appropriate window of tolerance; augment coping skills; enhance somatic and emotional literacy; and promote behavioral awareness in the child

2. trauma memory processing—somatic and emotional processing; trauma memory management and processing; addressing distorted beliefs and false attributions; and development of a coherent narrative and meaning-making

3. reconnection—making positive meaning of post-trauma self; integrating the new skills and resources to everyday life; and planning for future challenges. The goal is integration of the past, present, and future.

While this sequence of therapeutic tasks is necessary during play therapy with traumatized children to achieve integration and recovery, the process by which this occurs is often flexibly sequential in nature (Goodyear-Brown, 2010; Olejniczak, 2013).

This case study highlights movement through the PTDM quadrants and trauma therapy goals, examining who led this movement (i.e. child or therapist), and therapist use of self. Moreover, it highlights the role of the PTDM-R domain, Regulation and WOT, as a key mechanism in guiding clinical decision-making.

Trauma therapy phase 1: safety and stabilization

Phase 1 occurred between sessions 1 and 16, with the focus on ensuring Shyanne experienced a sense of safety in our therapeutic relationship and the physical environment. Thus, I utilized Quadrant III: Non-intrusive Responding as my orienting approach to play therapy during our first six sessions. This relationship provided the "safe container" (Winnicott, 1971) from which she could freely explore her experiences, test new ways of being, and progress towards healing (Oaklander, 1978). Repeated instances of interactive regulation supported Shyanne to learn that adults can be safe, predictable, responsive, and attuned (Schore, 2003).

Turning point 1

During session 1, Shyanne displayed a high degree of dysregulation and was chaotic in her play. Through my attunement to, and synchrony with, her mobilized physiological state, I responded by offering co-regulation. I immersed myself in the play, activating her mirror neurons (Berrol, 2006) with intentional use of my body energy to match Shyanne's, and then slowed down my body movements, all while remaining in the context of her play (Quadrant IV: Co-facilitation). I was able to assess her WOT for her relational capacity with me through her response to my co-regulation attempt. Could she use me as a resource for regulation or not?

Also during session 1, Shyanne demonstrated an innate drive to talk about her trauma experiences. She shared about some of the abuse she had witnessed between Karli and her former boyfriend and stated that "it's confusing when they're angry and scary and happy with me at the same time." However, the disclosures increased intensity of her dysregulation. Thus, following her initial lead, I witnessed and validated her story, assessing her capacity to tolerate exposure to her trauma content before co-regulating her again back into her WOT.

Following this, Shyanne engaged in sandplay for the remainder of the session. She connected with the sandtray, and over the course of therapy this became her primary play medium. Shyanne invited me into her sandplay, and staying in Quadrant III, I sought direction from her. She gave me clear directions about how she wanted the play to be carried out. From this backdrop, a process of "Struggle" (Allan, 1998) around the theme of safety emerged, and was played out repeatedly during sessions 2 to 7.

Turning point 2

Shyanne's sandplay "struggle" was clearly evident, with two different sides attacking each other and one side dying. Regardless of the miniatures used and variations on the theme of safety, Shyanne's side was repeatedly victorious over mine. As the sessions progressed, I immersed myself to a greater degree in her play, becoming more directive, increasingly working in Quadrant IV. Within the context of the play and metaphor I actively tested my hypotheses relating to Shyanne's sense of safety.

I explored Shyanne's WOT for conscious processing by offering interpretations via Quadrant I: Active Utilization, gently bringing her awareness to the similarities between her symbolic representations and her lived experiences of safety. Shyanne responded to these reflections with disclosures, stating that while she felt safe with Karli at contact visits, she "didn't feel safe when she left me" and that "it's scary when they are big screaming and I try to fix it." The disclosures continued to push Shyanne outside her WOT, although she learned to self-regulate by returning to her sandplay. Additionally, on two occasions my movement to Quadrant I using interpretive statements was misattuned, resulting in disruption to Shyanne's play. Thus, it was my task to repair these ruptures, which I did through re-attunement with co-regulation, and by returning to Quadrant III to allow her to direct the process again, while I followed her lead once again.

Given Shyanne's low self-regulation capacity at this stage of therapy, one of her primary therapeutic needs was for soothing and stabilization of her physiology. I knew this key phase 1 therapeutic task needed to be addressed early in therapy; however, it was essential that I first privileged Shyanne's need for control in our relationship. This trust would scaffold the rupture-repair process inherent in the therapeutic relationship, which by its very nature challenges a client's way of knowing, being, and relating. It would also enable Shyanne to effectively engage in more directive therapeutic interventions supportive of her recovery. I had been waiting for an invitation from Shyanne to do this, and it came in session 8.

Turning point 3

Shyanne had engaged in sandplay again, having created a "rubbish" site. This representation appeared to resonate deeply with her and she demonstrated a high level of energy and body movement in placing the rubbish—"the bad things"—into the garbage truck, emphasizing "how big" the rubbish was. As she worked the rubbish, she exclaimed, "It's turning into compost now. Compost is good for the garden. Worms help turn the rubbish into compost. Worms are the helpers." She then picked up a snake miniature and handed it to me, and looking me imploringly in the eyes said, "Here, you be the worm." This was the turning point in therapy when I sensed that Shyanne finally invited me to connect with her at a very deep level. The worm in her sandplay symbolically represented a helper in the renewal process, and she was communicating to me "Here I am...I trust you with me...I need you to help me...I want you to help me." Staying in Quadrant III, I deferred to Shyanne for direction of how I should proceed in her play, and she requested me to "do what the worm knows to do." In clarifying this instruction with her, she clearly gave me permission to proceed actively in facilitating the therapeutic process. She had expressed to me security and trust in our therapeutic relationship, and safety to be vulnerable. This enabled my greater degree of immersion as I facilitated progression through the therapeutic goal of safety and stabilization, enhancing her somatic, emotional literacy, and self-regulation skills. I engaged Shyanne in relational and sensorimotor play activities promoting this.

Turning point 4
I employed the play therapy mediums of movement, music, and creative visualization, as well as sensorimotor and breathing activities, working between Quadrant II: Open Discussion and Exploration and Quadrant IV: Co-facilitation. Shyanne's favorite activities were bubble blowing and music, especially drumming. With Shyanne drumming at a moderate pace (60 to 80 beats per minute), the brainstem was stimulated in a patterned and repetitive way—elements necessary for soothing the physiology (Perry, 2006).

Diaphragmatic breathing was another self-regulatory skill I supported Shyanne to develop working in Quadrant II. We practiced this breathing method and she explored her breath through different play activities including bubble blowing, singing, and wind instruments. Diaphragmatic breathing modulates the ventral vagus; the inhalation "turns off" the vagal brake and the heart rate increases, and the slow exhalation out "turns on" the vagal brake and the heart rate decreases (Porges, 2011). Hence, these activities served to exercise the vagal brake.

I worked in Quadrant II helping Shyanne understand how her body works and enabling her to look after her body when she has big feelings. She embraced learning about her "Inside your outside" (Rabe, 2008), particularly when she felt anxious and scared. Shyanne's "puppy dog" eyes grew wide in wonder on hearing her heartbeat through a stethoscope, and she delighted in gross motor activities to accelerate her heart rate followed by diaphragmatic breathing to slow it down again, listening with the stethoscope to the changes in her heart rate. "I can change my heart!" she exclaimed. She also learnt to reconnect with her senses when "time goes" and increase her arousal back within her WOT through her preferred method of drumming. This turning point was characterized by Shyanne's reconnection to self through discovery and awareness of her body.

Turning point 5

"I'm going to drum you my day," Shyanne announced. Shyanne was experiencing integration of self in relation to her physiology and emotions. Through play, she developed self-efficacy of her regulatory ability and needed me less for co-regulation. I observed her now holding her body posture more upright (Ogden *et al.*, 2006), and being more relaxed and considered in her approach to her play. Shyanne's dysregulation had stabilized and her WOT had widened. She had developed capacity to work at its regulatory boundaries, moving toward her trauma content from a safe foundation of relational safety and self-regulation skills to do so. This indicated to me her readiness for the more intensive trauma processing work of phase 2.

Trauma therapy phase 2: processing and management of traumatic memory

Phase 2 occurred between sessions 17 and 31; however, it is my view that trauma processing occurs at every stage of the play therapy process, because when a child is engaged in play she is using her unconscious self. In play, "children never leave themselves...they use more of themselves" (Oaklander, 1978, p.137). Play (particularly in Quadrants III and IV) not only triggers explicit (conscious) memories, it activates implicit (unconscious) memories and processes too (Cozolino, 2010), "connecting the here and now to the there and then" (Levy, 2011, p.51). This promotes integration of disintegrated sensations and experiences. Play therapy allowed Shyanne to experience her body in new ways, and with my presence she also experienced self-other in new ways too.

Throughout phase 2, I continued to approach sessions beginning in Quadrant III, given her personal need and style, and her play capacity (e.g. initiate, direct, and maintain the play). She frequently returned to the sand.

Turning point 6
From session 19, I observed a noticeable change in Shyanne's sandplay, from her process being primarily unconscious to increasing levels of conscious awareness. Her energy became more intense with her use of water and "sandstorms" moving across the sandtray. The theme of struggle that emerged during phase 1 progressed to "Resolution" (Allan, 1998) with the presence of restoration of order and greater organization: a reflection of what was happening in her internal world. Her play suggested that she was developing an ability to recognize and acknowledge external influences, and in her narratives, she began to relate to figures and objects as individuals from her lived experience, moving into Quadrant I at these times.

Turning point 7
"Playing in the sand is my favorite!" Shyanne told me in session 20. She undertook much of her trauma processing through this play medium, and throughout, I often utilized Quadrants I and IV, supporting titration of her exposure to her trauma content within or at the edges of her WOT. My role as both "partner in her dance" and as "titration agent" (Goodyear-Brown, 2010) provided the relationally rich context supportive of increasing affect tolerance. I observed Shyanne's WOT expand as she effectively regulated her arousal when it increased in response to the trauma content. In the sandtray, Shyanne played out experiences of being attacked, being alone and helpless, being helped by others, helping others, trying to get the help of another who is unable to help, and keeping the self safe when this occurred. It was also my role to hold the fragments of Shyanne's story to later help her piece these together into a coherent narrative of her experiences.

Turning point 8
In session 27, Shyanne abruptly abandoned her sandplay and, for the first and only time, engaged with the baby dolls. "Be quiet baby! You'll make him mad!" she shouted angrily, as she shook baby. Working in Quadrant IV immersed in the metaphor, I gently challenged this distorted belief that what was happening was baby's fault: "Baby is crying. I wonder what baby needs right now?" I was able to test my

hypothesis about the attribution of self-blame Shyanne may have been carrying and test her capacity to tolerate working at the edges of her WOT in undertaking cognitive restructuring work of cognitive distortions and false attributions.

Turning point 9

Shyanne returned to the sandtray in subsequent sessions. She appeared to reach resolution about her sense of safety and made the following statements: "My creatures are all safe…they don't get hurt anymore… the mummy birds know how to protect the baby birds… Why wouldn't there be safe places on my side?" Through play, Shyanne gained conscious awareness of these being her own experiences of her mother. As Shyanne's conscious awareness of her experiences increased, she actively directed therapeutic work, developing narrative around this. She led herself into Quadrant II: Open Discussion and Exploration, and explored the "job" of parents to protect their children, explicitly confronting the issue of feeling unsafe with her mother. I provided her with the narrative of her entry into out-of-home care as had been consistently communicated with her at various times by other Care Team members.

Turning point 10

I primarily led movement toward and focused my work in Quadrant II, facilitating the cognitive restructuring of the trauma narrative by addressing distorted beliefs and false attributions that had previously maintained her trauma experience, such as "It's my fault what happened."

Trauma therapy phase 3: promoting ongoing recovery

Phase 3 occurred over the final ten sessions—sessions 32 to 42. Shyanne had now returned to live with Karli and she visited her foster carer (Annie) every second weekend. Therapy during this final phase of intervention was aimed at consolidation and integration of the relational, somatic, emotional, and cognitive resources developed during therapy into her day-to-day life.

Turning point 11

Several sessions in this phase were dedicated to documenting the narrative of Shyanne's experiences (Quadrant II), culminating in her Life Story Book—"My Book about Me." Life story work (Rose, 2012) had primarily occurred during phase 2 alongside her disclosures, and this final part of the process enabled her to integrate the fragments of her story into a coherent whole in a way that the previous deficits in her autobiographical memory had prevented. Shyanne now knew "what school I went to in Prep and who my teacher was!"

Turning point 12

Alongside development of her life story book, Shyanne's ongoing sandplay process allowed her to direct her own movement towards the cognitive tasks of making positive meaning of her post-trauma self and identifying future challenges requiring planning and preparation. Shyanne identified the loss and grief of moving away from her foster carer as distressing; however, open discussion of this in Quadrant II enabled her to share these feelings with Karli, and together they could make plans for supporting Shyanne's ongoing relationship with Annie.

Turning point 13

Shyanne's reunification with Karli resulted in some regression in her newly emerging sense of self, due to an incident where she re-experienced threat to her safety. In her sandplay, she played out scenes of this disintegration—"I'm turning into a sand man... I am everywhere." During this brief period, I led Shyanne into Quadrant II, revisiting skills and qualities of her post-trauma sense of self previously learned, adapting them to the current situation. Through this process, Shyanne was able to differentiate her past experiences from the current situation.

Turning point 14

I had actively led Shyanne in preparing for our therapy ending some months before our scheduled final session. This preparation allowed Shyanne to experience the ending of a relationship in a planned and purposeful way, providing a new reparative experience rather than her previous experiences of abrupt and abusive relationship endings characterized by fear and unpredictability. In her final session, she stated, "I want to play in the sand one last time." Shyanne ran her hands through the sand, scooping it up into a mound in the middle of the tray. She created a lush forest surrounding the mound, and in finishing, she used one particular miniature which she placed on top of the mound. This symbol had emerged consistently in her sandplay during the latter half of therapy—it was the budgerigar. The dreamtime stories of Australian Aboriginal culture, which Shyanne had some connection with, view the budgerigar as representing "a heightened sense of integration…and by simply living in the present, Budgerigar effectively broadens our innate wisdom and learned knowledge, clarifies our life experiences, and heals our past…it is indeed a wise teacher" (King, 2007, p.124).

Turning points summary

Stage in process	Quadrant	Turning points	What contributed to the turning point?
Phase 1 Turning point 1 Session 1	Sessions 1–6 QIII as orienting approach Fluid movement between QIII, QII, QIV, and back to QIII	• Shyanne experienced herself as in control • Establishment of safety in the therapeutic relationship and physical environment • When a need for regulation was clinically indicated, I used myself to co-regulate • Shyanne discovered the sandtray, engaging with its sensory qualities, and this had a soothing effect on her hyper-aroused physiology	• Shyanne experienced acceptance, and of being witnessed and validated • I became attuned to her regulatory profile (especially hyper-aroused states), adaptive responses, and her WOT of her relational capacity with me and her exposure to her traumatic experiences • Shyanne identified a new self-regulation method
Turning point 2 Sessions 6–7	QIV, QI	• Playing out the battle/struggle	• I identified emerging themes of Shyanne's play, offering interpretations to test my hypotheses about these • This supported her conscious awareness of her feelings about safety and protection

cont.

Stage in process	Quadrant	Turning points	What contributed to the turning point?
Turning point 3 Session 8	QI, QIV, QII	• "You be the worm." Shyanne expressed security and trust with me • The emergence of greater complexity and more narrative in Shyanne's play	• Shyanne's feelings of trust and safety with me allowed her to be vulnerable • Stabilization in Shyanne's physiology resulted in progress in her play skills
Turning point 4 Session 10	QII	• "I can change my heart!" Shyanne's reconnection to self—awareness of her body	• Shyanne's trust enabled my greater degree of immersion, facilitating progress through therapeutic goals of somatic and emotional literacy skills
Turning point 5 Session 15	QIV	• "I'm going to drum you my day"—drumming body rhythms	• Integration of self—physiology and emotions • Enhanced self-efficacy of regulatory ability
Phase 2 Turning point 6 Session 19	QIII, QI	• Resolution of "the battle"—restoration of order in her internal world • Shyanne relating to sandtray miniatures as individuals from her lived experience	• Shyanne's meaning-making through play supported her awareness of external influences contributing to her trauma experiences, beginning to challenge her negative self-attributions
Turning point 7 Sessions 20–26	Fluid movement between all four quadrants	• "Playing in the sand is my favorite." Shyanne's sandplay allowed disclosure and processing of her trauma through non-verbal and verbal narrative	• I joined Shyanne in the therapeutic dance towards and away from her trauma content • I held fragments of her story to later help her develop a coherent whole
Turning point 8 Session 27	QIV	• "Be quiet baby! You'll make him mad!" I immersed myself in the metaphor of the play to test my hypothesis of self-blame and gently challenge this—"Baby is crying. I wonder what baby needs right now?"	• My immersion in the play enabled my hypothesis of self-blame to be tested, and to assess her tolerance for working at the edges of her WOT in undertaking cognitive restructuring work of cognitive distortions and false attributions

Turning point 9 Session 30	QIII, QI, QII	• "My creatures are all safe…they don't get hurt anymore…the mummy birds know how to protect the baby birds." Shyanne gained conscious awareness of these being her experiences with her mother	• Shyanne directed movement into QII, explored the role of parents in keeping children safe, and undertook development of a coherent narrative around this • Shyanne developing a felt sense of safety and security
Turning point 10 Session 31	QII	• "It's my fault what happened." Shyanne's enhanced self-regulatory skills and conscious awareness invited explicit trauma processing	• I followed Shyanne's lead and facilitated the cognitive restructuring of Shyanne's trauma narrative, and in addressing distorted beliefs and false attributions
Phase 3 Turning point 11 Session 32	QII	• "Now I know who my teacher was in Prep!" Shyanne's integration of her trauma narrative	• Life story work enabled a coherent narrative of key milestones in her life, and of her trauma narrative
Turning point 12 Session 33	QIII, QII	• Shyanne transformed her grief on leaving her foster carer as a support resource	• Shyanne making positive meaning of her post-trauma self
Turning point 13 Session 36	QIII, QII	• "I'm turning into a sand man… I am everywhere!" Disintegration/integration of self, due to experiencing perceived threat to safety	• I led progress of therapeutic goals, consolidating skills previously learned and adapting them to the current situation
Turning point 14 Session 42	QII, QIII	• "I want to play in the sand one last time." Budgerigar symbol—Shyanne experiences integration of self	• Preparation for final session allowed Shyanne to experience the ending of a relationship in a planned and purposeful therapeutic way

References

Allan, J. (1998) *Inscapes of the Child's World: Jungian Counseling in Schools and Clinics*. Washington, DC: Spring Publications.

Berrol, C.F. (2006) Neuroscience meets dance/movement therapy: Mirror neurons, the therapeutic process and empathy. *The Arts in Psychotherapy 33*, 4, 302–315.

Cloitre, M., Courtois, C.A., Ford, J.D., Green, B.L., et al. (2012) *The ISTSS Expert Consensus Treatment Guidelines for Complex PTSD in Adults*. Accessed on 03/08/2018 at https://www.istss.org/ISTSS_Main/media/Documents/ISTSS-Expert-Concesnsus-Guidelines-for-Complex-PTSD-Updated-060315.pdf

Cook, A., Spinazzola, J., Ford, J., Lanktree, C., *et al.* (2005) Complex trauma in children and adolescents. *Psychiatric Annals 35*, 5, 390–398.

Cozolino, L. (2010) *The Neuroscience of Psychotherapy: Healing the Social Brain* (2nd edn). New York: W.W. Norton & Company.

Dalai Lama Center (Producer) (2011) Parenting for the 21st century: Building the neural circuits for resilience and kindness [Video file]. Accessed on 03/08/2018 at https://www.youtube.com/watch?v=PGUEDtGSwW4

Drewes, A.A., Bratton, S., and Schaeffer, C. (2011) *Integrative Play Therapy*. Hoboken, NJ: John Wiley & Sons.

Ford, J.D. and Courtois, C.A. (2013) *Treating Complex Trauma: A Sequenced, Relationship-Based Approach*. New York: Guilford Press.

Gil, E. (2006) *Helping Abused and Traumatized Children: Integrating Directive and Nondirective Approaches*. New York: Guilford Press.

Gil, E. (2012) Trauma-Focused Integrative Play Therapy (TF-IPT). In P. Goodyear-Brown (ed.) *Handbook of Child Sexual Abuse: Identification, Assessment and Treatment*. Hoboken, NJ: John Wiley & Sons.

Golding, K.S. and Hughes, D.A. (2012) *Creating Loving Attachments: Parenting with PACE to Nurture Confidence and Security in the Troubled Child*. London: Jessica Kingsley Publishers.

Goodyear-Brown, P. (2010) *Play Therapy with Traumatized Children: A Prescriptive Approach*. Hoboken, NJ: John Wiley & Sons.

Ham, J. and Tronick, E. (2009) Relational psychophysiology: Lessons from mother-infant physiology research on dyadically expanded states of consciousness. *Psychotherapy Research 19*, 6, 619–632.

Hill, D. (2015) *Affect Regulation Theory: A Clinical Model*. New York: W.W. Norton & Company.

King, S.A. (2007) *Animal Dreaming: The Spiritual and Symbolic Language of the Australasian Animals*. Australia: Blue Angel Gallery.

Levy, A.J. (2011) Neurobiology and the therapeutic action of psychoanalytic play therapy with children. *Clinical Social Work Journal 39*, 1, 50–60.

Oaklander, V. (1978) *Windows to Our Children*. Utah: Real People Press.

Ogden, P., Minton, K., and Pain, C. (2006) *Trauma and the Body: A Sensorimotor Approach to Psychotherapy*. New York: W.W. Norton & Company.

Olejniczak, K. (2013) Applying the Play Therapy Dimensions Model to a Trauma Therapy Framework: A Retrospective Case Study Identifying the Neurobiological Mechanisms at Play. Unpublished masters thesis. Canterbury Christ Church University, UK.

Perry, B.D. (2006) Applying Principles of Neurodevelopment to Clinical Work with Maltreated and Traumatized Children: The Neurosequential Model of Therapeutics. In N.B. Webb (ed.) *Working with Traumatized Youth in Child Welfare*. New York: Guilford Press. Accessed on 23/05/2018 at https://childtrauma.org/wp-content/uploads/2013/08/Perry-Bruce-neurosequentialmodel_06.pdf

Perry, B.D., Hogan, L., and Marlin, S.J. (2000) *Curiosity, Pleasure and Play: A Neurodevelopmental Perspective*. Accessed on 03/08/2018 at https://childtrauma.org/wp-content/uploads/2014/12/CuriosityPleasurePlay_Perry.pdf

Porges, S. (2011) *The Polyvagal Theory: Neurophysiological Foundations of Emotions, Attachment, Communication and Self-Regulation*. New York: W.W. Norton & Company.

Rabe, T. (2008) *Inside Your Outside!* London: HarperCollins Publishers.

Rose, R. (2012) *Life Story Therapy with Traumatized Children: A Model for Practice*. London: Jessica Kingsley Publishers.

Schore, A.N. (2003) *Affect Dysregulation and Disorders of the Self*. New York: W.W. Norton & Company.

Schore, A.N. (2009) Right Brain Affect Regulation: An Essential Mechanism of Development, Trauma, Dissociation, and Psychotherapy. In D. Fosha, D. Siegel and M. Solomon (eds) *The Healing Power of Emotion: Affective Neuroscience, Development and Clinical Practice*. New York: W.W. Norton & Company.

Schore, A.N. (2017) Playing on the Right Side of the Brain: An interview with Allan N. Schore. *American Journal of Play 9*, 2, 105–142.

Siegel, D.J. (1999) *The Developing Mind: Toward a Neurobiology of Interpersonal Experience*. New York: Guilford Press.

Tronick, E. (2007) *The Neurobehavioural and Social-Emotional Development of Infants and Children*. New York: W.W. Norton & Company.

Tronick, E. and Beeghly, M. (2011) Infants' meaning-making and the development of mental health problems. *American Psychologist 66*, 2, 107–119.

Winnicott, D.W. (1971) *Playing and Reality*. New York: Routledge.

Yasenik, L. and Gardner, K. (2012) *Play Therapy Dimensions Model: A Decision-Making Guide for Integrative Play Therapists*. London: Jessica Kingsley Publishers.

10

THE CONTAINER

Piecing Together a Life Story

ADRIANA SORBO, VALERIE KENDALL, AND CASSANDRA WHITE

Case introduction

Like many children raised in the foster care system, the details of Carrie's early developmental history were scarce. A series of caseworkers, files and caregivers meant that no one person contained Carrie's history for her. What follows is an account of the journey the first author, Adriana Sorbo, made with this young person and the numerous turning points experienced along the pathway. From interviews with her caseworkers and foster parent, review of file reports and from Carrie's own reports, I was able to gather bits and pieces about her young life. Carrie was the fourth of five children and the only female child. She was born with serious and complex medical difficulties, experienced numerous surgeries and hospitalizations and required daily specialized medical care.

Carrie's family had a long history of involvement with child intervention services (CIS) and intervention was initiated for Carrie at birth due to concerns about parental substance abuse, domestic violence and neglect, complicated by the special medical care she would require. In infancy, along with her next eldest brother, Jordan, Carrie was placed in the care of her biological aunt where she resided off and on for approximately four years. During this time Carrie and her siblings spent periods of time in the care of their biological mother and father and, later, stepfather. However, parental rights were terminated when Carrie was approximately four years old and all contact between Carrie and her biological mother ceased shortly thereafter.

At approximately four years of age, Carrie was placed in the foster home of Janet and Eric. The foster parents had a biological daughter and a foster son, both three years younger than Carrie. Carrie's biological siblings were placed in other foster homes and with their family. Shortly after Carrie came to live with Janet and Eric they participated in brief attachment-focused therapy but had otherwise never engaged in any other therapy.

Janet described that although Carrie adjusted well to the family and quickly developed a close relationship with her, Carrie would sometimes have episodes of uncontrollable emotions. Janet described that during these meltdowns Carrie would often cry, scream, flail her body and sometimes throw things. Janet said that she was sometimes able to soothe Carrie and help to calm her down, but these "meltdowns" could last over an hour and, according to Janet, no trigger was typically apparent to her. In the year following her arrival to Janet and Eric's home, Carrie had regular contact with her brother Jordan. The day following an overnight visit in the foster home, Carrie disclosed to her foster mother that her brother had "hurt" her, later explaining that he had touched her genitals after they went to bed. Visits between Jordan and Carrie were terminated immediately. It is not entirely clear when this incident occurred, but it was my understanding that Carrie was approximately five years old at the time of the incident. Carrie's episodes of meltdowns increased significantly after the disclosure of sexual abuse. It appears that no therapeutic intervention was sought for either child after the incident, nor was any attempt made to further understand what occurred between the children.

Approximately two years after the disclosure, Carrie unexpectedly saw her brother in a playground close to her school. She was unaware that Jordan resided with a neighbor nearby and was completely surprised by this sighting. This incident triggered a significant escalation in her meltdowns, at which point Carrie's caseworker sought therapy for her. Also, around this time Janet and Eric separated and he moved away from the family.

Theoretical orientation

I would consider my theoretical orientation to be in constant evolution. However, there is a consistent set of scientific and theoretical underpinnings that shape my view of human development, my understanding of change and my role as a therapist. Drawing from a developmental perspective, I understand each child that I encounter in therapy as a constantly evolving human being. My approach to each child will, in part, be dependent on their age and stage of development and on how their experiences have impacted each age and stage of their development. A basic understanding of typical child development informs the interpretations I make regarding a child's presentation, their play and their ability to integrate experiences in therapy.

From a neurosequential perspective, I draw on Bruce Perry's (2006) evidence-based Neurosequential Model of Therapeutics (NMT), which considers the neurological development of the child when assessing child problematic issues. According to the model, during intake and history taking, the therapist would consider whether the child reached expected neurological functioning at the various stages delineated by the model. In addition, close attention would be paid during therapy to provide appropriate activities to rectify any shortcomings noticed during the child's growth periods, both in the past and currently. To understand more fully, one needs to know the developmental periods the model delineates. They are as follows: genetic, intrauterine, perinatal, infancy and childhood. At each of these levels parts of the brain are developing. Perry looks at the functions of predominant brain parts at each developmental period and assesses whether the child has presented as "Normal," "Mild Deficiency," "Moderate Deficiency" or "Severe Deficiency." Quickly reviewing, these are the principal brain parts we are looking at, along with the functions they control (as indicated by the brackets): *brain stem* (metabolism, arousal/self-regulation, attention/impulse, cardiovascular/physiological); *diencephalon/cerebellum* (sleep, feeding/appetite, coordination/balance, fine motor); *limbic* (affect/mood, threat response complex, attunement, play/pleasure, sharing/relational, short-term memory/learning); *cortex* (somatosensory integration, sense time/delay gratification, cognitive primary and concrete, self-awareness/self-image, speech/articulation, language expressive/receptive); and *prefrontal cortex* (motor activity/integration, module reactivity/impulsivity, planning/sequencing, abstract/conceptual, insight/reflective cognition, morality, values, spirituality).

Based on an accurate picture of the child's developmental trajectory (Perry, 2013, p.22), and revealing the present strengths and weaknesses of the child, a framework can be developed to include a sequence of various therapeutic strategies to answer the individual needs of the child. Hence, selecting the educational/therapeutic experiences provided is based not on the child's chronological age but on their neurological developmental level. Developmental level may vary across domains (e.g. cognitive, emotional, motor, social, spiritual). The NMT provides several assessment tools to address this.

In the case of Carrie, I do not know anything about the genetics of her biological parents but we do know that there was parental substance abuse and that Carrie was born with serious and complex medical difficulties. If the parents were neglectful in meeting Carrie's needs, as stated, was the mother inattentive to her health during pregnancy? Did she use street drugs during her pregnancy? Did she breast-feed? I also knew very little about the almost four years Carrie spent in the care of her aunt and how much of those years were spent in the direct care of her biological parents.

Referring to the NMT described above, I could expect negative outcomes within the brainstem function (self-regulation), within the diencephalon function (sleep difficulties as the child was moved from residence to residence; she had nightmares), within the limbic system (mood, threat response) and within the cortex (self-image, capability of delayed gratification). So, in all brain areas we could expect, and indeed saw, these various challenges for Carrie.

As much as possible, I attempted to address these issues through play therapy. Although I did not make use of the structured assessments and treatment planning tools that are part of the application of NMT, the knowledge that Carrie's brain functioning had very likely been impacted throughout her development informed the therapeutic decisions I made as well as the way in which I conceptualized her present-day behavior.

Most especially in working with children who experienced early disruptions in caregiving due to such things as trauma, parental addictions and mental illness, neglect, inconsistent caregiving, death or loss of caregivers, I draw on the vast area of research on attachment (Bowlby, 1973; Horowitz and Reidbord, 1992; Levy and Orlans, 1998;

Middleton *et al.*, 1993; Parks, 1965). Understanding that experience physically shapes our brain and that relationships with attachment figures in early years lay the foundation for the development of the self (Siegel, 2001) helps me to place a child's presenting behaviors in the larger context of their attachment needs. When children present in therapy with sub-optimal attachment experiences I see my basic role in therapy as being a caring, consistent adult who can act as a pseudo-attachment figure for a brief time in the child's life. For children involved with CIS who are moved from home to home, the opportunity to build sustained secure attachments to a small group of caregivers is often lost and with it the ability to develop a stable and unified sense of self.

Case study conceptualization

Carrie was a child who had not a care in the world, or that is how she attempted to present. She smiled all the time, was chatty and pleasant with everyone and went to great lengths to "forget" about the unpleasant things that happened to her. She was a child desperately trying to gain control of a life that almost always seemed out of control. Such a presentation reflects Judith Lewis Herman's introduction to *Trauma and Recovery* when she states, "The ordinary response to atrocities is to banish them from consciousness" (1992, p.1). Carrie's physical boundaries were impacted by the need for regular invasive medical intervention (she was permanently catheterized and required an adult to flush her medical equipment daily). Her emotional and psychological boundaries had been impacted by early experiences of neglect, witnessing domestic violence, sexual abuse and abrupt losses of important people in her life. Hence, on an almost constant basis, she tried to regain some control. She was bossy and demanding, she was charming and chatty. She had overwhelming emotional meltdowns that demanded the attention of her foster mother, a woman who had become her "one and only" and whom she called "Mom." As Herman says, "Atrocities, however, refuse to be buried" (1992, p.1).

Carrie was seven and a half when she began therapy at our office. She initially met with a male therapist who focused on: 1) play therapy and providing support to Janet, who was struggling to manage Carrie's emotional needs, and 2) safety and regulation strategies for Carrie. Janet reported that Carrie expressed fear about seeing her brother again and was especially fearful at bedtime, when she was most likely to have an emotional meltdown. Janet reported that Carrie expressed fear that Jordan would find their house and that she started to sleep with sticks and rocks under her pillow. After several months of therapy, the incidents of emotional dysregulation had decreased substantially, and Carrie reported feeling safer and in better control of her emotional states. Preparations were made to terminate therapy. However, Carrie had a second incident of running into her brother unexpectedly and she experienced a significant relapse. It was at this time that Carrie began to meet with me to continue her therapy as her previous therapist was no longer available.

When I first met her, Carrie was having weekly meltdowns and was fearful and clingy to her foster mother. In addition to seeing Jordan, she had recently experienced a series of major life events including the separation of her foster parents and another surgery.

Therapy process: stuck points

In therapy Carrie presented as a cheerful, curious and confident young girl. During her sessions, Carrie talked almost constantly and made attempts to negotiate getting her way when I introduced an activity instead of allowing her to direct the entire therapy session. During her initial session with me Carrie played with her back turned to me, but it was apparent that she was tracking me despite not looking at me directly. Her play included relational themes, themes of loss and transformation, and often involved an adult character that was in danger or incapacitated.

During initial sessions, I operated almost exclusively in Quadrant III: Non-intrusive Responding (Yasenik and Gardner, 2012). However, I began my first session with a here and now discussion reviewing the purpose for her therapy and talking about the impact of transition from one therapist to another (i.e. me) (Appendix A: Verbal Use of Self, 1.1 Here and Now Discussion). Although this was only a small part of the session, it was important that I was transparent with Carrie about what I already knew about her, minimizing any pressure she might have felt to tell me about the things that had happened to her. I was aware how the central theme of psychological trauma was "the conflict between the will to deny horrible events and the will to proclaim them aloud" (Herman, 1992, p.1). Once immersed in play, I used reflective and tracking comments of the play activity and restated content during play (Appendix A: 1.2 Reflecting and Tracking Statements and 1.3 Restating Content). On occasion, themes of nurturing, safety, trust and fear became evident and I took these opportunities to make soft interpretations in the play metaphor (Quadrant I: Active Utilization).

Stuck point 1: the family is falling apart

It was apparent that Carrie had formed an important and close relationship with Janet and used her as a co-regulator. Janet was committed to Carrie and expressed a desire to formally adopt her. However, Janet was feeling overwhelmed and taxed by Carrie's emotional needs, exacerbated by the turmoil in her personal life.

Because of the state of crisis in the home caused by Carrie's explosive emotions, my introduction to therapy with Carrie was not what it would typically be with a new client. After a brief introduction, I quickly jumped into the role of crisis intervener. While I would normally spend several sessions in Quadrant III (Non-intrusive Responding), I only spent the first session working in this quadrant because during her second session Carrie arrived significantly dysregulated and required direct intervention to help calm her (Quadrant II: Open Discussion and Exploration). I did return to Quadrant III for the third and fourth sessions but it quickly became apparent that the instability at home was reaching a crisis point and had to be addressed directly.

Much of my time was spent with Janet, providing emotional support, psycho-education and specific strategies to help her meet Carrie's emotional needs. I began to introduce structured play-based activities aimed at building trust and safety by establishing a hierarchical caring relationship between Carrie and I. During these sessions, I was highly physically involved in play (Appendix A: 3.1 Physical Self), using respectful touch and physical proximity to communicate caring and protection. Finally, a joint session between Carrie and Janet focused on repairing and strengthening their attachment relationship.

Stuck point 2: I'm fine, I'm fine, everything is okay

A brief return to child-led play suggested that Carrie's primary defense system of avoidance would prove a challenge to addressing trauma both in the play metaphor and consciously. I was faced with a dilemma:

work primarily in Quadrant I: Active Utilization and Quadrant III: Non-intrusive Responding, allowing the process of therapeutic play to unfold at Carrie's rate, or transition to a more directive approach in Quadrant II and Quadrant IV.

Although Carrie was still struggling emotionally, she had demonstrated the ability to tolerate conscious and direct discussion of the abuse she had experienced and, in fact, continued to talk on occasion about her brother and her experiences while living with her biological family with Janet. The abuse was "out in the open" and I decided it was therefore important to keep it in the open with the intention of minimizing the shame that often lurks when abuse is kept in the shadows. In addition, although Carrie was generally better regulated at home, her emotional state remained fragile and I worried that without directly addressing Carrie's feelings associated with her relationship with Jordan and practicing regulating strategies, she would become further destabilized.

Our sessions therefore were a balance of regulatory/safety-building activities and open exploration of the abuse by Jordan. I introduced the use of art, sandplay and movement as we explored the trauma (Quadrant II: Open Discussion and Exploration) and continued to be physically involved in play by using touch.

During these sessions Carrie could identify in the here and now her feelings related to Jordan, recount memories of her early childhood that were triggered by the memory of the sexual abuse by him, and describe the details of the days following the abuse. She quickly became dysregulated during these sessions but made use of several strategies to calm herself and stay with the material. These sessions were a constant balance of push and withdraw, ebb and flow whereby I was keenly attuned to my emotional self (Appendix A: 2.2 Emotional Self). I was sometimes highly impacted by Carrie's descriptions and need to withdraw into the safety of avoidance. I became aware of my own self-doubt and fear of pushing Carrie too far. I also became more attuned to Carrie's cues and began to trust that she would let me know when it was truly too much for her. I used play to provide psycho-education about sexual play, healthy touch and boundaries. For example, I used puppets to create stories about developmentally typical sexual play/curiosity versus inappropriate sexual touching. I gently placed the incident between Jordan and Carrie in the larger context of the chaos the two of them experienced together in their biological family, reminding Carrie that Jordan was also only a child when the incident had occurred.

After approximately seven weeks of weekly sessions, Janet reported that Carrie was increasingly emotionally unstable at home. Although she seemed to cope well at school, Carrie was having nightmares, was aggressive towards her foster brother and had what appeared to be dissociative "moments" when emotionally out of control. In collaboration with Janet, I decided to pull back on the trauma processing work Carrie and I had been doing and focus entirely on self-regulation and safety. Carrie responded especially well to the use of sensory-based strategies for regulating. For example, she was drawn to the exploration of different textures such as shaving cream, dry pasta and dry beans. We spent time exploring the sensory experience (i.e. How does it feel on your hands? What smells do you notice?) of a variety of textures. During these sessions, I gently tested Carrie's readiness to return to the trauma work focused on her brother. Although she acknowledged the need to talk about him, her body language (e.g. increased rate of speech) and reappearance of defense mechanisms (avoidance) suggested that she might not be ready to begin again. In later sessions, Carrie would gravitate to these "sensory bins" when processing challenging aspects of her relationships with her biological family.

As is often the case, external factors forced Carrie's therapy process to conscious processing of her relationship with her brother and offered an opportunity for growth. Carrie attended a holiday party with her foster family and was surprised to see her brother there. While debriefing with me, Janet explained that at first Carrie appeared terrified to see Jordan but that, with Janet's support, Carrie approached him directly and spoke to him. While telling me about the experience, Carrie used sensory-based strategies to remain regulated and explained that, although she had felt very anxious when she was in Jordan's presence, she was now grateful for the opportunity to speak with him. This incident inspired a plan to have a joint session with Carrie and Jordan, in collaboration with Jordan's individual therapist.

Carrie expressed polarizing feelings about her brother. Although there was fear, anger and helplessness associated with Jordan's perpetration on Carrie, there was also a deep sense of loss. Jordan was the only family member that Carrie had any connection to since being moved into foster care. She had what appeared to be simple curiosities about him such as how old he was now, what grade he was in and whether he had any contact with her family. The sexual assault was in and of itself traumatizing but it was also the reason she lost the only connection to her family that she had. The experience of seeing Jordan was empowering for Carrie and emboldened her in her healing. She planned a joint session, stipulating the boundaries she would accept in re-establishing a relationship with Jordan, and practicing exactly what she wanted to say to him and what she needed to hear back from him. When Carrie became overwhelmed by the direct processing of the sexual assault, a brief move into the play metaphor helped give her psychological distance, allowing her to continue processing in a safe and controlled way.

Stuck point 3: complete loss of control

After approximately six months of therapy, we took an abrupt turn. Over the course of a couple of days Carrie made several attempts at engaging in inappropriate sexual play with her foster siblings. The details of what occurred never became clear, but both siblings reported to Janet that Carrie had exposed her genitals to them and may have invited them to do the same. When describing what had happened Carrie disclosed that she heard Jordan's voice in her head telling her to do things and threatening her if she refused. She said that she'd been hearing his voice for months, maybe years, and was only now acting because she was feeling terrified and powerless.

Carrie was quickly able to face what had occurred and we met with her foster mother and foster siblings to talk about what had happened. We normalized sexual curiosity, reiterated the importance of privacy and the right to set boundaries for our bodies, and talked about how to play safely in the future. Carrie minimized her behavior but was able to stay present in the moment during this conversation. However, once alone with me Carrie became very distressed and insisted that she had to leave the home to go to her babysitter's because she could not trust herself around her foster siblings. We agreed to a safety plan that included staying closely connected to Janet when at home and Janet agreed to find a babysitter for Carrie for the following few days.

Unfortunately, because of concerns about the safety of the children in Janet's home, Carrie was quickly moved out of the home to an emergency children's group home by her caseworker. She was then moved to another group home where she was to remain. No advance plan for this move was put in place, and although she'd had sporadic visits with Janet, it was never made clear to Carrie that she was not moving back home. Three weeks after she had been moved I met with Carrie, her caseworker, Janet and the owner of the group home to tell Carrie that she would not be returning to Janet's home. Carrie was surprised and sad but quickly put up her defenses and tried to focus on other things. Carrie did not know this at the time but this would be the last time that she would see Janet for several months.

The following sessions with Carrie were focused on her most recent loss and adjustment to her new home and school. Carrie tried very hard to focus on the positives of being in the new group home, saying that "the voice" didn't bother her there because there were so many adults to help look after her. She expressed anger at Jordan for causing the loss of her foster family. She worried about her foster siblings and became preoccupied with whether she would ever get to see Janet again. Unfortunately, a decision had been made to terminate all contact between Carrie and Janet, but Carrie was unaware of this. I advocated strongly with child intervention services to reverse this decision, insisting that it would have a detrimental impact on Carrie. Eventually, the decision was reversed and Carrie began having regularly scheduled visits with Janet and her children, but until this occurred Carrie remained in the in-between space of not knowing and worrying that she had once again lost her family.

Our sessions returned to a combination of soothing activities and child-directed play. Themes of chaos, loss and incapacitated adults returned. It was also at this time that I introduced the activity that would become our final phase of therapy.

Stuck point 4: connecting the dots

I became increasingly aware that Carrie had developed a sense of self that existed in compartments, and although the compartments of her life had, on occasion, bumped into each other, Carrie kept them quite separate. She used controlling thoughts and controlling behavior to cope with the chaos and unpredictability of her life, and although this method had served to protect her along the way, it had also interfered with the development of a single, coherent self. Her early life with her biological family existed in one compartment, the incident of sexual abuse by Jordan in another, the life with Janet in a third, and now her "new" life in the group home became a new compartment. There were times during our work that memories from Carrie's early life would trickle into the present, suggesting an opening for larger processing of developmental trauma (as opposed to restricting therapy to the incident of sexual abuse). Johnson (1998, p.79) draws attention to Pynoos, Steinberg and Goengian (1996) who reference studies which suggest that trauma causes disruption in four areas, all affected differently according to the developmental level of the child. They include narrative coherence, emotional regulation, developmental transitions and transitions in peer relationships. Learning is compromised (Brody, 1993; Krystal et al., 1989; Ornitz and Pynoos, 1989; Pynoos, 1990; Pynoos, Nader and March, 1991).

Carrie's present life was by no means stable. She was getting adjusted to living in the group home, now with a rotating group of paid caregivers, and she still did not have any certainty about her relationship with Janet and her foster siblings. I struggled with the direction of therapy at this point. Although Carrie had opened the "therapeutic window" for exploring her early childhood, one could argue that there was a risk in pursuing this while her present life was still in limbo. Despite this, Carrie had shown great resilience, there was evidence that she was therapeutically ready, and the reality was that Carrie's life might never be ideally stable "enough." Therefore, I chose to introduce an art-based activity to help Carrie integrate the parts of her self that she had compartmentalized as epochs of her life. Using a variety of shoeboxes, I invited Carrie to turn each one into a house that represented a time of her life. For example, one box was decorated to represent Carrie's current home at the group home, another to represent Carrie's home with her birth mother and another the foster home she had recently moved from. Carrie also created people to live in each of the houses. She eventually added mailboxes to several of the homes and began to "send" letters from one to another, hence connecting these once separate parts of her existence.

Carrie was equally engaged and resistant to this work. My primary role during these sessions was to be Carrie's container, setting clear boundaries and providing safety. I pushed her to stay with the work while offering her space to self-regulate. This activity, which stretched over the course of several months, allowed Carrie to consciously and directly explore her current and past relationship with her biological mother. She explored memories of earlier abuse, witnessing domestic violence and the fear she experienced for her mother's safety. She wondered where her mother and siblings were presently and expressed a desire to have contact with them. It became apparent that, despite her very close relationship with Janet, Carrie yearned for her biological family.

It was during this time that a joint session was finally arranged with Jordan and his individual therapist. Carrie was both terrified and excited about seeing Jordan again. She was empowered by the fact that she would be in control of the session and carefully rehearsed what she wanted to say to him. During the session Carrie confronted Jordan about how she had felt when he sexually touched her and the resulting impact. He was able to extend an apology. With the support of Jordan's therapist, I facilitated a series of activities to discuss safe play, ways to ask for help and how to maintain healthy boundaries. Together the children shared their thoughts and memories about their biological mother, a powerful experience for Carrie given that she had had so few opportunities to have a shared memory with a family member.

This final phase of therapy was incredibly humbling for me. It was clear evidence that my role was to get out of Carrie's way while offering her a safe place to land. Despite the uncertainty in her life Carrie began to evidence the development of genuine stability within her self. She controlled her therapy process not from a place of fear but of power. Life was far from perfect. Carrie continued to experience emotional meltdowns at the group home and she had altercations at school with other students. She had begun regular visits with Janet but her "forever home" was still unknown. What became clear was that Carrie was developing a resilience that would allow her to better tolerate negative life experiences and to advocate for her needs in healthier ways.

As is often the case, my therapy with Carrie ended not because our work together was complete but because I changed jobs. Shortly after her joint session with Jordan, Carrie was transitioned to a new therapist and she and I had our final session together. Again, Carrie was closing the door on an important relationship, and although she relied on tried and true coping strategies (e.g. as soon as I told her I was leaving she withdrew from the joint activity we were doing and wanted to know all about her new therapist), she was able to consciously express her feelings in a way that I had not seen in the past. So, although there was yet another disruption in relationship, progress had been made.

Deblinger *et al.* (2011), who researched the impact of the trauma narrative and treatment length, found that with a narrative component and the use of cognitive behavioral components, eight sessions of treatment resulted in a reduction of abuse-related fear on the part of parents and a reduction of the children's abuse-related fear and anxiety. However, 16 sessions with no narrative portion was reported as increasing parenting skills and reducing externalized child behavior issues at post treatment.

While acknowledging that dealing with children like Carrie who have had multiple homes, multiple caregivers and broken attachments leading to disruptive behavior patterns can be challenging, using play therapy can let the child know that there is at least one person in their life who gives them a place where they are acknowledged and accepted. This can have a profound impact on that child's future life (Riviere, 2006). Despite the many stuck points I encountered on my therapeutic journey with Carrie, there were many important turning points as well. It is my hope that the time we spent together was an opportunity for Carrie to build resilience that will help protect her as she continues her life journey.

Summary of stuck points

Stage in process	Quadrant	Stuck points	What contributed to the stuck point?
Phase 1: Crisis Intervention/ Skill-building	QII: Open Discussion and Exploration	The family is falling apart	• Carrie's meltdowns are taking a significant toll on her foster mother, risking the stability of her placement
Phase 2: Relationship-building/ Identifying Goal and Intervention	QIII: Non-intrusive Responding; QI: Active Utilization	I'm fine, I'm fine, everything is okay	• In child-directed play, Carrie is often highly defended against exploration of uncomfortable or unpleasant feelings

Phase 3: Trauma Processing	QII: Open Discussion and Exploration	Complete loss of control	• Carrie exposes her genitals to her foster siblings, and discloses that she hears her brother's voice threatening her and directing her behavior • She is abruptly moved out of her foster home
Phase 4: Building Self-capacity and Reorganizing Life Story	QII: Open Discussion and Exploration; QIV: Co-facilitation	Connecting the dots	• Life may never be stable "enough" • Carrie is moved to a foster home and new school • Her contact with Janet is abruptly terminated

References

Bowlby, J. (1973) *Attachment and Loss: Separation, Anxiety and Anger*. New York: Basic Books.

Brody, V. (1993) *The Dialogue of Touch: Developmental Play Therapy*. Treasure Island, FL: Developmental Play Therapy Associates.

Deblinger, E., Mannarino, A.P., Cohen, J.A., Runyon, M.K., and Steer, R.A. (2011) Trauma-focused cognitive behavioral therapy for children: Impact of the trauma narrative and treatment length. *Depression and Anxiety 28*, 67–75.

Herman, J.L. (1992) *Trauma and Recovery: The Aftermath of Violence—from Domestic Abuse to Political Terror*. New York: Basic Books.

Horowitz, M. and Reidbord, S. (1992) Memory, Emotion and Response to Trauma. In S. Christianson (ed.) *The Handbook of Emotion and Memory: Research and Theory*. Hillsdale, NJ: Lawrence Erlbaum Associates.

Johnson, K. (1998) *Trauma in the Lives of Children: Crisis and Stress Management Techniques for Counselors, Teachers, and Other Professionals*. Alameda, CA: Hunter House.

Krystal, J.H., Kosten, R.R., Southwick, S.M., Mason, J.W., Perry, P.D., and Giller, E.L. (1989) Neurobiological aspects of PTSD: Review of clinical and preclinical studies. *Behavior Therapy 20*, 177–198.

Levy, T.M. and Orlans, M. (1998) *Attachment, Trauma and Healing: Understanding and Treating Attachment Disorder in Children and Families*. Washington, DC: CWLA Press.

Middleton, W., Raphael, B., Martinek, N., and Misso, V. (1993) Concepts of Normal Bereavement: A Response. In M. Stroebe, W. Stroebe and R. Hansson (eds) *Bereavement: A Sourcebook of Research and Intervention*. New York: Cambridge University Press.

Ornitz, E. and Pynoos, R. (1989) Startle modulation in children with post-traumatic stress disorder. *American Journal of Psychiatry 147*, 866–870.

Parks, C. (1965) Bereavement and mental illness. *British Journal of Medical Psychology 38*, 388–397.

Perry, B. (2006) Applying Principles of Neurodevelopment to Clinical Work with Maltreated and Traumatized Children: A Neurosequential Model of Therapeutics. In N. Boyd Webb (ed.) *Working with Traumatized Youth in Child Welfare*. New York: Guilford Press. Accessed on 23/05/2018 at https://childtrauma.org/wp-content/uploads/2013/08/Perry-Bruce-neurosequentialmodel_06.pdf

Perry, B. (2013) The Neurosequential Model of Therapeutics. In K. Brant, B.D. Perry, S. Seligman and E. Tronick (eds) *Infant and Early Childhood Mental Health: Core Concepts and Clinical Practice*. Washington, DC: American Psychiatric Publishing.

Pynoos, R. (1990) Post-Traumatic Stress Disorder in Children and Adolescents. In B. Garfinkel, G. Carlson and E. Weller (eds) *Psychiatric Disorders in Children and Adolescents*. Philadelphia: W.B. Saunders.

Pynoos, R., Nader, K., and March, J. (1991) Post-Traumatic Stress Disorder. In J. Weiner (ed.) *Textbook of Child and Adolescent Psychiatry*. Washington, DC: American Psychiatric Press.

Pynoos, R., Steinberg, A., and Goengian, A. (1996) Traumatic Stress in Childhood and Adolescence: Recent Developments and Applications. In B. van der Kolk, A. McFarlane and L. Weiseaeth (eds) *Traumatic Stress: The Effects of Overwhelming Experience on Mind, Body and Society*. New York: Guilford Press.

Riviere, S. (2006) Short Term Play Therapy for Children with Disruptive Behavior Disorders. In H. Gerard Kaduson and C.E. Schaefer (eds) *Short Term Play Therapy for Children* (2nd edn). New York: Guilford Press.

Siegel, D.J. (2001) Toward an interpersonal neurobiology of the developing mind: Attachment relationships, "mindsight," and neural integration. *Infant Mental Health Journal 22*, 1–2.

Yasenik, L. and Gardner, K. (2012) *Play Therapy Dimensions Model: A Decision-Making Guide for Integrative Play Therapists*. London: Jessica Kingsley Publishers.

11

TO KILL OR NOT TO KILL WHILE FIGURING OUT HOW TO LOVE ME FOREVER

A Child Loves Her Play, Not Because
It's Easy, But Because It's Hard

—— THERESA FRASER ——

Case introduction

Very early in my play therapy career, I received a referral to work with Samantha. Samantha's story was not unlike many of the children I had previously worked with when I wore the hat of child and youth care practitioner or CYCP. In North America, CYCPs through the Ontario Association of Child and Youth Care (OACYC, 2015, p.5) note:

> practice in a variety of service settings including: child welfare, youth criminal justice, child and family mental health, pediatric/adolescent health and mental health care, specialized education, youth shelters and mental health and substance abuse residential treatment.

CYCPs use the life space as the environment for interaction and make meaning of day-to-day interactions. For 25 years, there were many Samuels and Samanthas with whom I developed a therapeutic relationship. This time, however, I met Samantha as a play therapist in the role of mental health professional who introduced her to the therapeutic playroom for weekly appointments. The Association for Play Therapy defines play therapy as "the systematic use of a theoretical model to establish an interpersonal process wherein trained play therapists use the therapeutic powers of play to help clients prevent or resolve psychosocial difficulties and achieve optimal growth and development." Play therapy is a way to work with individuals at their developmental level using the universal language of play, recognizing that in play we can be little or big, vulnerable or strong, happy or angry and so on.

Samantha was big but also so very little. She tried to be strong so her vulnerability wouldn't show through. She wore the armor of happiness and silliness to hide the anger, sadness and rejection she had experienced. She resided in a group home for latency-aged children. She was 11 years of age and understandably angry. She was rejecting of caregivers and had many primary caregivers in her life before I had the privilege of meeting her. She was apprehended into the care of the state after being abandoned.

Babies are abandoned on fire station doorsteps. Children are sometimes abandoned in child welfare offices. Samantha had been repeatedly abandoned, first by her birth mother who had abandoned her at a friend's home when she was four. Her mother had gone to get groceries and never returned. The friend later adopted Samantha. It was a private adoption that appeared to go well until she was dropped off at a hospital in her ninth year. She stayed in an adult psychiatric ward until the local child protection agency picked her up when no one came to either visit or claim her after two weeks of inpatient care. She didn't know her birth name and her adoption records were sealed. She was placed in a foster home for six months until she made threats against the unborn child of the foster mom when she sensed they were going on vacation without her. She was right. There was no intention for Samantha to join the family on vacation. Her threats just ensured that she rejected them before they could reject her.

Samantha arrived home from school one day to find a child protection worker with the trunk (boot) of her car open at the front of the house. All of Samantha's belongings were in the trunk. Yet again, for the third time in her life—the primary caregiver didn't say goodbye nor warn her of an impending move. Instead, the next person just picked her up. The next person (who promised yet again) to protect her and to keep her safe moved her from a foster home setting to a more intrusive setting—a group home. It was here where other children came and went. Staff usually worked 12-hour shifts and Samantha changed her elementary school yet again. The only relationship she verbalized grieving was the school crossing guard from her previous foster home. She experienced the crossing guard as a Nana who greeted her daily with no expectation from her except that she only walk when the safe sign was held up.

I met with the group home staff first without Samantha. They shared a narrative of a little girl who could be kind to younger children but was also rejecting of any adults in her life who attempted to demonstrate kindness or nurturance. She would demonstrate aggressive interactions towards other children both in her residence and at school if challenged or overshadowed. She would use weapons such as knives or sticks if they were within reach. She used animated language with sexual overtones and themes. She would publicly masturbate and pretend to "hump" staff when she walked up behind them. She made verbal threats that all members of the treatment team feared would get her charged when she became 12 years of age. She verbalized and demonstrated feeling anxious. She was hyperactive, hypervigilant, impulsive and at other times demonstrated signs of depression and had difficulty sleeping.

Staff and her child protection worker weren't sure what therapeutic goals they wanted for her regarding counseling. There were so many symptoms and behaviors they were concerned about that impeded her relationship building and day-to-day functioning in her many life spaces. They knew that she needed help and support, and given her reluctance to talk play therapy made sense as the model of intervention.

Samantha's externalizing behaviors communicated that she didn't feel safe, wasn't connected to others and had difficulty regulating her emotions (Bath, 2008).

This was no surprise given her complex trauma history. Dr. Bruce Perry describes trauma as "a psychologically distressing event that is outside the range of usual human experience, often involving a sense of intense fear, terror and helplessness" (Perry, 2007, p.15). The definition that is attributed to Beverly James's work is that trauma "refers to overwhelming, uncontrollable experiences that psychologically impact victims by creating in them feelings of helplessness, vulnerability, loss of safety, and loss of control"

(James, 2009, p.1). Samantha's repeated rejections created a little girl who felt helpless and vulnerable and felt that she had no control or power over her day-to-day life or future.

The challenge with Samantha's history was that her childhood stories were held by those who had disappeared and her private adoption records were sealed. Her hospital admission was precipitated by self-harming behaviors such as head banging, and while there was a disclosure that her adoptive older brothers and their friends had penetrated her, she later recanted this disclosure. Samantha's child protection worker also indicated that there was concern at the time about auditory hallucinations. Those who work with trauma recognize that a stress response can include responses such as fight, flight or freeze. Freeze develops in a state of perpetual stress in which the stress chemicals simply do not stop and the reward chemicals never or seldom come. In the state, fight/flight cortisol flood eventually leads to "freeze" dissociation (Roelofs, 2017). It appeared that Samantha's stress response both precipitated and perpetuated all of these symptoms.

Theoretical orientation

Working with children who have complex trauma histories means that we try to intervene ensuring that those impacted by an "event" have opportunities to feel empowered, feel strong, feel safe and that we provide opportunities for the children to have some decision-making power. They may not have the opportunity to make their legal day-to-day living decisions, but in the play therapy room they can choose how to express their feelings using the healing tools (play objects and materials) that they also get to choose. While play cannot change the external realities of children's lives, it can be a vehicle for children to explore and enjoy their differences and similarities and to create, even for a brief time, a more just world where everyone is an equal and valued participant (Evans, 2010).

Integrative Play Therapy

Drewes, Bratton and Schaefer (2011) share that complex and difficult treatment cases often require a more comprehensive treatment approach. This integrative play therapy approach may involve the blending of theories and techniques. Leblanc and Ritchie (2001) and Bratton *et al.* (2005) agree that the optimal play therapy treatment effect falls within 30–40 sessions specifically when the treatment is provided by a mental health professional (cited in Lin and Bratton, n.d.).

Case study conceptualization

Samantha is a child with a complex trauma history who had few current people supporting her in her various life spaces while she engaged in the therapeutic process. This was important to be mindful of as she proceeded through the phases of therapy. She could not be rushed, and the play therapy approach needed to be integrative to meet Samantha's current and unmet needs that included helping her to remember her stories, visit her stories, share her stories and rewrite her future story. She had no one to call an attachment figure and no one who was interested in becoming one for her.

Samantha was vulnerable and angry and she communicated this with anyone who interacted with her. As already noted, to begin the process while creating a therapeutic alliance (with someone who has been wounded and faced rejection far too often), the work would need to follow child-centered play therapy principles (Axline, 1947; Landreth, 1991), while understanding Dr. Bruce Perry's Neurosequential Model of Therapeutics (Perry and Szalavitz, 2006). Samantha would require activities that would assist her when she was ready to rewire, bottom up and inside out (primitive, limbic or cortical brain).

Samantha's play therapy process often reminded me of the Dr. Benjamin Spock quote where he states that "a child loves her play, not because it is easy but because it is hard." Samantha bravely worked hard while allowing me the privilege of holding space for her therapeutic journey.

Therapy process: turning points and emergence of self

When introduced to Samantha, the first goal was to attempt to create a therapeutic alliance so that Samantha could risk demonstrating her feelings over the course of play therapy sessions. A child-centered approach (Axline, 1947; Landreth, 1991) was therefore utilized for an initial 12 sessions. A short solution-focused approach would not have provided Samantha with the opportunity to build trust with any clinician given her many abandoning experiences. Thankfully, Samantha's legal guardian recognized that she needed to be worked with both intentionally and carefully.

Samantha challenged the development of our therapeutic relationship by beginning and ending each session with swear words, usually directed at me. This intensive swearing always "bookmarked" the play. My clinical play therapy supervisor questioned for two months if Samantha was treatment ready. She appeared too angry. My sense as a play therapist was that the reinforced and multiple experiences of abandonment precipitated these weekly tests of commitment of myself and the play therapy process. On one occasion I was ill and had to cancel an appointment and she refused to even swear at me for two sessions. She came in and sat down. She made no eye contact and stared at her shoes.

Her (*first* appointment of the day) sessions were re-scheduled to become end-of-the-day appointments for my own self-care. Beginning the day being verbally abused precipitated exhaustion like no other. Recognizing that these attempts to attack and disengage were self-protective strategies was helpful in not personalizing the attacks while creating a milieu that was healing. Cuskelly, Poulsen and Ziviani (2013) state: "The most relevant aspects of the therapy environment are those that support or interfere with the person's ability to engage and participate successfully in activities that meet their need satisfaction within a particular context" (p.236).

Understanding Samantha's chronosystem or the events in her lifetime that impacted her at different stages of time (Bronfenbrenner, 1989) helped to depersonalize the violence. Coming to therapy was hard. It touched parts of her memories that she hoped to board up. It became clear that end-of-the-day sessions also helped Samantha to be able to meet and review memories in the play therapy room and sometimes even leave them there. This was significant, given a discussion or play of her past always triggered a restraint with Child and Youth Care staff when Samantha arrived home. After 12 sessions she was given permission to quit therapy, but she continued to self-advocate, so she had ongoing sessions. Gradually the swearing times shifted from 15 minutes to ten and then five. Her swear words became less violent and angry. She then moved to swearing at puppets and could dialogue with them, confronting them on the mean things that they did to children.

It was surprising in the moment that at the end of the session the angry Samantha would return, but now it is clear (reflectively) that her anger was about the endings and the goodbyes that she had to endure weekly.

Turning point 1

Samantha got to a point where she made a list of people who had wronged her. It took her a few weeks to get the list just right. She didn't know the names of her brother's friends who had raped her and she stated that she didn't care what the policy was, as it wouldn't get her help to catch the perpetrators.

One day she bounced in without swearing and stated that she had been thinking all night about what she wanted to play *with* and she knew what she needed. She had decided to sword fight with foam swords that were carefully stored in the playroom. Before picking up the sword she used the chalk and the chalkboard door to list the many people who had ever wronged her. The list was long. Using swordplay she would ask me to play a role. It was my job to be one of the people who had abandoned and hurt her. In each circumstance, she told the person how she felt about their actions towards her. She then (depending on the perpetrator) would cut their ears, eyes, arms or feet off, ultimately killing them before we moved on to the next perpetrator. Her articulate confrontation before killing the person seemed to calm her down. She also would thank me for helping her to "tell them off" as I pretended to die over and over again.

When her list was completed (and it took almost the whole session) she asked me to use the chalkboard to share my list of people that I wanted to kill. I didn't have a list. I explained that I was an adult who had already told all the people that had hurt me how I felt. We had a Here and Now Verbal Use of Self discussion (Appendix A). Samantha incorporated this sharing into her reactions.

Samantha was crushed. She verbalized that she had shared her most vulnerable experiences and I needed to reciprocate. She threw himself down to the ground weeping and could only tolerate me sitting beside her quietly. I intentionally didn't touch her. I didn't talk. I just sat beside her and offered her tissues and some water.

Turning point 2

At this point, my golden retriever was whining at the door. I opened the door to my play therapy office (which happened to be a home office with a separate entrance). I allowed our golden retriever, Patch, to come through the door, and she came down the lower level stairs ever so gingerly and laid beside Samantha on the floor. They had never met, though Samantha had heard Patch barking when the group home van pulled up into the parking area of the building. Patch placed her paw on Samantha's arm and reciprocally Samantha wrapped her arm around Patch while she sobbed until the session ended. At this point in the session I was utilizing non-intrusive responding and co-facilitation. Dog and girl lay quietly touching each other without looking at each other or me. There was no evidence of Samantha wanting to engage in a conversation or wanting me to encourage her to chat more. As soon as Samantha heard the group home staff knock on the door, she got up and then stormed out of the play therapy room. She didn't say goodbye or hug Patch for the last time.

I contacted the group home staff and explained that we had an intense session and to contact me if she appeared to be moving into crisis. Ironically there was no conflict and no restraints. Staff reported that she wasn't excited to do her chores but we all agreed that this was an age-appropriate act of resistance. She also didn't mention the session nor voice any concern about coming to the next session.

Samantha came back to the next session still angry, though she allowed me to explain that, at that point in my world, I had come to terms with those who had wronged me as I had done my own "killing" in my own way when I was younger. We talked about how the metaphor of killing had helped her to feel like she could verbalize how angry and sad she felt about being left behind and rejected as well as the hurt she had experienced. She then talked about forgiveness, stating that she couldn't forgive her mom(s) yet. I acknowledged that no one could ask her or tell her when to forgive but that she would know if she was ever ready to do so. Older teens and adults may identify that they are in a place of forgiveness, but this should never be forced on a child.

Turning point 3

Prior to this session I had prepared some arts materials hoping that I could engage her in creating a safe place drawing. She was not willing to engage in any activities that I had prepared. Instead she chose to pick up a toy doll and asked to bathe the doll. We filled a plastic doll bath with warm sudsy water and lavender-scented bubbles. Samantha bathed the doll all the while asking repeatedly if anyone might see her doing so. When she was finished she wrapped the doll up and then proceeded to rock it back and forth.

Doll bathing occurred in two more sessions before she came into the office and then initiated a "go fish" card game. Cards became her focus for a few sessions. We took turns dealing cards and we took turns putting them away. Card playing became the theme for a few more subsequent sessions.

Turning points 4 and 5

Her next request was that I read her the book *Love You Forever* by Robert Munsch (1986). This story is about the reciprocal love that a mother has for her child and a child has for their mother. It was not a book that I would have chosen as it does not appear that this child has received much nurturing during her early years. Once I read her the book it prompted her to talk about a few special people she had met in her past. This list included the crossing guard.

In a subsequent session, she would ask to wrap herself in a blanket lying sideways on a wooden rocking chair while I read her this book. The blanket had to be soft and fleecy. Her request was always so specific and evident of her ability to plan and identify what she needed to feel heard and happy. During this time, I began to make linking interpretations (Yasenik and Gardner, 2012) between actions taken and unmet needs. As Samantha gets older she will find people whom she feels are safe.

The repetitive book reading reminded me of reading to my children when they were preschool age. It appeared that we were "growing up" Samantha. This intervention is an example of using a neurosequential approach. In this approach Dr. Bruce Perry (2007) talks about the Neurosequential Model being:

> a developmentally-informed, biologically-respectful approach to working with at-risk children. The Neurosequential Model is not a

specific therapeutic technique or intervention; it is a way to organize a child's history and current functioning. The goal of this approach is to structure assessment of a child, the articulation of the primary problems, identification of key strengths and the application of interventions (educational, enrichment and therapeutic) in a way that will help family, educators, therapists and related professionals best meet the needs of the child.

It was clear that Samantha enjoyed the vestibular input that the rocking chair provided. She required sensory reassurance that all was well in her world. She wasn't moving residences and had time to let her guard down. Storytelling and chair rocking happened for at least four additional sessions. She was able to move from angry feelings directed to those who had caused her deep hurt to loving feelings for those from whom she could accept kindness (these people included some group home staff and myself as well as Patch the dog).

The dog provided Samantha with a safe outlet in which to share affection and support when she felt most vulnerable. As sessions continued, I gave Samantha a Robert Munsch tape, so she could listen to the *Love You Forever* story while settling at bedtime. She was so appreciative of this gift and was able to express a goal, which was that she would fall asleep as easily as the other kids did in the group home.

While therapy was going on, I also expressed concern about finding someone to "tell" the little girl's life story. The child protection worker reported that there truly was no one who could connect Samantha or her parents to each other. With permission, I went into Samantha's school and reviewed her school file. In this file were the addresses of all of the schools that Samantha had attended. For each school, a letter was drafted to the principal requesting that the staff team attempt to locate:

- photos that Samantha might be in (class photos, special events and even individualized pictures)

- staff who would remember her enough to write her a letter

- a letter describing what was going on in the school at the time Samantha attended.

Letters were sent out and, within a month, return letters made their way back to the child protection agency. The letters were then forwarded to me so we could use them to begin to do some life story work. Samantha, however, was not in a place where she could accept the photos. She wasn't sure that she even wanted to talk to anyone from her past. She was worried about seeing herself as a little person. The letters were put aside and instead we worked on building current connections with adults she began to feel safe with at school and home.

With her worker's permission, I also purchased her a cell phone so she could contact me or other staff at her group home because she was being moved out of town to an adolescent program. This was not a regular gift from a therapist, but for a little girl who had no one in her life, it was decided that she needed a lifeline.

Samantha is in her early 20s now. She attends college and plays some team sports. She checked in a few years ago to say that she had found a family to spend time with in her town of origin. It isn't her biological or foster family, but she is happy. She is working at a job that she wants. She has begun to date but is determined that men will never hurt her again. She also thanked me for the tape but said that she is still trying to figure out how to "love you forever." I told her that she didn't need to but if she ever wanted to talk that I would love to see her.

Turning points summary

Stage in process	Quadrant	Turning points	What contributed to the turning point?
Establishing therapeutic rapport: swearing at therapist—testing therapist for relational safety	QII, III Child led and therapist led		• Therapist invites Samantha to use healing tools in the way she chooses to
Samantha stops swearing—feels rejected and isn't sure if she will invest in therapeutic process	QIII Child led		• Therapist cancels session; child feels rejected
Swearing decreases	QIII Child led		• Therapeutic relationship is developing

cont.

Stage in process	Quadrant	Turning points	What contributed to the turning point?
Swearing at puppets	QIV, II Child led and co-facilitation	Making a list of those who had wronged her	• Catharsis (Schaefer and Drewes, 2014)
Sword fighting	QIII	Patch joins Samantha	• Child can accept caring from pet
Nurturing toys	QII, I Directive and non-directive	Bathing baby dolls in the playroom	• Allowing herself to care for "others"
Bibliotherapy and vestibular input	QII Therapist led	Reading *Love You Forever* (Munsch, 1986) while Samantha rocks in the rocking chair	• Open to experiencing/ receiving nurturance from a distance • Practicing with what relationally "*could be*"
Separation preparation and therapeutic ending	QI, II Therapist-led interpretations	Samantha says goodbye	• Therapist purchases a cell phone so Samantha can call if she needs to • She never calls

References

Axline, V. (1947) *Play Therapy*. New York: Ballantine Books.
Bath, H. (2008) The three pillars of trauma-informed care. *Reclaiming Children and Youth* 17, 3, 17–21.
Bratton, S., Ray, D., Rhine, T., and Jones, L. (2005) The efficacy of play therapy with children: A meta-analytic review of treatment outcomes. *Professional Psychology: Research and Practice 36*, 4, 367–390.
Bronfenbrenner, U. (1989) Ecological Systems Theory. In R. Vasta (ed.) *Annals of Child Development: Vol. 6*. London: Jessica Kingsley Publishers.
Cuskelly, M., Poulsen, A.A., and Ziviani, J. (2013) *The Art and Science of Motivation: A Therapist's Guide to Working with Children*. London: Jessica Kingsley Publishers.
Drewes, A., Bratton, S., and Schaefer, C. (2011) *Integrative Play Therapy*. Hoboken, NJ: Wiley.
Evans, J. (2010) *Playing: Christian Daily Living*. Minneapolis, MN: Fortress Press.
James, B. (2009) *Treating Traumatized Children*. New York: Free Press.

Landreth, G. (1991) *Play Therapy: The Art of the Relationship*. Muncie, IN: Accelerated Development Inc., Publishers.

Leblanc, M. and Ritchie, M. (2001) A meta-analysis of play therapy outcomes. *Counseling Psychology Quarterly 14*, 149–163.

Lin, Y.W. and Bratton, S. (n.d.) *Summary of Play Therapy Meta-Analyses Findings*. Accessed on 03/08/2018 at http://evidencebasedchildtherapy.com/meta-analysesreviews

Munsch, R. (1986) *Love You Forever*. Toronto, Ontario: Firefly Books.

OACYC (2015) *Safeguarding the Other 23 Hours: Legislation of Child and Youth Care Practice in Ontario*. Toronto, Ontario: Ontario Association of Child and Youth Care. Accessed on 23/05/2018 at www.oacyc.org/uploads/File/Safeguarding_FINAL_WEB_VERSION.pdf

Perry, B. and Szalavitz, M. (2006) *The Boy Who was Raised as a Dog and Other Stories from a Child Psychiatrist's Notebook*. New York: Basic Books.

Perry, B.D. (2007) *Stress, Trauma and Post-Traumatic Stress Disorders in Children*. Accessed on 23/05/2018 at https://childtrauma.org/wp-content/uploads/2013/11/PTSD_Caregivers.pdf

Roelofs, K. (2017) Freeze for action: Neurobiological mechanisms in animal and human freezing. *Philosophical Transactions of the Royal Society B: Biological Sciences, 372*(1718), 20160206.

Schaefer, C.E. and Drewes, A.A. (2014) *The Therapeutic Powers of Play: 20 Core Agents of Change* (2nd edn). Hoboken, NJ: Wiley.

Yasenik, L. and Gardner, K. (2012) *Play Therapy Dimensions Model: A Decision-Making Guide for Integrative Play Therapists*. London: Jessica Kingsley Publishers.

12

SYMBOLIC SOLUTIONS

Establishing a Sense of Safety for Relationship Repair

SONIA MURRAY

Case introduction

Carl is a child who taught me to fully appreciate the essential therapeutic element of establishing and maintaining the relationship between child and therapist and the child's play. Carl came to play therapy with a small grain of hope, but with an entrenched internalised sense of threat and mistrust in himself, others and the world around him. This chapter will present Carl's therapeutic process through humanistic and integrative play therapy. Carl had experienced nine years of severe relational trauma, complex developmental trauma (van der Kolk, 2005) and neglect, including sexual abuse, loss and bereavement. Carl's play therapy process extended over a period of four years and he attended over 100 sessions. Due to his complex traumatising experiences, the therapist knew it would be a long process and the initial goal was to establish a sense of safety; from there, connections and trust could begin. The play therapy was initially individual, but later in the process incorporated Carl's foster carer (June). Through the therapeutic relationship and process, Carl began to develop an internalised sense of safety that enabled him to begin to incorporate a healthier internal working model of himself and relationships. He was able to develop a more balanced view of himself, his experiences and his capabilities. Additionally, he developed a more coherent narrative about himself and his experiences. Carl's journey was at times slow and complex as his behaviour responses would require him to be placed within a school environment with other children who were unpredictable and expressed their distress through their behaviours. Unfortunately this unpredictable and at times volatile environment would continuously require Carl to stay in a state of alarm, fear or terror (Perry, 2006). This impacted on his therapeutic process.

To ensure anonymity, some elements have been changed to protect the child's identity.

Theoretical orientation

In considering Carl, his complex needs and his life experiences, my approach was based in Norcross's (2005) assimilation integration. The therapeutic methodology was grounded in a humanistic approach incorporating trauma-informed and attachment-aware theories and knowledge to create a therapeutic environment to facilitate change. The overriding belief of a humanistic approach is that the children have a fundamental drive for self-actualisation and know what they need to do to realise this, but sometimes need a therapeutic environment and therapeutic relationship to be able to achieve this. The use of Axline's (1947) non-directive principles of accepting the child where they are at developmentally, socially and emotionally, creating a permission/accepting environment and respecting the child's self-discovery, as well as the therapist working in Quadrant III: Non-intrusive Responding (Yasenik and Gardner, 2012), formed the basis of the therapeutic relationship and environment to bring about change. However, as the therapy progressed and Carl developed, it was appropriate to incorporate working in the different quadrants to facilitate growth and change.

The therapeutic relationship is an essential requirement to facilitate change with children who have experienced relational trauma (van der Kolk, 2005). There is accumulating evidence that the quality of the therapeutic relationship is a strong predictor of change, increasing the likelihood of better effects (Flückiger *et al.*, 2012; Karver and Caporino, 2010). As Carl had experienced relational trauma by his primary caregivers throughout his childhood until he went to live with his foster carer, it was necessary to establish a therapeutic relationship. As noted by Herman (1992, p.133):

> The core experiences of psychological trauma are disempowerment and disconnection from others. Recovery therefore is based upon the empowerment of the survivor and the creation of new connections. Recovery can take place only within the context of relationships; it cannot occur in isolation.

The characteristics of the therapeutic relationship are similar to the attachment purposes as noted by Divecha (2017) in providing a sense of safety and security, regulating emotions by soothing distress, creating joy and supporting calm, and providing a secure base from which to explore. It mirrors a healthy child/parent secure attachment of having attuned engagement, emotional connections and a predictable environment. Often attuned engagements and emotional connections involve playful interactions. Also it is within the compassionate attunement within the therapeutic relationship that new neural pathways can be developed (Cozolino, 2010).

The relational trauma caused both psychological and physiological conflict for Carl as children's drive is to seek comfort from their caregivers. When feeling frightened they seek to connect, but the child is faced with a dichotomy as their source of comfort is also the threat, and therefore their innate drive is to flee. It ruptures trust in relationships and develops an internal working model that relationships are sources of threat and unpredictable: "The most pernicious trauma is deliberately inflicted in a relationship where the traumatized individual is dependent—at worst, in a parent/child relationship" (Allen, 1995, p.7).

An aspect of creating a therapeutic relationship is playful interactions. It was deemed that the therapeutic powers of play would provide Carl with a developmentally appropriate medium to safely explore, develop and gain mastery over some of his experiences. The majority of Carl's experiences had occurred in his first few years of life, when he was preverbal and with limited cognitive ability. He had little capacity to process the traumatic and terrifying experiences, thus leaving him in a state of toxic stress and functioning from his lower brain (brain stem) (Perry, 2004). Additionally, Carl had not experienced persistent good enough emotional scaffolding to be able to learn to understand and regulate his emotional states. Carl was underdeveloped in his emotional understanding and his cognitive ability, thus making verbal therapy developmentally inappropriate. The play provided the vehicle for turning points to occur and, as noted by Hong and Mason (2016, p.38), "counterbalanced the alarm system in his brain".

My theoretical orientation for Carl was further informed by child development with particular reference to the impact of trauma on all aspects of the child, physically, relationally, socially, emotionally and neurobiologically. Due to the lack of safety, Carl had not been able to use his social engagement system (Porges, 2011). He presented as hypervigilant to sound, movement and smell and was nearly always operating in either sympathetic or parasympathetic vagal responses. Due to being in these responses, as noted earlier, he was functioning from his lower brain and constantly seeking sources of potential threat. This was his overriding need and this impacted on his ability to access his prefrontal cortex or higher brain (Perry, 2004). Prichard (2017) concludes that "the part of the brain developing at the time of the trauma is where treatment must start". Therefore my starting point was working in the lower brain and limbic brain as these were the areas where he was functioning by establishing a sense of safety and building a relationship (Perry, 2006). Only once he had begun to establish an internalised sense of safety, and his social engagement system was online, was he able to access his higher brain to process, conceptualise and understand.

Furthermore it was essential for me to have an understanding of myself and my states as he was dependent on me increasing co-regulation actions and behaviours.

Case study conceptualization

Nine-year-old Carl had something about him (an inner resilience or drive) to keep striving forward. Looking back on his experiences, it is a wonder that he still wanted to connect with anyone or anything. At the time of the referral, Carl was residing with a therapeutic foster carer and attending a specialist educational provision for children experiencing social, emotional, mental health and behavioural difficulties. His needs were not met in a mainstream setting. He displayed his distress through significant emotional and behavioural regulation challenges both within his foster home and in school. He had only been residing with his foster carer for approximately six months at the time of the referral and he was in the early stages of developing an attachment relationship with her.

It was clear from the information gathered and my observations that Carl had developed an impoverished sense of self that was incompetent and perceived as not valued (Harter, 2012). His self-esteem was fragile as he struggled to manage change, cope with frustration and regulate his responses. He had internalised how his caregivers had treated him and developed a sense of self that he was at fault and he was "bad" (Harter, 2012).

Having gathered a comprehensive history about Carl's experience and having observed him around school, I knew the therapy would be a long process, and the initial goal was to establish a sense of safety both externally and internally; from these connections trust could begin. As Perry (2000) states, "A sense of safety comes from consistent, attentive, nurturing and sensitive attentions to each child's needs. Safety is created by predictability and predictability is created by consistent behaviours."

The predictable nature of play therapy begins the process of creating a sense of safety; however, the predictability of the therapist and the therapeutic relationship is the corrective factor.

Therapy process: turning points and emergence of self

Carl's experiences of relational trauma impacted on all aspects of his development, particularly his sense of self, and this was apparent in the play therapy. His play content and recurring themes were often linked to mistrust and trust (Ryan and Edge, 2011). Initially Carl's themes were related to constant exposure to danger, vulnerability, absence of protective factors, hopelessness, despair, threat, abandonment and loss of self. I will now explore specific play elements that were turning points in the therapeutic process.

Turning points 1–3: hide-and-seek play

Throughout Carl's play therapy, hide-and-seek play was a common element and this play initiated turning points in the change process. It came in different forms from hiding objects to persons being hid and being sought. Hide-and-seek is a form of relational play and can be seen as a way of mastering anxiety about separation, plus developing a positive sense of self. Being separated can initiate a life-threatening response and potentially trigger a sympathetic or parasympathetic vagal response. The play of being separated and being quickly reunited helps children learn to soothe and regulate their responses (Frankiel, 1993). Hide-and-seek play helps develop a secure sense of self, by developing an internal perception of their caregiver's presence (Israelievitch, 2008). In addition, the development of a secure sense of self comes from the experience of first being reunited as they are worthy of being found, but second from being reunited by someone who is expressing joy and delight at finding them. The play can have high levels of emotional activation, but because it is play, it is not seen as life threatening, so it does not trigger a fear or terror state in the child. As the child is determining the play, then they with the support of the therapist (if needed) can determine the level of activation. For neurodevelopment, a level of emotional activation is required for neuropathways to be formed.

When hide-and-seek occurs in play therapy, it is an opportunity to re-experience and rework early attachment experiences and loss (Frankiel, 1993; Israelievitch, 2008). It is often a sign that the child has formed a sense of safety within the therapeutic environment, but more importantly it is an indicator that the therapeutic relationship is developing.

Unfortunately for Carl, he had repeatedly experienced the terror of his caregivers both physically and emotionally disappearing for long periods of time. Additionally, on their return he could not guarantee their response towards him and at times they would be dismissive, rejecting and/or aggressive. Therefore, undertaking hide-and-seek in the therapy sessions represented significant risks for Carl. Would the therapist react as per his previous experiences, would she be bothered to find him, would she be pleased to find him? As noted by Bergman (1993, p.364), "to risk playing Hide-and-Seek one has to be able to take for granted the reunion will occur and will be pleasurable".

The hide-and-seek play took different forms, with differing levels of risk. Initially Carl tested the risk by hiding things in the sandtray and checking to see my response about finding them. I was very conscious of the importance of engaging in the joy of finding them. He would repeatedly check to see if we were "just playing". Therefore I was very conscious of my own emotional state and my body language and intonations in my communications. The whole of me needed to portray that we were "just playing" and there was no danger. This enabled us to both use our social engagement systems. The "just playing" process allowed Carl to rework his previous experiences of being abandoned and being in hyper-aroused and hypo-aroused states (Kestly, 2014). Initially he would struggle to allow me to find the objects, so he would point them out. I reflected that it was difficult for him to trust that I would be able to find them. Steadily, as he became more confident in my responses, he would make it harder to find the objects by placing them around the room and would be checking my persistence in finding them.

Carl's hide-and-seek play continued until he had experienced enough predictable instances to take the risk of hiding himself in the playroom. This shift from object use to embodiment play represented the first turning point and opened up varying levels of risk, starting with hiding in plain sight to actually hiding inside cupboards and so on. Kestly (2016) suggests that the role of hiding is linked to the child using the play within the context of the therapeutic relationship to experiment with low arousal aspects of the parasympathetic zone. Unfortunately in Carl's early traumatic experiences, he would often have been forced into a parasympathetic response of immobilisation as he was unable to mobilise due to his age and ability to move/escape from the threat. Therefore, this play may have provided Carl with the opportunity to re-experience, rework and gain mastery through him being able to mobilise in the play.

First, he was unable to tolerate the risk of me not finding him, so he would say "here I am" or make a sound to indicate where he was. I would then delight in the joy of finding him. At this point I was working in Quadrant IV: Co-facilitation (Yasenik and Gardner, 2012) and, having been asked to find him, entered the play with the hypothesis that he was beginning to trust that I would find him and that he was ready to develop a tolerance of waiting for the reunite. So with careful attuned responses, my portrayal of safety and observations of his emotional and behavioural states, I was gradually able to extend his tolerance of waiting before going into a stress response by giving commentaries about my actions and taking slightly longer to find him. For example, "Is he under this table? I am going to keep looking for Carl. Is he beside this cupboard? Oh no, I can't wait to find him." Initially this play generated very little joy in Carl, but as the play was repeated, he began to experience the excitement and joy of being found.

The next turning point incorporated a greater risk as Carl wanted to get inside the cupboard. In the therapy room there were cupboards with roll-down shutters to close them. Initially he wanted to make a den in the cupboard, so we removed all the toys and he placed a blanket in the bottom and climbed into the space with a flashlight and biscuits. Then when he felt safe enough in there, he asked for me to close the shutter. This was a significant risk as he could not be sure that I would remain; however, the therapeutic relationship was significantly stronger and the previous experiences of hide-and-seek play had established an internalised sense of trust and permanency so that he was able to take the risk. Through the repeated experience of the therapist being there even when out of his sight, he had developed the concept of object permanence in connection to relationships. This had not been his experience in early childhood. I gradually closed the shutter under his direction and immediately opened it when he asked as it had become intolerable for him. This was repeated until he was able to manage with the shutter completely down. I remained beside the cupboard and narrated that he was right inside and that he was safe. This was a real sense of immobilisation as he was reliant on me to open the shutter.

I noticed that, when Carl asked for the shutter to come down, my heart rate accelerated, and my thought processes were: "Should I let him do this? How might it be perceived by others?" Some of my responses may have been Carl's emotional transference to me, but the rest were my own doubts and worry. Having noticed this, I knew I needed to regulate myself by taking a few deep breaths to portray the sense of safety to Carl. This play appeared to be highly significant to Carl, and therefore my doubts needed to be put aside and I reminded myself to trust his process.

Initially the shutter was required to go up quickly and then back down, repeatedly. This enabled Carl to stay within his window of tolerance, but also extend it. The length of time with the shutter down increased and a sense of peacefulness emerged. The need for verbal connections for safety reduced, and when the shutter went up I noticed Carl appeared relaxed. This play continued for over ten sessions and then his play changed.

During this play I was working in Quadrant III: Non-intrusive Responding as the majority of Carl's play was stimulated by implicit memories. The turning point of this embodied play was that Carl's implicit memories were being re-experienced within the safe context of play, but also with someone who was truly present and supportive, which had been missing in his early life experiences.

The next hide-and-seek play incorporated me having a blanket over my head and not being able to see, but needing to find Carl in the playroom. Carl would move around the room whilst I was trying to find him and the play involved a chase and escape element. The play had moved from immobilisation to mobilisation and would suggest that now Carl was working in the sympathetic zone. With this somatosensory play, he was gaining mastery of being in control and experienced the power of being able to escape. I would repeatedly search for him as he continuously moved out of my reach. Thankfully the playroom was large and allowed for lots of movement. As the play progressed Carl became more skilled at stealthily moving around the playroom and I was reliant on not only attuning my senses but also my instinct about where he was. I would regularly comment that even though I could not see or hear him, something in my body was telling me which direction he was in. Carl as a young child had had to override/disregard his instinctive responses as his drive was to seek comfort from his caregiver at times of threat, but unfortunately his source of comfort was also at times the cause of threat, so his drive was to flee. Therefore, my hypothesis was that Carl needed support with understanding and using his body/senses to recognise threat and sources of comfort. In addition, his limited emotional intelligence needed further development and required another's modelling of this. I worked in Quadrant IV: Co-facilitation (Yasenik and Gardner, 2012) and narrated what I noticed about my body reactions and feelings when trying to find him. By using myself and my attuned bodily awareness I was able to facilitate Carl's therapeutic process (Geller, 2013). Therapeutic presence requires the therapist to bring their whole self into the therapeutic relationship, including understanding and using their "own bodily experience in order to access the knowledge, professional skill, and wisdom embodied within" (p.209).

As with the previous hide-and-seek play, initially he would require being found quickly, but as the play progressed he was able to extend the time before he let me find him, until during one session, I was unable to find him or catch him until the last minute of the session. During this play I was immensely immersive as I was fully engaged and wholly reliant on my body and all my senses other than sight to stay connected to him. This play was also recreated later in the therapy with his foster carer.

Turning point 4: rescuers were able to rescue

The next turning point came from the incorporation of embodiment play and projective play (Jennings, 2006). Carl used objects in the sand to create story narratives and explored themes of mistrust, helplessness and hopelessness. The play involved a vehicle which needed to be rescued, but the rescue vehicles were repeatedly destroyed in accidents or disasters before getting to Carl's vehicle. They were blown up, sunk in the sand, crashed, pushed into ponds or fell into deep holes and were covered. Sometimes other rescue vehicles attempted to rescue some of the wrecked rescue vehicles, but then they were destroyed. Carl's internalised sense of self was that he was not worthy of help or that no one could help him, or as Harter (2012) suggests, he was a child who had developed an impoverished sense of self. He had been let down on numerous occasions by the adults around him, including perceived protectors. He was rejecting of any help and was resistant to building relationships with people around him.

It was necessary to use the safety of Carl's symbolic play at this point, and therefore I remained in Quadrant III: Non-intrusive Responding, reflecting on the actions and that every time the vehicle thought it was going to be rescued but the rescuers were unable to get there. Occasionally I would test if Carl was ready to bring the symbolic material into conscious thinking by using the occasional interpretive reflections; however, each time this was ignored or rejected (Quadrant I: Active Utilization). Remaining in the metaphor provided the distance for Carl to explore the unconscious defence of not being able to accept help. This repeated play was symptomatic of post-traumatic play (Gil, 2017; Terr, 1990) and was Carl's way of working through his unresolved experiences. It took the form of dynamic post-traumatic play (Gil, 2017) as the play was energetic, engaging and flexible, even though the themes remained the same. It enabled him to rework the sensations and negative emotions linked to his experiences of being neglected, abandoned and no one helping him. In addition to Carl's sense of self being reorganised, the play may also have been representative of trying to understand the traumatic death of a family member. Unfortunately the rescuers had been unable to get there in time and no one had been able to help them.

This repeated play went on for about two months before the play expanded to include a rescue vehicle being able to reach Carl's vehicle. I reflected that someone had made it to Carl's vehicle and were trying to rescue it. However, at this point, the rescue vehicle had not got all the equipment it needed to rescue Carl's vehicle, so it sunk in the sand. I reflected that even when help arrived, it could not help. However, it was the tentative stage of realising the possibility that there are people who can get through to help that likely contributed to the next turning point, and the beginning of the reworking of the sense of hopelessness and helplessness. This play continued for the next couple of sessions and I continued to reflect the hope of someone arriving to help, but then the disappointment of them not being able to help. I also reflected that the rescuers did not give up; they kept trying to get to Carl's vehicle.

The turning point occurred when the rescuers arrived and they had all the equipment they needed, but also they had made a path for other rescuers to come. Carl's vehicle was able to be rescued. I reflected that the rescuers had got there and rescued him, but also a path had been made so that other rescuers could come in the future if needed. Alongside this I modelled the emotional responses of relief, joy and gratitude of being rescued. This play had enabled Carl to modify cognitive distortions related to his early life experiences and develop a sense of worthiness. Plus he was able to organise his experiences and memories. This symbolic change represented an actual change in Carl's responses to accepting help from his foster carer and school staff. Carl was developing a strong relationship with his foster carer and he was more willing to allow school staff to help him both emotionally and academically. However, it was still fragile and, at times of stress, he would revert to defensive strategies of rejecting help.

Turning point 5: genogram

Another turning point involved working in Quadrant II: Open Discussion and Exploration (Yasenik and Gardner, 2012). This occurred about three years into Carl's play therapy. He was in his early teens and had moved to a secondary specialist provision but was struggling to regulate his emotional and behavioural responses in this setting. He was also testing the strength and persistence of his relationship with his foster carer, who had become his permanent carer. June is a highly skilled, attuned parent who is consistent and persistent in her parenting, but his mistrust in parental relationships was pushing her tolerance. Therefore, we concluded that it would be beneficial for Carl, his relationship skill development and his sense of self-worth that June joined the therapy sessions. Additionally, Carl had requested that she attend. The aim of the work was to strengthen Carl's trust in relationships, particularly parental caring relationships, and provide him with a different perspective. Involving June would provide her with additional skills, understanding and ways of responding to help further meet Carl's needs, but furthermore it would provide some completely focused time together that everyday life does not always allow for. As noted by Guerney and Ryan (2013, p.17), "the parents (carers) would not only be given positive skills, but this role would create a new perception of their parents (carers) on the part of their children."

Prior to entering the process, June and I had spent some time exploring the child-centred context of the sessions and the reflective responding. Primarily the sessions involved both of us following Carl's directions and the play was representative of the sessions with myself. He recreated the hide-and-seek play, this time involving June, and a significant element of the play was accepting June's nurture on being found. They both delighted in the joy of finding him. This play continued for a number of sessions and they would often end up in a hug on the sofa, smiling and laughing.

In the midst of this work, June raised that Carl appeared to have a confused view of his birth family and a conflict in his emotions towards himself within the context of June's family. Carl had an internalised view that he was to blame for all the events, experiences and others' actions that had occurred in his early life. Therefore he did not believe he was worthy of receiving the love and care June and her family were providing. Following further exploration in supervision it was concluded that Carl was cognitively developed enough to explore this with a more directive technique. As noted by Yasenik and Gardner (2012, p.51), "The therapist is primarily utilizing a developmentally sensitive, cognitive play therapy approach, and will engage in conscious process of the child's presenting issue."

I was also conscious that the complexities of Carl's birth family may need the symbolic distance of play materials to enable him to feel safe enough to be able to further explore and process. Therefore, I introduced a genogram activity using miniature objects (adapted from Carey, 2010) with Carl and June. The aim was to explore his internalised view of his birth family and his now forever family.

With two large sheets of paper, one for each family, every family member was identified and Carl was then asked to find miniatures to represent each family member. Carl engaged with the symbolic representations of both his birth family and his now forever family. He included miniatures that represented the issues that impacted on the individuals including alcohol and drug misuse. Whilst focusing on his birth family, he was able to identify both positive and negative aspects of the different individuals, which enabled him to have a more realistic view of them and differentiate what was real and what he fantasised and hoped they were. He also identified significant others who had been protective figures for him and his mother in his early years. He was able to articulate his feelings and thoughts regarding them and begin to develop a narrative of the self with the supportive scaffolding of June and myself and the therapeutic powers of play.

Amidst the process, Carl identified himself as a knight who wore strong armour, and in the dialogue about the function of the armour, he identified that it was to keep people away. This was symptomatic of Carl's developed safety defences in relationships. He had strong armour to keep people away, so therefore I tentatively tested his capacity to bring this into his conscious thinking by voicing that this armour had served him well when he was little, but wondered if it was needed so much now. He gave a small nod of acknowledgement, but no comment. This was enough to raise the thought process of an alternative way of being now that he was in a safe, supportive and nurturing environment. June asked if she could add some symbols to represent Carl from her perspective, and Carl agreed. She included a wizard, a brain and a ray of sunshine, as he had been so clever and wise at trying to look after himself and others when he was little and he was a ray of sunshine. Unfortunately, at the time of his traumatic life experiences, he was at the age where he was only cognitively able to think in terms of opposites (Harter, 2012) and he was only able to conceptualise things as all good or all bad. Consequently, he had internalised that he was all "bad" and that he was to blame. Unfortunately, his life experiences had obstructed his I-self construction, particularly his self-awareness, but alongside this his Me-self of positive self-perceptions was impacted. This activity enabled him to understand that there were longstanding issues that had begun long before he was born that had impacted on the care he had received. He was able to have a view that he was the product of the issues, not the cause, and was thus able to develop a more coherent narrative about himself and his family. Throughout this activity, there was a sense of heaviness and sadness. I was very conscious of carefully attuning to Carl, June and myself through this activity to ensure the play remained within his window of tolerance and that he did not experience traumatic intrusive memories. The play and the safety of the therapeutic relationship enabled the painful feelings, thoughts and understanding to be examined carefully.

Together, Carl and June developed a symbolic representation of their family. Carl and June co-created their family genogram, agreeing on the symbols and identifying different characteristics for each family member. This play felt different; there was a light-heartedness, playfulness and freedom about it. On completing the activity, he stood back and then moved the two symbolic representations far apart and verbalised that he did not want his new family to be "infected" by the sadness and anger of his birth family. He then went to June and relaxed against her as she hugged him. For that moment he was able to see that he was not the reason for their anger and sadness. Whilst he cared deeply for them, he was unable to change them and they could not meet his needs. However, with June he was cared for deeply and she could meet his needs and provide a nurturing, supportive and safe environment.

This session was a turning point, but unfortunately his ingrained self-protective strategies and his sense of self was so impacted upon that at times he would fall back into his old safety behaviours and would react before he was able to think.

Conclusion

Working with Carl was one of the most significant experiences in my role as a play therapist. He and his play therapy process taught me so much, particularly the necessity of the therapeutic relationship, the use of self and the need to go at the child's speed. To be trusted enough by Carl for him to be able to take the risks to explore his mistrust in relationships within the play therapy was a privilege and an honour. The therapeutic relationship, therapeutic environment and the therapeutic powers of play enabled Carl to explore, rework and repair from his early life experiences. The turning points enabled Carl to have a level of awareness that was not previously accessible to him and provide him with opportunities to view himself and others differently. I have met with Carl on a number of occasions into his adulthood and his life journey has had its ups and downs, but with the persistent loving support of June he is thriving. Carl and June have both given permission for this chapter to be written, and this may also be a turning point for him.

Turning points summary

Stage in process	Quadrant	Turning points	What contributed to the turning point?
Early stages	QIV: Co-facilitation	Hide-and-seek play involving the child	• Child experiencing himself as in control within sessions • The embodiment play • The child experiencing the anticipation and joy of waiting and then being found • The predictability of the therapist's reactions • The therapist's use of self, particularly her internal understanding of herself and her playfulness • The safety of the play • The child experiencing being able to tolerate the risk of not being found
Early stages	QIII: Non-intrusive Responding	Hide-and-seek play in the cupboard	• Child experiencing himself as in control within sessions • The therapeutic relationship • The embodiment play • The child re-experiencing the sense of immobilisation • The therapist's use of self, particularly her internal understanding of herself and keeping herself in her ventral vagus state • The safety of the play • The child experiencing that someone would help

cont.

Stage in process	Quadrant	Turning points	What contributed to the turning point?
Early stages	QIII: Non-intrusive Responding	Hide-and-seek play involving chase and seek element	• Child experiencing himself as in control within sessions • The embodiment play • The child being mobilised • The child being able to physically escape • The child being able to externalise the ability to run and escape • The therapeutic relationship • The predictability of the therapist's reactions • The therapist's use of self, particularly her internal understanding of herself and keeping herself in her ventral vagus state • The safety of the play • The child experiencing being able to tolerate the risk of not being found
Middle stages	QIII: Non-intrusive Responding QI: Active Utilization	Rescuers were able to rescue	• The symbolic nature of the play (projective play) • The safety of the play • The therapeutic relationship and reflective responding • The reworking of post-traumatic play • The therapist understanding the child's need to stay within the symbolism of the play
Ending stages	QII: Open Discussion and Exploration	Genogram	• Child experiencing himself as in control within sessions • The therapeutic relationship • The symbolic safety of the visual representation of his families • The relationship with his foster carer

References

Allen, J. (1995) *Coping with Trauma: A Guide to Self-Understanding*. Washington, DC: American Psychiatric Press.

Axline, V. (1947) *Play Therapy*. New York: Ballantine.

Bergman, A. (1993) To be or not to be separate: The meaning of hide-and-seek in forming internal representations. *Psychoanalytic Review 80*, 3, 361–376.

Carey, L. (2010) Family Genograms Using Miniature Objects. In L. Lowenstein (ed.) *Creative Family Therapy Techniques*. Toronto: Champion Press.

Cozolino, L. (2010) *The Neuroscience of Psychotherapy: Healing the Social Brain* (2nd edn). New York: W.W. Norton & Co.

Divecha, D. (2017) What is a Secure Attachment? And Why Doesn't "Attachment Parenting" Get You There? *Developmental Science Blog*, 3 April. Accessed on 30/12/2017 at www.developmentalscience.com/blog/2017/3/31/what-is-a-secure-attachmentand-why-doesnt-attachment-parenting-get-you-there

Flückiger, C., Del Re, A., Wampold, B., Symonds, D., and Horvath, A. (2012) How central is the alliance in psychotherapy? A multilevel longitudinal meta-analysis. *Journal of Counseling Psychology 59*, 1, 10–17.

Frankiel, R. (1993) Hide-and-seek in the playroom: On object loss and transference in child treatment. *Psychoanalytic Review 80*, 3, 341–359.

Geller, S.M. (2013) Therapeutic Presence: An Essential Way of Being. In M. Cooper, P.F. Schmid, M. O'Hara and A.C. Bohart (eds) *The Handbook of Person-Centred Psychotherapy and Counselling* (2nd edn). Basingstoke: Palgrave.

Gil, E. (2017) *Posttraumatic Play in Children: What Clinicians Need to Know.* New York: Guilford Press.

Guerney, L. and Ryan, V. (2013) *Group Filial Therapy: The Complete Guide to Teaching Parents to Play Therapeutically with their Children.* London: Jessica Kingsley Publishers.

Harter, S. (2012) *The Construction of the Self: Developmental and Sociocultural Foundations* (2nd edn). New York: Guilford Press.

Herman, J.L. (1992) *Trauma and Recovery.* New York: Basic Books.

Hong, R. and Mason, C.M. (2016) Becoming a neurobiologically-informed play therapist. *International Journal of Play Therapy 25*, 1, 35–44.

Israelievitch, G. (2008) Hiding and seeking and being found: Reflections on the hide and seek game in the clinical playroom. *Journal of Infant, Child and Adolescent Psychotherapy 7*, 1, 58–76. Accessed on 24/05/2018 at www.tandfonline.com/doi/full/10.1080/15289160801946783?scroll=top&needAccess=true

Jennings, S. (2006) *Creative Play with Children at Risk.* Milton Keynes: Speechmark.

Karver, M.S. and Caporino, N. (2010) The use of empirically-supported strategies for building a therapeutic relationship with an adolescent with oppositional defiant disorder. *Cognitive and Behavioral Practice 17*, 2, 222–232.

Kestly, T.A. (2014) *The Interpersonal Neurobiology of Play: Brain-Building Interventions for Emotional Well-Being.* New York: W.W. Norton & Co.

Kestly, T.A. (2016) Presence and play: Why mindfulness matters. *International Journal of Play Therapy 25*, 1, 14–23.

Norcross, J.C. (2005) A Primer on Psychotherapy Integration. In J.C. Norcross and M.R. Goldfried (eds) *Handbook of Psychotherapy Integration.* New York: Basic Books.

Perry, B. (2000) *Creating an Emotionally Safe Classroom.* Scholastic Early Childhood Today, Vol. 15. Accessed on 24/05/2018 at http://teacher.scholastic.com/professional/bruceperry/safety_wonder.htm

Perry, B.D. (2004) How the Brain Develops: The Importance of Early Childhood. In *Understanding Traumatized and Maltreated Children: The Core Concepts* [Video]. Houston, TX: Child Trauma Academy.

Perry, B.D. (2006) Applying Principles of Neurodevelopment to Clinical Work with Maltreated and Traumatized Children: The Neurosequential Model of Therapeutics. In N.B. Webb (ed.) *Working with Traumatized Youth in Child Welfare.* New York: Guilford Press. Accessed on 23/05/2018 at https://childtrauma.org/wp-content/uploads/2013/08/Perry-Bruce-neurosequentialmodel_06.pdf

Porges, S. (2011) *The Polyvagal Theory.* New York: W.W. Norton & Co.

Prichard, N. (2017) The Biology of Play Therapy: At the Heart of Play [PowerPoint presentation].

Ryan, V. and Edge, A.M. (2011) The role of play themes in non-directive play therapy. *Clinical Child Psychology and Psychiatry 17*, 3, 354–369.

Terr, L. (1990) *Too Scared to Cry: Psychic Trauma in Childhood.* New York: Harper & Row.

van der Kolk, B. (2005) Developmental trauma disorder. *Psychiatric Annals; Thorofare 35*, 5, 401–408.

Yasenik, L. and Gardner, K. (2012) *Play Therapy Dimensions Model: A Decision-Making Guide for Integrative Play Therapists.* London: Jessica Kingsley Publishers.

13

FROM ISOLATION TO INVIGORATION

Five Canadian Play Therapists Share an Emergence of Selves through the Power of Finding Belonging in a Professional Community

IRENE A. BARRETT, BRUCE A. BEAUDET, KATHARINE CHAPMAN, DANA DIAMOND, AND TAMMY REIS

> I think it's a matter of intention in relationships. When you're on the same journey you tend to gravitate towards a sense of closeness.
>
> Bruce A. Beaudet

There are periods in one's professional life when there is an awareness that something exceptional is occurring that will have a deeper impact than merely vocational growth. For the authors of this chapter, the journey in finding one another while seeking professional development as integrative play therapists has not only been enriching but also grounding. The journey towards becoming a registered or certified play therapist in Canada can be a unique experience, given our vast geographic nature accompanied by the fact that it is a growing profession in our country. For some play therapists and play therapist interns, these two factors can be a barrier to pursuing the profession or completing the registration or certification process. For those who do attempt to proceed in spite of these barriers, the profession itself can oftentimes feel isolating, leading to professional insecurities. Through the use of hermeneutical and critical interpretive lenses, this chapter will unpack the narratives of five Canadian play therapists/play therapist interns in their journeys to move beyond the impasse of practicing in isolation to a discovery of self, facilitated by an emergence into a professional community. In highlighting personal experiences and the power of the development of collegial connection, the authors will share how issues such as isolation due to proximity and limitations to collegial consultation were navigated, leading to professional growth in the clinicians' sense of professional self. The chapter will also explore experiences of empowerment through professional development and how the discovery of the Play Therapy Dimensions Model (Yasenik and Gardner, 2012) informed clinical practice, addressing impasses with clients and often resulting in therapeutic successes.

It is important to note that the authors' narratives are interwoven to capture a collective voice from written narratives as well as discussions occurring during a focus group. This style of data collection is purposeful in the effort to merge individual and group narratives within a unified context to capture the "I" and "We" within hermeneutical and critical interpretive research methods. Together, we celebrate each stage in the journey and hope to provide insight to others who may be considering a similar career path.

Theoretical orientation

The theoretical foundation of this chapter rests with the conceptualization of levels of consciousness or self-awareness, something that has been examined from various theoretical frameworks as far back as William James and Sigmund Freud (Morin, 2006). A critical aspect of the development of self is the growth of the private self, which is conceptual and abstract in nature. Another domain of self-awareness is our public self. The professional self forms a core or central part of the public self. Newen and Vogeley's (2003) concept of meta-representational self-consciousness, one of the highest forms of self-awareness, identifies that iterative self-referential processes occur whereby an individual tries to imagine what other people think of them, and attempts to construct a model of the models. As Morin (2006) notes, reaching this level of meta-self-awareness requires time spent in self-reflection as well as quality of self-information.

As will be discussed, the development of our professional selves, as play therapists, occurred as a result of the interaction of our existing mental models of our professional selves with colleagues who were on a similar journey of growth and self-reflection. Through connections within this group, as well as during training based on an integrative conceptualization framework, a recursive process of thinking and reflection about our professional selves occurred. An important outcome was a shift from an isolated experience of the professional self, to a newly consolidated conceptualization of the professional self as play therapist. The depiction of this unique experience within Morin's (2006) framework of levels of awareness, particularly public/professional awareness at the meta-representational level, highlights how the authors experienced this journey.

In search of belonging

Experiencing isolation in the play therapy field was a collective thread within the authors' narratives. There are different noted experiences of isolation, such as difficulty in finding information regarding professional development and difficulties in establishing collegial relationships with fellow play therapists. The professional self was also stunted due to a lack of opportunities for mirroring, relationship development, and a vulnerability in the self-exploration process with peers and supervisors.

Once a practitioner makes the decision to become a play therapist, there are a number of isolating factors that can be experienced, particularly for those who do not work near play therapy colleagues in the Canadian play therapy scene. In the authors' experiences, the commonality was the sense of aloneness, oftentimes leading to feelings of self-doubt. This section highlights the dissonance experienced when play therapist interns face discrepancies between external feedback and the self when developing a play therapist mental model. Each noted experience required moments of reflection and thoughtful navigation to address. For the first author, the journey in finding training in play therapy was a difficult experience:

> I was isolated from the point of finding play therapy. I had no idea where to look. Where do you go? What do you do? Obviously you go to the websites of organizations and try to find a place. I remember quite clearly that when we first met I felt like I just needed someone to talk to who gets play therapy or who would want to talk to me about my work.

Discovering play therapy is different than finding play therapy training offered in our country. For those who do not have a colleague who has taken the journey, website searches can be a confusing and overwhelming experience.

The next author highlights that her employment in "the North" provided a geographical and communication barrier that is not often experienced by mental health practitioners working in more developed parts of the country:

> I was on the road a lot traveling to remote communities so I wasn't in the office on Mondays, and of course that day was spent getting things organized for next day's travel and service delivery. It was during a time when cellphones and the Internet were not readily available so you're pretty much out there by yourself. When I started I didn't feel like I had a lot of people that I could connect with about my work.

Hastings and Cohn (2013) noted that practitioners who work in rural areas face many challenges, leading to feelings of isolation, such as the lack of opportunity for collegial consultation, challenges due to travel demands, as well as issues with ensuring confidentiality. For those who provide mental health services in "the North," the large land mass accompanied by a lower population density results in traveling clinics where workers commute long distances to isolated communities on fixed schedules, leading to intermittent service delivery for clients. Even the most basic levels of collegial connectivity are limited for those in these positions, which only intensifies the experience of isolation. This form of service delivery also resulted in challenges regarding one's capacity to provide consistency in treatment:

> There are a few issues that concerned me as a counselor responsible for supporting children in remote communities, particularly for those who had experienced complex trauma. First, based on the geography of the Yukon and the vast area that I covered, I was only able to get to each community about once every three or four weeks. This didn't provide for a lot of continuity in service and increased the time it took to build a therapeutic relationship with the children and families that I was working with.

Another isolating experience for those providing play therapy services in the rural areas of our country is the inability to provide these services in a manner that aligns with play therapy best practices due to time and travel constraints. Having to modify the therapy process or interventions in ways that do not align with information provided in the play therapy literature or supervision is polarizing and can be experienced as a "them vs. me" circumstance. The concept of "them" refers to those who can practice in an ideal setting versus the concept of "me," the clinician who must accommodate the best way I can in my current circumstance. These experiences in turn can result in dissonance within oneself due to the lack of cohesiveness in acquired knowledge.

The lack of collegial connection not only exists for those working in rural Canada but also in urban settings as well:

> I don't have a lot of people even being in the Edmonton area where I work who I can talk about my play therapy practice. At my job I spend time educating my colleagues about my work so I'm isolated from that point.

Even in larger centers in our country, play therapists are not necessarily connected in a community of colleagues that are accessible for peer consultation. A prevalent theme in our focus group was that collegial communities are not solely about like-mindedness but also a sense of connectivity when working in a field of practice. Accordingly, limitations are placed on one's ability to enter into self-reflective processes necessary to attain the autobiographical knowledge needed for the development of the conceptual self (Newen and Vogeley, 2003).

A lack of connectivity was not only highlighted within collegial interactions but also within play therapy supervisory interactions. Many supervision sessions occur remotely, either over the phone or using video conferencing technology. For some, the manner in which these working alliances are created can be a barrier to an enriched supervisory experience:

> Although I valued my clinical supervision, being on the phone just wasn't the same. Even when you can see each other on Skype it's a bit different, but being on the phone where it is just a voice makes it hard to connect. I felt like my supervision was good and I got some things out of it but I didn't feel like that relationship formed enough for me to put myself out and be vulnerable in the way I needed to be able to grow clinically. So I can say in the beginning I felt isolated more so because

there were not too many people in my area that I could connect with and I didn't necessarily feel safe enough to ask the questions that I really wanted to ask in my clinical supervision. And it's harder early on, like for instance if you developed a working relationship face to face and then have to move it to over the phone that's different, but developing that relationship early on is very difficult.

For this author, developing a working alliance with a supervisor over a medium of connection that she did not like created a barrier to engagement. Furthermore, the lack of opportunity to develop a working alliance in person, prior to the distance supervision process, led to barriers in personal exposure the author believed was necessary for personal and professional growth. This in turn impacted the author's experienced cohesiveness of self-identity with the information they were seeking to inform their play therapist mental model.

Working in different cultural and societal contexts than their play therapist supervisor further contributed to isolation, particularly if cultural and community dynamics were misunderstood:

I just feel like in the beginning when you're new and you're doing supervision by the phone it was hard to know if my supervisor would understand my context, like for instance working as a white person with first nations people and the remoteness of my rural setting. When you're talking to someone who resides in downtown Toronto and that is the farthest from your reality, it's hard to know for certain if it was really understood completely.

For those of us pursuing supervision in remote settings, the need for personal connectivity, as well as the supervisor's contextual understanding of our cultural and vocational worlds, is essential for cohesiveness in one's personal practice model as a play therapist, which may also be thought of as a mental model (Morin, 2006).

Isolation was also noted to occur for those who work as a lone discipline within a multi-disciplinary context, as well as a lone play therapist amongst peers with similar mental health backgrounds, such as social work or psychology:

On one hand I'm a lone psychologist amongst social workers at my work. We work incredibly well together but there are times when I feel like we speak a different language. On the other hand, my Psychology colleagues all work in adult mental health so I sometimes feel like my practice and approach does not coincide with their perspective of our discipline, so I don't really feel like I fit in anywhere in my work context.

Within this author's clinical context, the lack of collegial mirroring resulted in feeling isolated and misunderstood. The desire for mirroring not only was noted to be desired based on discipline but also in regards to one's gender as well:

I showed up for the first time for Green Stream [training program] and Ken and I were the only guys there. We had to put a sign up for the men's room because there were 30 women and just the two of us. It's not that I don't jive with you ladies or any other women, but it is just interesting being a male in what I think is a female-dominated profession.

Following suit with the gender isolation noted by Simpson (2004), the author above provides another context regarding the need for mirroring during the skill development stage. Having the capacity to understand oneself within the context of the craft is vital in grounding oneself in the play therapist role. Thus, not only do play therapist interns seek contextual understanding, there is also a desire to interact with peers and supervisors who align in terms of our demographic context. Mirroring literature notes how these sought-after experiences enhance knowledge comprehension and integration through social cognitive processes (Gallese, 2009; Kuhbandner, Pekrun and Maier, 2010; Marshall, 2006). These desired interactions help shape our understanding of selves in these newfound roles, thus informing our professional self.

Another area of isolation was the general lack of understanding of play therapy itself in areas of the country where it has not been an established practice. For one author, the move from a province with an established play therapy community to another that was underdeveloped in the area was a difficult and emotional transition:

I did a stint in Alberta where I saw others partake in play therapy and I was drawn into the joyous experiences my colleagues were experiencing. Then I returned home and the reality broke my heart. I transitioned from an office with established play therapy practices to another where they were just exploring the concept. My early years of practicing were met with questions and uncertainty by those around me. Those days were hard for me because I knew what was needed but I felt so alone in trying to build these services in my program area. I truly felt lost in the trenches.

The collective voice of the authors highlights the importance of collegial contact during the development of one's identity as a play therapist as well as the difficulties experienced when one is aware of discrepancies between external feedback and one's private and professional self.

When the gates opened: transitioning from isolation to belonging

The transition from isolation to belonging was a powerful transformation for the authors, which helped solidify an understanding of one's role as a play therapist. Collectively, in finding one another during advanced play therapy training, the authors highlight how the sense of belonging fostered an emergence of our professional self.

The experience of acknowledging like-mindedness was an initial shift in discourse, where the enthusiasm of finding each other was described as a sense of homecoming:

> I felt like the little bee girl in the Blind Melon "No Rain" video where I was going around dancing for people and not quite feeling as though I was being understood or accepted. Now I am the little bee girl standing at the gate with my mouth open in awe that you all exist and I can come on in.

For those who have been practicing play therapy in isolation, having the experience of being immersed in opportunities to connect with play therapy colleagues can be an exciting and overwhelming experience. This is particularly true for those who yearned for collegial relationships like the author above.

A major stepping-stone in the development of the professional self was experiencing a collective knowing through our discourse in play therapy. This commonality provided continued opportunities to consult and feel understood by those on a parallel journey in the play therapy certification/registration process:

> It is special to have the opportunity to talk things through even though you may have the answer. It solidifies the clarity of the answer

when you can talk it through with somebody and when someone knows what you're talking about. Because we all have education and a background in play therapy we don't have to say a lot to have that common language to consult and brainstorm.

Another author who voiced comfort in experiencing a "knowing" echoed this sentiment:

It feels a little bit like when you go to a foreign country and you try to fit in and it works out okay but when you go home communication feels effortless. Other people fully understand and you can even speak in partial sentences and they can finish them for you because of that same understanding.

Coming together in advanced training provided an opportunity to foster peer relationships that could extend beyond time spent during the training itself. The return to practice in the once experienced isolated environments was experienced differently because of the capacity to reach out during times when clinical team support was needed. For others, the value of resource sharing was a noted shift from working in isolation to feeling collegial connectivity:

Although I found the answers myself, there was something about having you as a part of that process that made it feel less isolating. It meant the world to me to have someone who would help me think the situation through and have those same sorts of resources to brainstorm because sometimes we don't have the answers though, like for instance when you sent the resource of the sensory tools. I have books on supporting sensory issues but I didn't have the resource that you sent.

The sharing of vocational experiences and knowledge not only was experienced as a support to an understanding of the self as a play therapist, it also navigated us away from isolation. Providing a context to understand the professional self, within a validating context, fosters the ability to reach a level of meta-self-awareness during one's identity formation as a play therapist. In a focus group discussion, the collegial bond was discussed in terms of feeling safe to be oneself in a vulnerable manner and feeling accepted, while exploring how one's play style aligned with play practice and theory:

Author 1: For me I felt like I could be myself in this group as well. I know when I went through Green Stream [training program] and I just tore up their playroom and they were accepting of that. It's good to have that acceptance of who I am. It was great to be myself in a situation.

Author 2: But that's really what teamwork is, right? For me the emergence of self really has been in parallel with our relationships and this team experience.

Positive feedback, acceptance and mirroring from one's peers are important experiences in one's journey in discovering the self as a play therapist. For these two authors, the acceptance of each other fostered a rich group experience. There was also a noted development of a "We" self amongst the authors, where mutual learning from each other's strengths resulted in an internalization of the group play experience, which then informed clinical practice:

The thing I craved the most was to be on a team. I wanted to be able to talk about my clinical practice and to receive feedback. In finding you guys I've actually internalized our collective selves. When I am shifting my play style to one that aligns with one of your strengths, I think about the way I witnessed whichever one of you it may be and then try to mirror what I witnessed in our practice with one another. So although we are so far away from each other we really are a team.

The formation of a play therapy community was a turning point for the authors individually as well as collectively. These experiences align with Gallese (2009) who highlighted that social identification, empathy and "we-ness" are fundamental for personal and social development. Experience of collegial mirroring provides what Marshall (2006) references as "social glue" that promotes social connectivity. This author gives voice to Morin's (2006) concept of meta-self-awareness, where complex conceptual self-representations inform the private self and enrich the development of the public self.

Turning points and emergence of the professional self

Following initial growth in the professional self, the authors sought to extend their newfound awareness by examining an integrative conceptualization framework: the Play Therapy Dimensions Model (Yasenik and Gardner, 2012). This also became a transformational process as the authors were challenged to integrate play therapy theory and practice, as well as master the conceptualization of the self and others. In so doing, another recursive process of self-reflection was initiated, further extending their meta-self-awareness. This was noted in the authors' acknowledgment of a common language embedded in the Play Therapy Dimensions Model that afforded group members with the ability to converse with one another regardless of their theoretical underpinnings:

> We have a structure that helps us think about the play therapy process and then communicate with peers, to obtain supervision, feedback and guidance. I've found it helpful to consistently look for circumstances, developmental considerations, worldview, transference, countertransference, child factors, therapist factors, ethical concerns, etc., and to be able to share these efficiently in supervision because we are working from the same model. This works even when we practice from very different orientations, are situated in diverse organizations and are separated by thousands of kilometers.

Conceptual frameworks such as the Play Therapy Dimensions Model also provided a structure to clinical processing, enhancing supervision efficacy within the group:

> We had a common way of presenting cases and it was always in a certain order, which was really effective. I found having that structure helped us process files as a team and it got better and better over time.

The collective mastery of the model enriched growth and reflection by offering members a structure for jointly examining the play therapy process:

> I like the model because I can be adaptable to what is happening in front of me. The dimensions model gives me a structure in case I need to be a little more directed to meet the child's needs in my playroom. It's a phenomenal conceptual piece of decision-making, and that's so helpful for me in that regard. It's highlighted my adaptability. I think it supports the play therapist to be authentic but still have that structure and encouragement to consider what is not just inside of you in terms of your play preferences or who you are.

Prior to exposure to an integrative framework there was a noted uncertainty about how one's natural play style would align with client needs. Having the opportunity to explore oneself within the model's framework, then understanding where one's natural play style fits within it, provided this play therapist with a newfound confidence in her practice. Two authors echoed this during the focus group, stating that the internalization of the model was a significant turning point in their professional development:

> Author 1: Rather than solely listening to my gut, I now have a systematic way of taking that instinct and asking myself "Is this accurate? Does it make sense?" It has given me more confidence because I have a process to work through to help guide my work.

> Author 2: I have had the same experience. I now have the ability to walk through the model in my own mind and process its components while the session is occurring. For me, the model has shifted from something that took me a long time to ponder to something that I have internalized as an automatic check-in.

The model provided objectivity to the authors' subjective clinical judgment, referred to as the "gut" above. The ability to merge theory and practice within a practical systemic framework was empowering for the above authors, enhancing confidence in their clinical work with clients. These narratives highlight how an integrative conceptualization framework can meet the clinicians where they are in their clinical practice rather than the reverse, where clinicians need to change or adapt their natural play styles to align with a specific framework.

The shift from clinical insecurity to a sense of knowing one's private and public self is a vitalizing and necessary part of the growth process for play therapists. The shift from understanding play therapy strictly from a theoretical standpoint to integrating the theory in clinical practice is also an essential component of the process. The following author describes how her discovery of the concept of co-facilitation, as outlined in the Play Therapy Dimensions Model, played a critical role in her theory-to-practice journey:

> One significant area I felt stuck was with children who experienced trauma who would emotionally flood during non-directive play. I felt immobilized to help them. While presenting one of these stuck files during a training in the model I had an aha moment when learning about the co-facilitation dimension which was a new play style for me. I realized that the model itself provides a language to explain my shifts in theoretical underpinnings to meet the child where they are

and that is perfectly okay. This gave me more confidence because I had a concrete conceptualization of what I was doing and it helped me to grow to be a competent play therapist.

The authors note a sense of empowerment occurred when they saw opportunities to expand their clinical choices by considering other therapeutic interventions, based on the client's moment-to-moment presentation:

It also gives the ability to add one too. When I look at the moderating factors for example and there are some things that the model would guide me to and then I would say "I'd like to add to that based on situations where I've worked and the people that I've worked with." When you have a structure you can modify those structures to something that can fit the specific circumstance for whatever you want it to fit for you, right?

The foundation of professional development is the ability to learn new concepts and techniques that build upon one's current skillset. The author above notes how his mastery of the model gave permission to expand his clinical repertoire in an informed manner. This narrative also highlights how understanding the therapist's use of self enhances the emergence of a professional self by offering objectivity and discourse to subjective clinical experiences.

"Turning it all around": how our invigoration of selves provided movement in the play therapy process

The journey from isolation to invigoration positively impacted clinical competency. The first author notes how the Play Therapy Dimensions Model, along with a newly secured understanding of the professional self, supported ten-year-old Russell in his therapeutic process:

When I first started working with Russell (a pseudonym), a ten-year-old boy, I was told that his mother was nowhere to be found and that his father was low functioning and unable to care for him. Russell had nowhere to go but a group home. There were reports from the group home that Russell often isolated himself when he was upset and tended towards depression. Naturally, given my "free range" background, I took a child-centered play therapy approach, which I quickly discovered wasn't going to work with Russell. Sessions seemed to be going nowhere as Russell repeatedly made sandtray army battles while I tracked and reflected (Quadrant III). He was listless and matter of fact; so was I. We both needed a jolt, so I decided that in our next session we would have a swordfight. When Russell arrived for our session, I immediately threw him a foam sword and engaged him in battle (Quadrant IV). He didn't have a chance to think about it and quickly defended himself. We had a spirited battle where we thrusted and parried, making metal sword clanging sounds. As we were fighting, he talked about his friends (Quadrant II) and the positive experiences he had with them at a camp he attended. Russell was alive and I felt alive as we engaged both physically and relationally. We continued sword fighting over the ensuing sessions and I added other physical activities to keep it from getting stale. Sometimes we had puppet fights and other times we would simply go for a walk. Over time, Russell was able to express his feelings of being left alone by his parents and the accompanying sadness. Russell had internalized his world; it was out of sight from the world around him. After all, who could he trust when his parents let him down? I equally love my internal world, so it would have been comfortable for me to stay there as well, but to do so would have no benefit for Russell. Russell and I were in a parallel process that moved from the internal to the external. I had taken the battle in the sandtray and brought it to life. We were no longer surrounding ourselves with ourselves.

The relationship between the author, the client and the Play Therapy Dimensions Model highlights how the emergence and use of self as a therapist translates into supporting an emergence of self with the client. The author's narrative illustrates the beauty of navigating the dimensions to shift from clinical impasses to successes.

The next author shares a narrative of supporting Lila (a pseudonym), a child who shifted from being frozen within her self to finding her external self:

> I was asked to work with Lila because she was painfully shy and quiet. She rarely spoke in class, froze when asked questions, and shied away from any kind of direct attention. The school personnel feared she was not performing to her potential. A review of Lila's file showed me that she was a very intelligent child with superior non-

verbal skills and underdeveloped verbal skills. English was not her first language and this explained some of the discrepancy. Lila had a very traumatic early start and continued to have an unstable home life. She was polite and cooperative; however, it was not surprising that she was cautious and reluctant to talk. I asked questions and she whispered almost inaudible responses. We played games and she quietly played along. I read books and she listened to every word. The sessions felt long and painful. I attended my first play therapy training with the Rocky Mountain Play Therapy Institute early into the work with Lila. The Play Therapy Dimensions Model helped me to conceptualize the therapeutic process with her. I recognized that the direct and conscious approach (Quadrant II) was not working for Lila. Given her developmental stage, strong non-verbal skills, weak verbal skills and traumatic background, I hypothesized that moving to a less directive approach while using metaphor and non-verbal symbols might help her engage in therapy. While I thought this change would help, switching to symbols and metaphor through the use of miniatures and storytelling produced a response that surprised even me. I introduced the task, but from there Lila led the session (Quadrant III). She created a rich story full of details. Beyond crafting the picture using symbols, she told her story with a loud, brave voice. The metaphorical work caused a shift in Lila. Over time she started engaging in activities at school, and as her voice became louder in sessions, she also started to speak up in the classroom and in extracurricular activities. I observed tremendous growth in her that was driven from the inside out.

This author highlights how integrative practice can provide inhibited children with a variety of therapeutic options and experiences, which in turn supports therapeutic growth. Each child may have different needs and desires on a moment-to-moment basis in a therapy session. An attuned play therapist, with a foundation in an integrative framework such as the Play Therapy Dimensions Model, is better equipped to understand the underlying moderating factors to align need with clinical practice.

Words of wisdom

The sharing of our collective narrative depicting our journey from isolation to invigoration was purposeful and was meant to inform the play therapy community of barriers that exist. We also wish to highlight how we addressed these impasses and found our way to an enriched and satisfying career. For those who are in a position to make change, we hope our collective voice can be considered to make informed choices for change. For those who may be considering entering the field, we wish to pass along personal words of wisdom as food for thought:

> Author 1: For any therapist out there considering learning more about play therapy, I encourage you to jump in with both feet and undertake study and supervision. I have seen hundreds of children grow, move forward and bring about change in their lives through play therapy. It is a rich and rewarding field. I would encourage people if they go to a training and it feels like it fits their needs to stay with that training body for a while and build that circle of support around them.

> Author 2: There's a line in the song "I've Seen All Good People" by the rock band Yes that says: "Don't surround yourself with yourself." When it comes to play therapy, it's sound advice. Read everything you can about play therapy and get a sense from all those who came before you. Take the journey with like-minded people and enjoy the ride. Don't be too uptight about getting it right or wrong, that's just the way life is, but you'll get through. Chime on.

References

Gallese, V. (2009) Mirror neurons, embodied simulation, and the neural basis of social identification. *Psychoanalytic Dialogues 19*, 519–536.

Hastings, S.L. and Cohn, T.J. (2013) Challenges and opportunities associated with rural mental health practice. *Journal of Rural Mental Health 37*, 1, 37–49.

Kuhbandner, C., Pekrun, R., and Maier, M.A. (2010) The role of positive and negative affect in the "mirroring" of other people's actions. *Cognition and Emotion 24*, 7, 1182–1190.

Marshall, R.J. (2006) Suppose there were no mirrors: Converging concepts of mirroring. *Modern Psychoanalysis 31*, 2, 289–312.

Morin, A. (2006) Levels of consciousness and self-awareness: A comparison and integration of various views. *Consciousness and Cognition 15*, 2, 358–371.

Newen, A. and Vogeley, K. (2003) Self-representation: Search for a neural signature of self-consciousness. *Consciousness and Cognition 12*, 529–543.

Simpson, R. (2004) Masculinity at work: The experiences of men in female dominated occupations. *Work, Employment and Society 18*, 2, 1–35.

Yasenik, L. and Gardner, K. (2012) *Play Therapy Dimensions Model: A Decision-Making Guide for Integrative Play Therapists.* London: Jessica Kingsley Publishers.

14

DISCUSSION AND SUMMARY

—— LORRI YASENIK AND KEN GARDNER ——

What can be understood by focusing on turning points in play therapy? What are we looking for when evaluating growth and development when working with children in play therapy? We became acutely aware after reviewing the many case examples that there is a confluence of factors that are important to consider when answering these questions. More specifically, factors related to therapist use of self, timing of interventions, degree of directiveness and consciousness, the child's emerging self, degree of consistency and safety in the play therapy setting, and the therapist/child relationship have been exemplified. No one factor stands alone to aid in the understanding of movement that stimulates change in play therapy. Although each author identified a different theoretical approach to their work with a child, each practitioner followed similar pathways to identifying important pivotal moments. Practitioners looked for nuanced changes in a child's behavior, attitude, tone, language, use of objects, play themes, emotional intensity, sense of empowerment, self-understanding, and self-awareness. These subtle changes tended to lead the child towards a relief of symptoms and, moreover, an identified reorganization and resolution of issues impacting the child. Therapist awareness and ability to observe and identify turning points in the play therapy process go beyond what many of us also view as the "magic" and wonder of play therapy.

Turning points and therapist decision-making

The Play Therapy Dimensions Model emphasizes a therapist's need to continually ask "*What* am I doing?" "*How* am I doing it?" and "*Why?*" when working with children. It is not enough to make use of a technique or a theory without answering "why?" and why with *this* child *now*? Following the child's lead is an important consideration, but it is not the only consideration. If we turn our attention to Chapter 2, "Emergence of Self through Learn to Play Therapy," a number of decision-making points were identified in the work with "Billy." Billy was assessed through Learn to Play (Stagnitti, 1998) and notably was operating at a level of play that was lower than other children his age and stage of development. His awareness of himself and others was limited and he was described as "floating" into the room. In this case, only following the child's lead would not have benefited Billy. The therapist, having identified missing play skills, chose the type of play (sensory motor) in order to engage Billy emotionally and began where he may be able to join. Through the use of a large doll with long arms a ball game was introduced. Billy had to focus on the doll which encouraged "other-related" play, which the author described as a place to begin before a child can engage in self-related play activities. The therapist directed and introduced all the play activities during Billy's first session. For children who present with low play skills, it is important to find ways to engage at "the child's" level and to increase connection and enjoyment. As the play moved from scripts including everyday life activities, Billy began to incorporate some of his own ideas into the play. By the next session, the therapist identified what she determined as the first turning point: Billy no longer floated into the room seemingly unaware of self and other, but he entered in an excited, engaged manner. He was happy and knew why he was there. *Turning point type 1: a change in thought, behavior, affect, or understanding about something* was identified by the author. Both behavior and affect were observed as significant and Billy's focused attention and enjoyment continued and helped in the evolution of subsequent turning points indicating an increased ability to sequence and organize play scenarios (a skill previously unavailable to him).

Play therapists are aware that play skills are essential to overall child development (cognitive, physical, social-emotional, and moral). Taking note of Billy's subtle increase in independently organizing play scenes and his emerging sense of self in relation to others was essential to the decision-making of the therapist. She had to adapt her use of self, moving from highly directive with a focus on scaffolding play to less directive. There was a weaving back and forth between following the child and providing direction for the child through therapist interaction and through the offering of play materials.

Moving to Chapter 3, "Just Like a Kid!" we reflect on an Adlerian play therapist's decision-making process as related to turning points. Eight-year-old "Lonny" had come from a disrupted abusive family background, and although now living with his grandmother, "Lonny" presented with many emotional and behavioral difficulties. The author used the Adlerian model of intervention (Kottman and Meany-Walen, 2016) that identifies four phases of counseling: 1) building an egalitarian relationship with the client, 2) investigating the client's lifestyle, 3) helping the client gain insight into their lifestyle, and 4) reorienting/re-educating the client. The author worked in the school setting and knew of Lonny's social-emotional and behavioral problems before working with him. Lonny needed a lot of control during the therapy process, and although Adlerians are both directive and non-directive in their practice, "how" to be directive was one critical decision-making issue when working with Lonny. The author viewed the first observed turning point to be Lonny's request to attend counseling as she viewed this as a plea for help. Previously, Lonny tended to reject others and their attempts at trying to help him. His personal request to "play with" the therapist was viewed as *turning point type 1: a change in thought, behavior, affect, or understanding about something*. It was his drive to connect with the therapist who he knew was working with other children that struck the therapist as important. The next turning point was a small interpersonal behavior: a moment of direct eye contact (*turning point 1*). Many therapists might miss this moment of contact and therefore miss viewing it as a turning point. As small as this might seem, it is the beginning of connection and of a therapeutic relationship. Incrementally, various small or more obvious behavior(s), affect, or understanding about something signal the therapist in how to make use of self. As important as this moment was, the therapist had to make a decision not to over-respond and to temper her own emotional excitement about the potential of contact with highly defended Lonny.

The therapist then identified another turning point in her description of "changing the rules." Lonny began to drive and direct the play through the game of Uno. He started to position himself differently moving from repetitive and restricted play to an elaborated form of the game where he took some control and at the same time offered some choice to the therapist. Changing the rules led to greater proximity to the therapist and greater opportunity for the next phase of therapy (*turning point type 3: a moment in time where the child makes use of themselves or play objects in a way previously not observed, such as a change in the drive and direction of the play or the positioning of themselves in the play*). How quickly to engage in the change in the game was one decision the therapist had to make. How directive should she be? Does she make any interpretations? Should she be working in Quadrant III: Non-intrusive Responding? These are critical therapeutic decision-making points.

In Chapter 9 we are introduced to a seven-year-old girl, Shyanne, who has experienced trauma. An integrative approach, within a trauma therapy framework, is used to develop an understanding of the child's regulatory profile. Through the Window of Tolerance construct the therapist carefully assesses the child's moment-to-moment functional abilities associated with her arousal state, assisting her to move through the first phase of treatment: Safety and stabilization. During the second treatment phase: Trauma memory processing, a therapist might anticipate brief movement to higher levels of conscious awareness, which is characteristic of *turning point type 2: the emergence of a level of awareness not previously available to a child.* Through mediums such as sandplay, which provide distance from the discomfort of the potentially negative appraisals from the I-self to the Me-self, the child has an opportunity to recover and positively shift their schematic representations of self and others.

During session 19 the therapist observed a shift in Shyanne's sandplay, with apparent movement from her process being primarily unconscious to increasing levels of conscious awareness. This shift is illustrated by Shyanne's energy becoming more intense and focused through her use of water and "sandstorms" moving across the sandtray. An earlier theme of struggle, which emerged during phase 1, shifted to resolution, with the thematic presence of restoration of order and greater organization. As hypothesized by the therapist, this ordering and restoration mirrored what was happening in her internal world. More specifically, Shyanne's play suggested that with emerging awareness she was developing an ability to recognize and acknowledge external influences. This awareness was further exemplified in her narratives, as Shyanne began to relate to figures and objects as individuals from her lived experience. This shift in awareness, which contributed to brief moments of processing in Quadrant I, was in turn accompanied by a return to less conscious processing in Quadrants III and IV, where experiences and feelings were once again disclosed through metaphor and re-ordered.

Yet another example of turning points in relation to decision-making is exemplified in Chapter 6, "Shame Can Get Stuck in Your Throat." Five-year-old "Freddy" came to therapy to address past sexual abuse. Following the Flexibly Sequential Play Therapy (FSPT) model, the therapist identified six turning points during a single session. Some pivotal moments are observed over time while others may occur during a single session. This chapter identifies multiple turning points during one session. Of interest is the incremental and/or intermittent movement children make towards self-growth and change. Freddy had a lot of social support and enough ego-strength to move quickly once given an opportunity to work with disowned thoughts and feelings in therapy. As the session progressed, Freddy provided numerous indications of moving closer to consciousness about his past sexual abuse experience. The therapist had to adjust her use of self (physical and emotional) and level of directiveness with each turning point. Of interest is that close to the end of the session Freddy, through the use of the dragon, moved from projecting feelings and actions onto the dragon to making self-referencing statements such as "It was scary, and it really, really happened" and said "I was *scared*," with a great emphasis placed on the word "scared." This point in the process exemplified *turning point type 4: a change in what is illuminated or seen in the play; a change in the way of viewing self or others.*

In this case, Freddy was able to bring his past experiences into the domain of direct discussion and exploration. Even with this being the case, decisions had to be made about how long and in what way to "stay with" Freddy's view of self in relation to what had happened "to" him. His disowned feelings had a reference now and he could later make use of "I-self" to inform the "Me-self." It was a significant point in the therapy process and one that many therapists may feel is the "end" of the symbolic and projective play. Chapter 6 helps the reader understand the weaving process and that, although Freddy is more capable of making use of a conscious reference to "self," he will at times throughout the process need to take distance in order to eventually incorporate the many dissociated parts of his experience.

We can see the value in identifying what *type* of turning point is emerging when highlighting a few of the chapter examples. The four types of play therapy turning points can inform the play therapist in many ways. The use of words is not the only way in which children tell us what is happening in play therapy. Play therapy is a complex practice that requires the play therapist to hold many constructs at the same time. The skill goes beyond the effective use of theory and includes the ability to observe small changes embedded in play behavior, emotional expression, and play themes.

Turning points in supervision

In a broad sense, supervision provides a relationship in which professional values, commitments, and even one's professional identity are formed. It also provides "tacit training" in the practice of supervision itself (Falender and Shafranske, 2004). From this perspective, turning points in supervision, which create new levels of awareness and understanding for the practitioner, contribute over time to potential tipping points in the entire developmental trajectory of a profession.

In addition to the critical role of the supervisory relationship, where an alliance of individual and shared responsibilities is formed, there is an underlying inquiry process that facilitates understanding of the therapeutic process and fosters in the supervisee a rich awareness of their profession and personal contributions to it (Falender and Shafranske, 2004). Although different models of supervision emphasize distinct learning strategies, including direct instruction, observation, and role playing, most supervisors would agree that the real challenge is getting at the "soft stuff"—the supervisee's awareness of self as a practitioner. Even if the supervisee and supervisor share similar theoretical orientations, unless there is a process for inquiry and reflection, embedded in a decision-making framework, there is the potential for numerous collision points in supervision (Gardner and Yasenik, 2008).

Therapist use of self is a challenging area to address in supervision, as it is part of the "soft stuff" that is not readily accessible to examination and reflection. The danger lies in scrutinizing such a complex construct in overly general terms or in an ad-hoc manner, leaving the supervisee confused by ambiguous or changing terms and inconsistent feedback. What is required is feedback on specific types and degrees of immersion, described as specific behaviors reflecting therapist use of self and occurring on a moment-to-moment basis during child/client interactions. The Degree of Immersion: Therapist Use of Self (Appendix A) was developed to strengthen therapist awareness of impact on the child client and to support appropriate decision-making. This scale should be completed by the supervisee in advance of a supervision session. To explore the degree to which they are immersed in play, supervisees examine specific categories and sub-categories of immersion, rating the level to which they were immersed as well as the child's response to their immersion. This follows from the core assumption that it is the child's needs that drive the therapy process. When used regularly in supervision, the scale keeps the supervisee on track by continually reflecting on the interaction between them and the client, building the supervisee's attunement to the child and strengthening their decision-making. In many cases, it also supports the supervisee's awareness of transference and countertransference issues, and the impact of these issues on the play process.

The Supervision Form for Therapist Use of Self: Degree of Immersion for Next Session Plan (Appendix B) is designed to assist the supervisee in targeting specific forms of immersion, based on supervisory feedback obtained during review of self-ratings on the Degree of Immersion form. By identifying areas of immersion to increase or decrease, it is hoped that the supervisee will enter the next session with their personal radar tuned to the child's drive and direction in the therapy process. Recognizing that one's use of self must be continuously adjusted in the therapy space, the therapist will of course need to make alterations as necessary.

Stoltenberg, McNeill, and Delworth (1998) and other developmentally focused supervisors have conceptualized therapist development as occurring in levels, stages, or phases. After reviewing various conceptualizations, a three-phase approach was adapted by the authors for supervising play therapists (Yasenik and Gardner, 2012). Utilizing a developmental framework, in combination with the Play Therapy Dimensions Model, provides the play therapy supervisor with a way to: 1) identify the stage of development of the supervisee; 2) design activities that match the needs of the supervisee; 3) assist the supervisee in reflecting on the play therapy process; and 4) support the supervisee to avoid the practice of random eclecticism (Gardner and Yasenik, 2008).

The first phase of play therapist development, termed Phase 1: Beginning Play Therapist, is characterized by time spent learning about the power of play and the symbolic nature of children's communication. Therapist self-awareness is typically limited at this initial stage, while self-focus in sessions is high as therapists are worried about how they are managing (Yasenik and Gardner, 2012). This phase of development cannot be rushed as play therapy requires a unique skillset and, because of its expressive nature, a high degree of personal awareness.

When working with Phase I play therapists, supervisors should utilize bridging activities designed to increase the skills, knowledge, and experience of the supervisees. Bridging activities during supervision include theoretical discussions, exploring personal practice models, reviewing play therapy sessions on videotape, introducing play therapy techniques, and practical skill demonstration by the supervisor in the play therapy room. They also include introducing self-development exercises using expressive play-based modalities, such as puppets and sand, and providing positive feedback. An excellent resource for play therapy supervisors is the edited book by Drewes and Mullen (2008).

Phase II: Imitation of Experts is characterized by supervisees who are more aware of the child's needs and more capable of identifying the child client's worldview. Increased overall awareness means that supervisees will also be more vulnerable to their own fragility. In this phase the supervisor learns about the supervisee's tolerance, patience, and capacity for empathy. One of the most confusing aspects of Phase II is that the expectations for integration of broad-based knowledge are much higher, accompanied by pressure to keep adding to the learning experience. Supervision bridging activities to enhance growth include: encouraging risk taking and creativity, shifting from a "tell me" to "show me" approach, decreasing the level of supervision structure by encouraging more independence, emphasizing the therapy *process* versus therapy techniques, and providing more supportive confrontation. This is a challenging phase of development for both supervisors and supervisees, but perhaps more so for the supervisor (Yasenik and Gardner, 2012).

The Phase III supervisee is considered an advanced play therapist. During this phase the supervisee often begins to identify an area of specialization. At this level a play therapist has a broad knowledge base and is focused on diverse ways of conceptualizing cases. By this level of development the play therapist understands how they are making use of the self in play therapy sessions and how to quickly identify the needs of the child and appropriately respond. The Phase III therapist is capable of simultaneously keeping in mind the unique qualities of the child, the presenting problem, and the numerous ways to address specific referral issues.

By focusing on the unique needs of the child and markers of therapist immersion, supervisors and supervisees can jointly conceptualize movement in the play therapy process, particularly those brief yet instructive turning points. Over time, the supervisee will move from a practitioner who is highly focused on the next best technique or approach, to a self-reflecting practitioner who critically examines approaches in relation to their use of self and the unique needs of the child (Yasenik and Gardner, 2012). This shift, in itself, represents a significant turning point in practitioner development.

References

Drewes, A.A. and Mullen, J.A. (2008) *Supervision Can Be Playful: Techniques for Child and Play Therapist Supervisors.* Lanham, MD: Jason Aronson.

Falender, C.A. and Shafranske, E.P. (2004) *Clinical Supervision: A Competency-Based Approach.* Washington, DC: American Psychological Association.

Gardner, K. and Yasenik, L. (2008) When Approaches Collide: A Decision-Making Model for Play Therapists. In A.A. Drewes and J.A. Mullen (eds) *Supervision Can Be Playful: Techniques for Child and Play Therapist Supervisors.* Lanham, MD: Jason Aronson.

Kottman, T. and Meany-Walen, K. (2016) *Partners in Play: An Adlerian Approach to Play Therapy* (3rd edn). Alexandria, VA: American Counseling Association.

Stagnitti, K. (1998) *Learn to Play: A Program to Develop the Imaginative Play Skills of Children.* Melbourne: Coordinates Publications.

Stoltenberg, C., McNeill, B., and Delworth, U. (1998) *IDM Supervision: An Integrated Developmental Model for Supervising Counselors and Therapists.* San Francisco, CA: Jossey-Bass Inc.

Yasenik, L. and Gardner, K. (2012) *Play Therapy Dimensions Model: A Decision-Making Guide for Integrative Play Therapists.* London: Jessica Kingsley Publishers.

The Editors

Lorri Yasenik, PhD, RSW, RPT-S, CPT-S, is a Registered Clinical Social Worker specialized in working with children and families in the areas of treatment of trauma, high conflict separation and divorce, and child development. In addition to being a Certified Supervisor of Child Psychotherapy and Play Therapy, Lorri is a Registered Family Mediator and a Registered Parenting Coordinator. As Co-director of the Rocky Mountain Play Therapy Institute (RMPTI), Lorri delivers approved play therapy training programs for those who wish to become registered or certified as play therapists nationally and internationally.

Lorri has a keen interest in legal issues that affect children's lives and has completed research in the area of "Including the voices of children in the legal system." As a follow-up to this study, she has (with colleagues from Australia) developed the *Meeting with Children* training program (a non-evaluative child-inclusive approach for ADR practitioners and Child Consultants) and the accompanying *Meeting with Parents* program, which are offered nationally and internationally related to Child Inclusive Practice. Lorri is focused on safe and appropriate child inclusion balanced with children's rights. Lorri has co-authored three books, and many book chapters and articles, related to child psychotherapy, play therapy, and children and family law. Lorri is the 2016 recipient of the Monica Herbert Award for outstanding contribution to Child Psychotherapy and Play Therapy Research, Academic Writing and Clinical Work awarded by the Canadian Association for Play Therapy.

Ken Gardner, MSc, R Psych, CPT-S, is a Registered Clinical Child Psychologist with a background in clinical, school, and community psychology. As a Certified Child Psychotherapy and Play Therapist/

Supervisor, Ken specializes in the areas of play therapy for children with developmental, emotional, and behavioral concerns. Ken was a director of a service continuum for dually diagnosed children and adolescents with complex behavioral issues, as well as a long-standing consultant to school-based behavioral programs. With nearly 30 years of clinical experience, his practice currently includes evaluations for students experiencing learning and/or developmental difficulties.

As Co-director of the Rocky Mountain Play Therapy Institute (RMPTI) in Canada, Ken has extensive experience as a consultant and as a play therapy trainer, working both nationally and internationally. Ken has co-authored two books and several chapters on play therapy. In 2011 Ken was the recipient of the Monica Herbert Award for outstanding contribution and dedication to Child Psychotherapy and Play Therapy in Canada, awarded by the Canadian Association for Play Therapy.

Lorri and Ken are the authors of *Play Therapy Dimensions Model: A Decision-Making Guide for Integrative Play Therapists* (2012).

The Contributors

Carolina S. Araya, PhD, MSc, MFT, is a Child and Family Psychotherapist. She has vast experience as a professor and researcher in educational and clinical psychology in Chilean universities. She is currently a member of the Metáfora Centre, an institution that provides training in play therapy for child psychologists and psychiatrists in Chile. Additionally, she assists children and their families in her private practice, and is involved in research regarding playful learning in the elementary school years.

Irene A. Barrett, MEd, R Psych, is a Registered Counseling Psychologist and play therapist intern. She has worked for the past eight years as a child and adolescent psychologist on the west coast of Newfoundland and Labrador.

Bruce A. Beaudet, MTSC (Clinician), currently works in a residential treatment facility and does play therapy with children ages six to twelve. Bruce completed advanced play therapy training at the Rocky Mountain Play Therapy Institute (RMPTI) in Calgary, Alberta.

Katharine Chapman, MSW, RSW, is a Clinical Social Worker who specializes in attachment-focused interventions that incorporate: expressive arts, play therapy, Theraplay®, cognitive behavioral therapy, and mindfulness. She is pursuing her designation as a Certified Play Therapist specializing in Theraplay®. Katharine's passion is in supporting a therapeutic experiential integration through a highly personalized approach tailored to each client's needs.

Dana Diamond, MEd, R Psych, RPT, is a Registered Psychologist in Newfoundland and Labrador and a Registered Play Therapist with the

American Play Therapy Association. She enjoys hiking the gorgeous East Coast Trails of NL with her husband and two children.

Athena A. Drewes, PsyD, RPT-S, is a licensed Psychologist and Registered Play Therapist. She is Director of Clinical Training and APA-Accredited Doctoral Internship at Astor Services for Children and Families, a large multi-service non-profit mental health agency in New York. She has over 40 years of clinical experience in supervision and clinical work with sexually abused and traumatized children and adolescents in school, outpatient, and inpatient settings. She is a former Board Director of the Association for Play Therapy and Founder and President Emeritus of the New York Association for Play Therapy. She has written extensively on play therapy and is an invited guest lecturer in the US, Taiwan, England, Ireland, Argentina, Mexico, Denmark, Canada, and Italy. She has edited/co-edited 11 books, including: *School-Based Play Therapy*; *Cultural Issues in Play Therapy*; *Supervision Can Be Playful: Techniques for Child and Play Therapy Supervisors*; *Blending Play Therapy with Cognitive Behavioral Therapy: Evidence-Based and Other Effective Treatments and Techniques*; *Integrative Play Therapy*; *The Therapeutic Powers of Play*; *Puppet Play Therapy*; and *Play Therapy in Middle Childhood*, published by the American Psychological Association, with a companion of Dr. Drewes' integrative prescriptive play therapy work.

Theresa Fraser, MA, CPT-S, is a Certified Canadian Play Therapy Supervisor and an approved Supervisor for the British Association for Play Therapy. She is the author of two books on foster/adoption and attachment. She is also a Professor of Child and Youth Work and has presented play therapy and trauma-focused parenting workshops worldwide. Theresa and her life partner, Kevin, have been treatment foster parents for over 25 years to over 200 children.

Paris Goodyear-Brown, MSSW, LCSW, RPT-S, is a Licensed Clinical Social Worker and a Registered Play Therapist-Supervisor with 20 years of experience in treating traumatized and attachment-disturbed children and families. She is the Clinical Director and Senior Clinician of Nurture House, serves as the Executive Director of the Lipscomb Play Therapy and Expressive Arts Center, is an Adjunct Instructor of Psychiatric Mental Health at Vanderbilt University, and has an international reputation as a dynamic speaker and innovative clinician. She is best known for developing clinically sound, play-based intervention models that are used to treat a variety of childhood problems. She has received the APT award for Play Therapy Promotion and Education and is the author of multiple books, chapters, and articles related to child therapy. Her newest books include: *Tackling Touchy Subjects*; *Handbook of Child Sexual Abuse: Identification, Assessment, and Treatment*; *Play Therapy with Traumatized Children: A Prescriptive Approach*; and *The Worry Wars: An Anxiety Workbook for Kids and Their Helpful Adults*. Other publications can be found at www.nurturehouse.org

Linda E. Homeyer, PhD, LPCS, RPT-S, is Professor of Professional Counseling at Texas State University where she developed their play therapy program. Linda served several years on the Texas Association for Play Therapy Board of Directors and served two terms as President of the Association for Play Therapy Board of Directors. She is a recipient of APT's Lifetime Achievement Award and designated Director Emerita. Linda presents training on play therapy throughout the world, including her most recent work in Lebanon, Jordan, and Malaysia. She has numerous publications, including: *Sandtray Therapy: A Practical Manual* (third edition) and *The Handbook of Group Play Therapy*. Her publications are available in Chinese, Russian, Korean, and Spanish. Linda is the director of the Door of Hope, a faith-based counseling center in New Braunfels, Texas. She also provides clinical services including play therapy, sandtray therapy, family therapy, and clinical supervision.

Francisca Jenschke Smith, MSc, MFT, is a Child and Family Psychotherapist. She is a certified psychotherapist supervisor and has broad experience as a child psychotherapist trainer in different universities and Chilean institutions. Currently, she works as a trainer of play psychotherapists in the Metáfora Centre, attending children and their families in her private practice. Her contemporary interest topics are sandplay and Jungian psychology.

Valerie Kendall, PhD, R Psych, has been counseling for 20 years. She has run a private practice for 18 years in Calgary, Alberta. In addition her experience includes clients from a number of Employee Assistance Programs and non-profit agencies. Val has play therapy certifications with the Association for Play Therapy in the United States and with the Canadian Association for Child and Play Therapy. An ex-Physical

Education teacher and team coach, play therapy proved a natural outgrowth, and basic training at the Rocky Mountain Play Therapy Institute, and a further two-year certification in Expressive Arts, set her on her path to work with children, an occupation she loves.

Terry Kottman, PhD, NCC, RPT-S, LMHC, founded The Encouragement Zone, where she provides play therapy training and supervision, life coaching, counseling, and "playshops" for women. Terry developed Adlerian play therapy, an approach to working with children, families, and adults that combines the ideas and techniques of Individual Psychology and play therapy. She regularly presents workshops and writes about play therapy, activity-based counseling, and life coaching. She is the author of *Play Therapy: Basics and Beyond*, co-author (with Kristin Meany-Walen) of *Partners in Play: An Adlerian Approach to Play Therapy*, and has written several other books. In 2014, she won the Lifetime Achievement Award from the Association for Play Therapy.

Sonia Murray, DipSW, BAPT, full member, holds a Diploma in Social Work and is a Registered Play Therapist. She has over 25 years' experience as a practitioner in the fields of child abuse, social, emotional, and behavioral difficulties, children's mental health, childhood trauma, parenting programs, and play therapy. Sonia trains nationally and internationally on topics related to play therapy, understanding behavior, play, communicating with children, behavior management, and positive parenting. Her work history includes employment as a childcare social worker, parent worker, and play therapist in education, social care, and health settings. Sonia provides consultation, supervision, and training in both statutory and voluntary fields of children's services. Sonia has also contributed to many publications, including *The Use of Therapeutic Stories*. Sonia served on the Board of Directors for the British Association of Play Therapists in a variety of capacities including Treasurer and Chair of Business and Research sub-committees for nearly ten years.

Katherine Olejniczak, MA, RPT-S (APPTA), CPT-Approved Supervisor (PTI), currently works in private practice and is the Director of Psychology and Play Therapy Australia. She is a Psychologist, a Certified Play Therapist with Play Therapy International, a Registered Play Therapist with the Australasia Pacific Play Therapy

Association, and an approved supervisor with all these bodies. She has completed a Masters in Practice Based Play Therapy and currently holds appointments with Deakin University, Australia—as a member of the Course Advisory Board for the Master of Child Play Therapy course—and as a Fieldwork Supervisor for these students. She is an experienced clinical supervisor, consultant, and trainer in the areas of childhood trauma and play therapy.

Magdalena S. Oyanedel, MFT, is a Child and Family Psychotherapist. She is the Director of the Metáfora Centre in Santiago, Chile, an institution that provides training in play therapy for child psychologists and psychiatrists. For the past eighteen years she has been working in the fields of childhood trauma. Additionally, she is dedicated to training play psychotherapists, and assists children and their families as a private practitioner. Her ongoing interest topic is the psychotherapeutic approach to relational trauma through play.

Eileen Prendiville is the Course Director for the MA in Creative Psychotherapy and Play Therapy (Humanistic and Integrative Modality) and the Postgraduate Diploma in Play Therapy at the Children's Therapy Centre in Co Westmeath, Ireland. Eileen was a founder member, and National Clinical Director, of the Children at Risk in Ireland Foundation, Ireland's specialist treatment service for children and families affected by child sexual abuse. Eileen is a psychotherapist, play therapist, supervisor, and trainer. Eileen co-edited *Play Therapy Today: Contemporary Practice with Individuals, Groups, and Carers* and contributed chapters to this and other books. She was Chairperson of the Irish Association of Humanistic and Integrative Psychotherapy from 2012 to 2014 and is the current Chairperson of the Irish Association for Play Therapy and Psychotherapy. Eileen devised "The Therapeutic Touchstone," an innovative approach for use when working with vulnerable and dependent clients.

Tammy Reis, MSW, RSW, CPT, has, since the early 2000s, worked with children and families in Whitehorse and remote Northern communities in the Yukon with both government agencies and non-profit organizations. Currently, she works with children under the age of five and is passionate about child and infant mental health.

Adriana Sorbo, MA, is a Registered Psychologist in Calgary, Alberta, and Registered Play Therapist with the Association for Play Therapy.

She has worked with children, adolescents, and parents in numerous settings, including inpatient and outpatient mental health, non-profit agencies, and private practice. She is currently in private practice where she works with children and their caregivers and has recently begun to offer consultation and training to caseworkers and caregivers of foster children.

Karen Stagnitti, PhD, is a professor with a personal chair in the School of Health and Social Development at Deakin University, Australia. She teaches on the Master of Child Play Therapy course. Karen has over 100 publications, both national and international, which are composed of peer-reviewed journal articles, invited journal articles, book chapters, and books. She developed the first norm-referenced standardized assessment of a child's ability to self-initiate play called the *Child-Initiated Pretend Play Assessment*. She has also developed two further play assessments: the *Pretend Play Enjoyment Developmental Checklist*, which assesses pretend play ability, enjoyment of play, and self-representation; and the *Animated Movie Test*, which is designed for use with young people.

Cassandra White, MSc, R Psych is the Director of Rocky Mountain Psychological Services, a private psychology clinic in Calgary, Alberta. Her career spans over 20 years and has focused primarily on working with children and families. Cassandra is passionate about her work; she loves to learn and seeks to bring play into the "serious work" of life. Cassandra is also a mother of four children who are her greatest teachers.

Appendix A

DEGREE OF IMMERSION: THERAPIST USE OF SELF SCALE

Immersion relates to ways and degree to which you use yourself during a play therapy session with a child. Using the scales below, mark on the line the degree to which you evaluate your "immersion" on the following factors.

1 Verbal Use of Self

1.1 Here and Now Discussion (Open Discussion and Exploration)

During the session, what was the degree to which you were involved in verbal discussion "about" the child's life or with the child outside of the play activity?

1	2	3	4	5
LOW		MODERATE		HIGH
Almost not at all. Stayed in play activity and/or followed child's lead.		Some discussion observed, usually led by the child. Discussion included spontaneous information sharing about school and activity, a family member, etc.		Spent significant part of session outside of metaphorical play in direct discussion.

Child's Response: Please rate the effectiveness of **your use of** *Here and Now Discussion*

- ☐ **Low** (Play was shut down. Child pivoted away as a defensive response)
- ☐ **Medium** (Child elaborates play, i.e. adds verbalizations and/or play themes/actions)
- ☐ **High** (Child incorporates/assimilates language or actions facilitated by therapist, indicating a greater awareness of self or circumstances)

Provide an example that supports your rating of the child's response:

1.2 Reflecting and Tracking Statements (Non-intrusive Responding/Co-facilitation)

During the session, to what degree were you using reflecting and tracking statements? Tracking refers to what the client is doing or what the play objects are doing. Reflecting statements refer to the guesses or statements about what the therapist thinks the client is experiencing, such as *"you seem really happy right now,"* or what the character is experiencing: *"that one is very angry."*

1 LOW	2	3 MODERATE	4	5 HIGH
Used few or no reflecting or tracking statements.		Some use of reflecting or tracking statements. Reflections included feelings or non-verbal actions in play.		Primarily used reflecting and tracking statements related to child's emotions, non-verbal behavior play actions, verbal content play sequences, or metaphors.

Child's Response: Please rate the effectiveness of **your use of** *Reflecting and Tracking Statements*

- ☐ **Low** (Play was shut down. Child pivoted away as a defensive response/ or child annoyed by your use of reflecting and tracking statements)

- ☐ **Medium** (Child elaborates play, i.e. adds verbalizations and/or play themes/actions)

- ☐ **High** (Child incorporates/assimilates language or actions facilitated by therapist, indicating a greater awareness of self or circumstances)

Provide an example that supports your rating of the child's response:

1.3 Restating Content (Non-intrusive Responding/Co-facilitation)

During the session, to what degree did you paraphrase what the child said during the play without adding meaning or interpretation? Children talk in therapy directly about the play media and through the play media.

1	2	3	4	5
LOW		**MODERATE**		**HIGH**
Used few or no restatements of verbal content.		Some/ moderate use of restatements or paraphrases made to child after child's comments.		Frequent use of restatements/ paraphrases of child's verbalizations during the play.

Child's Response: Please rate the effectiveness of **your use of** *Restating Content*

- ☐ **Low** (Play was shut down. Child pivoted away as a defensive response/ or child annoyed by your use of reflecting and tracking statements)

- ☐ **Medium** (Child elaborates play, i.e. adds verbalizations and/or play themes/actions)

- ☐ **High** (Child incorporates/assimilates language or actions facilitated by therapist, indicating a greater awareness of self or circumstances)

Provide an example that supports your rating of the child's response:

1.4 Interpretations (Active Utilization)

During the session, to what degree did you utilize interpretive statements? Interpretations are verbal comments made by the therapist (after observing repetitive play themes and play scenarios). It is a function of utilizing play material to assist a child to develop new understanding/meaning by bringing a link between play and the child's lived life to conscious awareness. Types of interpretations may include: reflective interpretations, linking interpretations, and/or bridging interpretations (Yasenik and Gardner, 2012).

1	2	3	4	5
LOW		**MODERATE**		**HIGH**
No use of interpretations/ too soon to utilize an interpretation. Tracking and restatements used. Still formulating hypotheses/ child not ready or able to work at high levels of consciousness.		Some/ moderate use of interpretations. First level: reflective interpretations used. Some soft hypotheses are formed and use of characters to test hypotheses observed. Interpretations made primarily through the play metaphor.		Used one or more types of interpretative statements (reflective, linking, or bridging). A child's current or past experience embedded in play is raised to a higher degree of consciousness through the interpretation made by therapist to child.

Child's Response: Please rate the effectiveness of **your use of** *Interpretations*

☐ **Low** (Play was shut down. Child pivoted away as a defensive response/ or child annoyed by your use of reflecting and tracking statements)

- ☐ **Medium** (Child elaborates play, i.e. adds verbalizations and/or play themes/actions)
- ☐ **High** (Child incorporates/assimilates language or actions facilitated by therapist, indicating a greater awareness of self or circumstances)

Provide an example that supports your rating of the child's response:

2 Emotional Use of Self

2.1 Emotionality (Non-intrusive Responding/Co-facilitation)

During the session, what was the degree of the emotional intensity that you assigned to either reflective statements or by inserting an emotion or emotional meaning to a character or characters in the play metaphor? If you were in role play, also consider your intensity of use of emotions regarding the character that was assigned the emotion(s), including tone, prosody, duration, volume, and facial expressions (therapist).

1	2	3	4	5
LOW		**MODERATE**		**HIGH**
Primarily observed the child/ rarely reflected emotions of the child or the characters in the play.		Some/moderate emotional intensity utilized and focused on one or more characters or emotionality mirrored the child's emotional expression.		High use of emotionality. Many reflective statements or inserted emotional comments noted (both verbal comments and vocalizations). The overall use of self was intense on several levels and was either therapist led or directed by the child.

Child's Response: Please rate the effectiveness of **your use of** *Emotionality*

- ☐ **Low** (Play was shut down. Child pivoted away as a defensive response/ or child annoyed by your use of reflecting and tracking statements)
- ☐ **Medium** (Child elaborates play, i.e. adds verbalizations/emotions and/ or play themes/actions)
- ☐ **High** (Child incorporates/assimilates language or actions facilitated by therapist, indicating a greater awareness of self or circumstances)

Provide an example that supports your rating of the child's response:

2.2 Emotional Self (all quadrants)

During the session, what was the degree to which you were personally emotionally involved during the session? This may include your awareness of feeling a particular intense emotion or that you notice yourself shut down or become numb or that you may temporarily lose track of following the client. You may become aware of a personal experience or be triggered to a personal memory.

1	2	3	4	5
LOW		**MODERATE**		**HIGH**
I did not feel particularly emotionally involved but remained empathic and had a clear sense of neutral but present feeling.		I felt moderately emotionally involved. I noticed I had some of my own feelings related to the client material.		I felt highly emotionally involved and affected by the client's presentation or play scenario and/or child's disclosure. I felt flooded or shut down during some part of the session.

I became aware of one or more of the following emotions:

☐ Anger

☐ Sadness

☐ Fear

☐ Confusion

☐ Joy

☐ Worry

☐ Frustration

☐ Other _____

Child's Response: Please rate the effectiveness of **your use of** *Emotional Self*

☐ **Low** (Play was shut down. Child pivoted away as a defensive response/ or child annoyed by your use of reflecting and tracking statements)

☐ **Medium** (Child elaborates play, i.e. adds verbalizations/emotions and/ or play themes/actions)

☐ **High** (Child incorporates/assimilates language or actions facilitated by therapist, indicating a greater awareness of self or circumstances)

Provide an example that supports your rating of the child's response:

3 Physical Use of Self
3.1 Physical Self (all quadrants)

During the session, what was the degree to which you were physically involved during the session? Physical self includes: physical movement in play activities, physical proximity or touch, and level of physical energy.

1	2	3	4	5
LOW		**MODERATE**		**HIGH**
Very little physical involvement. Primarily observed the child and followed child in the space. Did not engage in activities even when approached by the child.		Engaged in physical play only when directly invited to do so. Some physical play and movement with moderate contact.		Fully engaged in the play. Physical contact part of the play. High energy output. You may consider touch therapies as high, such as Theraplay®.

Child's Response: Please rate the effectiveness of **your use of** *Physical Self*

☐ **Low** (Play was shut down. Child pivoted away as a defensive response/or child annoyed by your use of reflecting and tracking statements)

☐ **Medium** (Child elaborates play, i.e. adds verbalizations/emotions and/or play themes/actions)

☐ **High** (Child incorporates/assimilates language or actions facilitated by therapist, indicating a greater awareness of self or circumstances)

Provide an example that supports your rating of the child's response:

4. Self-System
4.1 Embodiment (all quadrants)

During the session, what was the degree to which you were aware of your self-system in the presence of the child? Self-system includes: your body/energy awareness in relation to "other" (the child). It is the ability to be consciously aware of your internal state(s) of being.

1	2	3	4	5
LOW		**MODERATE**		**HIGH**
Disembodied: I was mostly operating from a cognitive space. I was not specifically aware of my internal state(s) of being during much or most of the session. **Lost in embodiment:** I became unaware of my body and internal states of self and self responses during the session.		Moderate and intermittent awareness of self-system. There were points during the process where the I-self/Me-self were operating in a reflexive and conscious way. I could identify at least one point in the session where I could identify my internal experience in relation to the child.		Highly aware of my self-system. I was mostly aware of a reflexive process of the back and forth of the "Me-self" informing the "I-self" and vice versa. Body-mind awareness "on-line."

Child's Response: Please rate the effectiveness of **your awareness of your** *Self-System*

- ☐ **Low** (Play was shut down. Child pivoted away as a defensive response/or child disengaged from you or the play)

- ☐ **Medium** (Child elaborates play, i.e. adds verbalizations/emotions and/or play themes/actions and appears to connect non-verbally)

- ☐ **High** (Child appeared highly connected in a non-verbal or verbal way)

Provide an example that supports your rating of the child's response:

TOTAL IMMERSION SCORE ☐ _____

8–16 ☐ Low Immersion   17–24 ☐ Moderate Immersion   25–40 ☐ High Immersion

IMMERSION SUMMARY
1 Verbal Use of Self

Here and Now Discussion	☐ Decrease	☐ Increase	☐ On track
Reflecting and Tracking Statements	☐ Decrease	☐ Increase	☐ On track
Restating Content	☐ Decrease	☐ Increase	☐ On track
Interpretations	☐ Decrease	☐ Increase	☐ On track

2 Emotional Use of Self

Emotionality	☐ Decrease	☐ Increase	☐ On track
Emotional Self	☐ Decrease	☐ Increase	☐ On track

3 Physical Use of Self

Physical Self	☐ Decrease	☐ Increase	☐ On track

4 Self-System

Embodiment	☐ Decrease	☐ Increase	☐ On track

Provide a rationale that supports your rating:

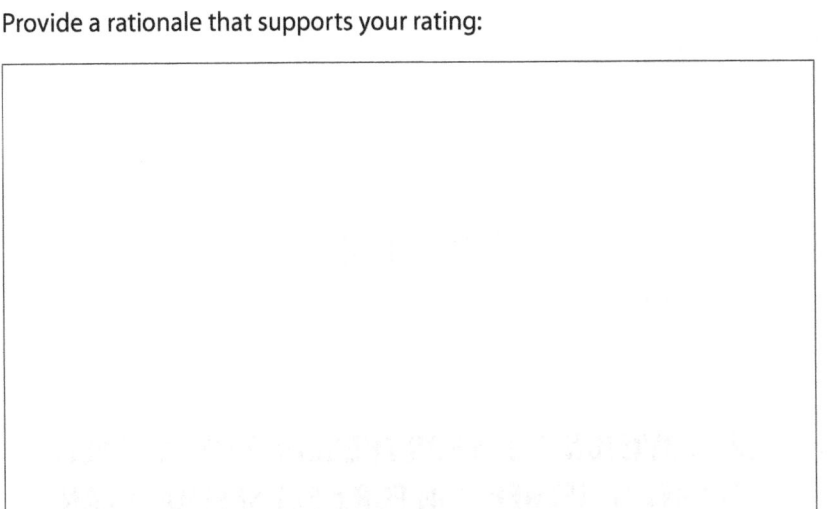

References

Yasenik, L. and Gardner, K. (2012) *Play Therapy Dimensions Model: A Decision-Making Guide for Integrative Play Therapists.* London: Jessica Kingsley Publishers.

Appendix B

SUPERVISION FORM FOR THERAPIST USE OF SELF: DEGREE OF IMMERSION FOR NEXT SESSION PLAN

For each area of immersion that you plan to either increase or decrease in degree, describe ways you will change your "use of self."

1 Verbal Use of Self

1.1 Here and Now Discussion

_____

_____

_____

1.2 Reflecting and Tracking Statements

_____

_____

_____

1.3 Restating Content

_____

_____

_____

1.4 Interpretations

2 Emotional Use of Self

2.1 Emotionality

2.2 Emotional Self

3 Physical Use of Self

3.1 Physical Self

4 Self-System

4.1 Embodiment

Follow-Up Supervision Session Date _____ Time _____

Supervisor _____ Supervisee _____

Subject Index

Sub-headings in *italics* indicate figures and diagrams.

Adlerian play therapy (AdPT) 10, 27, 30, 275–6
    case study 59–60, 147–8
    case study conceptualization 65–71, 151–2
    theoretical orientation 60–5, 148–50
    therapy process 71–81, 152
    turning point 1 71–3, 153–4
    turning point 2 73, 154–5
    turning point 3 73–4, 155–6
    turning point 4 74–5, 156–7
    turning point 5 75–7, 157–8
    turning point 6 77, 158
    turning point 7 78
    turning point 8 78–9
    turning points summary 80–1, 159
affective regulation 166–7
    affective synchrony and affect regulation in psychotherapy 190–2
assets 70
assimilation integration 238
Association for Play Therapy 223–4
attachment theory 131–2, 149–50, 191, 210–11
autism 48

behavior 18–19
    behavior which needs to change 70
    goals of misbehavior 68–9, 148, 149
birth order position 66–7

brain function 46–7, 84, 86, 127, 129, 150, 196, 240
    Neurosequential Model of Therapeutics (NMT) 209–10, 227

Changes in Behavior Checklist 151
changes in play 21–2
    self-awareness 19–21
    self-concept 23–4
    thought 18–19
chapter overview 10–12
Child Behavior Checklist 151
Child Sexual Behavior Checklist 151
child-centered play therapy 10
    case study 207–8
    case study conceptualization 211–12
    stuck point 1 213
    stuck point 2 213–16
    stuck point 3 216–17
    stuck point 4 217–20
    stuck points summary 220–1
    theoretical orientation 209–11
    therapy process 212–21
Child-Initiated Pretend Play Assessment (ChIPPA) 44
Circle of Security Project 128, 139
cognitive behavioral therapy (CBT) 119
Cognitive-Behavioral Play Therapy 27
comfort 69–70
consciousness 25, 27–9
control 69–70
Crucial Cs (connect, capable, count, courage) 69, 79, 148–9, 157

Deblinger, Esther 139
Degree of Immersion: Therapist Use of Self Scale 10, 12, 32–3, 152, 279
　tracking therapist immersion and impact on turning points 34–9
Diagnostic and Statistical Manual of Mental Disorders (DSM-5) 43
dialogical hermeneutics 163
directiveness 25–7
disordered play 21

ecosystemic play therapy 27
Embodiment-Projection-Role (E-P-R) 10
　E-P-R paradigm and overcoming trauma linked to child sexual abuse 87–8, 96
emergence of self in play therapy 15–16
　Adlerian play therapy 71–81, 153–9
　Flexible Sequential Play Therapy (FSPT) 133–44
　integrative play therapy 90–100, 229–34
　intersubjective and relational psychoanalysis 168–85
　Learn to Play Therapy 48–56
　Play Therapy Dimensions Model—Revised (PTDM–R) 194–204
　prescriptive play therapy 114–22
　therapeutic relationship 241–52
　turning points and emergence of the professional self 264–7
Ericksonian theory 31
eye movement desensitization and processing (EMDR) 142

family 67–8, 149
　family atmosphere 67
　family constellation 66–7
Flexible Sequential Play Therapy (FSPT) 10, 277–8
　case study 125
　case study conceptualization 129
　Components of FSPT 127
　theoretical orientation 126–8
　therapy process 130–2
　turning points 1 and 2 133–4
　turning point 10 138–40
　turning point 11 140–3
　turning points 3 and 4 134–5
　turning point 5 136
　turning point 6 136–7
　turning points 7 and 8 137–8
　turning point 9 138
　turning points summary 143–4

Freud, Sigmund 256
friendship 68–9
functioning at life tasks 67–8

gestalt play therapy 27
grounding 112–13

I-self 15, 16, 19–20, 28, 45, 98, 174, 181
immersion 32–3
　Embodiment 117, 153, 158
　Emotional Use of Self 33, 112, 158, 214
　Physical Use of Self 33, 114, 120, 153, 157, 158, 213
　Self-System 33, 93
　tracking therapist immersion and impact on turning points 34–9
　Verbal Use of Self 33, 153, 212, 229
integrative play therapy 10, 24–5, 188, 226–7
　case study 83, 223–6
　case study conceptualization 86, 227
　E-P-R paradigm and overcoming trauma linked to child sexual abuse 87–8, 96
　emergence of true healing play 92–4
　theoretical orientation 84–6, 226–7
　therapy process 88–90, 227–34
　turning point 1 90–2, 229
　turning point 2 92–4, 230
　turning point 3 94, 231
　turning point 4 94, 231–3
　turning point 5 94–5, 231–3
　turning point 6 95
　turning point 7 95
　turning point 8 and 9 96
　turning point 10 97
　turning point 11 97–8
　turning points summary 98–100, 233–4
Intersubjective and Relational Psychoanalysis 10
　affective regulation 166–7
　case study 161–3
　case study conceptualization 167–8
　final remarks 182–3
　intersubjectivity 164–5
　play and object-presenting 165–6
　relational trauma 165
　theoretical orientation 163–7
　therapy process 168–81
　turning point 1 168–71
　turning point 2 171–4
　turning point 3 174–7
　turning point 4 177–9

Subject Index

turning point 5 179–81
turning points summary 183–5
isolation, professional 257–62
  transitioning from isolation to belonging 262–4
  working in remote areas 258–9

James, William 256
Jungian play therapy 31

Learn to Play Therapy 10, 45–7, 274–5
  case study 43–4
  case study conceptualization 47–8
  theoretical orientation 45–7
  therapy process 48–50
  turning point 1 50–1
  turning point 2 51–2
  turning point 3 52–3
  turning point 4 53
  turning point 5 53–4
  turning point 6 54–5
  turning points summary 55–6
life tasks 67–8
lifestyle convictions 70

mastery play 21
Me-self 15, 16, 19–20, 28, 45, 98, 181
metacommunication 27, 62–4, 75, 76, 77, 117
mirroring 128, 137, 194, 257, 276
  collegial mirroring 257, 261, 264

Neurosequential Model of Therapeutics (NMT) 209–10, 227, 231–2

only children 66–7
ordered play 21

personality priorities 69–70
phenomenology 163
play and object-presenting 165–6
play therapy 9–10
  play therapy materials 112–13
Play Therapy Dimensions Model (PTMD) 9, 10, 12, 152
  directiveness and consciousness 25–9
  four quadrants 29–31
  integrative conceptualization framework 24–5
  invigoration of professional selves 267–9
  Play therapy dimensions diagram 26
  turning points and emergence of the professional self 264–7

Play Therapy Dimensions Model—Revised (PTDM–R)
  affective synchrony and affect regulation in psychotherapy 190–2
  case study 187–8, 276–7
  case study conceptualization 192
  Play Therapy Dimensions Model—Revised 189
  theoretical orientation 188–90
  therapy process 193–204
  trauma therapy phase 1 193–7
  trauma therapy phase 2 197–9
  trauma therapy phase 3 199–201
  turning point 1 194
  turning point 2 194–5
  turning point 3 195–6
  turning point 4 196–7
  turning point 5 197
  turning point 6 198
  turning point 7 198
  turning point 8 198–9
  turning point 9 199
  turning point 10 199
  turning point 11 200
  turning point 12 200
  turning point 13 200
  turning point 14 200–1
  turning points summary 201–4
power 68
prescriptive play therapy 10, 27
  assimilative integration 107–8
  case study 103–6
  case study conceptualization 110–14
  common factors 107
  final remarks 121
  middle phase of treatment 116–18
  technical eclecticism 106–7
  theoretical integration 107
  theoretical orientation 106–10
  therapy process 114–21
  turning points summary 121–2
pretend play 45–7
professional development 254–5
  invigoration of professional selves 267–9
  isolation 257–62
  professional selves 256–7
  turning points and emergence of the professional self 264–7
psychodynamic play therapy 30–1, 109, 110

quadrants 12, 29–31
Play therapy dimensions diagram 26
Quadrant I: Active Utilization 25, 30–1, 91, 93
    Adlerian play therapy 62, 63, 64, 65, 75, 76, 77, 152, 153, 156
    child-centered play therapy 213, 214
    Flexible Sequential Play Therapy (FSPT) 130, 134
    integrative play therapy 93
    intersubjective and relational psychoanalysis 168, 173, 174, 182
    Play Therapy Dimensions Model— Revised (PTDM–R) 195, 198
    prescriptive play therapy 119
    therapeutic relationship 246
Quadrant II: Open Discussion and Exploration 25, 32, 36, 89, 92, 94
    Adlerian play therapy 62, 63, 64, 65, 72, 74, 75, 76, 78, 152
    child-centered play therapy 213, 214
    Flexible Sequential Play Therapy (FSPT) 130, 138–9
    integrative play therapy 89, 92, 94
    intersubjective and relational psychoanalysis 176, 177, 182
    Play Therapy Dimensions Model— Revised (PTDM–R) 196, 199, 200
    prescriptive play therapy 111, 112, 114, 115, 118, 120
    therapeutic relationship 247
Quadrant III: Non-intrusive Responding 25, 29, 30, 38, 89, 90, 91
    Adlerian play therapy 62, 63, 73, 152, 154
    child-centered play therapy 212, 213, 214
    Flexible Sequential Play Therapy (FSPT) 130, 132, 133–4, 135, 136, 142
    integrative play therapy 89, 90
    intersubjective and relational psychoanalysis 177, 182
    Learn to Play Therapy 52, 54
    Play Therapy Dimensions Model— Revised (PTDM–R) 193, 194, 195, 196, 197–8
    prescriptive play therapy 110, 111, 114, 115, 119
    therapeutic relationship 238, 244, 246
Quadrant IV: Co-facilitation 25, 30, 38, 91
    Adlerian play therapy 62, 63, 64, 65, 75, 76, 77, 78, 156, 158
    child-centered play therapy 214
    Flexible Sequential Play Therapy (FSPT) 130, 133, 135, 136, 137, 138, 141, 142
    intersubjective and relational psychoanalysis 174, 177, 182
    Learn to Play Therapy 47, 49, 52, 54
    Play Therapy Dimensions Model— Revised (PTDM–R) 194, 195, 198
    prescriptive play therapy 110, 111, 112, 115, 116, 117, 120
    therapeutic relationship 243, 245

Reflecting and Tracking Statements 37, 39, 51, 152, 154, 156, 213
Regulation and window of tolerance (WOT) 188–90, 191–2, 193–5, 197–9
relational trauma 165
Restating Content 51, 52, 54, 62, 121, 152, 154, 156, 213
Rogerian theory 46

safe play 21, 22
school 67–9, 97
self-awareness 19–21, 28
self-concept 23–4, 68–9
self-development 10
    emergence of self 15–16
skills 71
soothing 112–13, 196
spirituality 68
Spock, Benjamin 227
stuck points 212–21
supervision 259–60
    Supervision Form for Therapist Use of Self 279
    turning points in supervision 278–81

therapeutic relationship 227–8
    case study 237–8
    case study conceptualization 240–1
    theoretical orientation 238–40
    therapy process 241–52
    turnings point 1, 2 and 3 241–5
    turning point 4 246–7
    turning point 5 247–50
    turning points summary 251–2
Therapeutic Touchstone 89
therapists 10, 255–6, 278–80
    immersion 32–3
    in search of belonging 257–62
    invigoration of professional selves 267–9
    play therapist development 280–1

theoretical foundation 256–7
therapist decision-making 274–8
tracking therapist immersion and impact on turning points 34–9
transitioning from isolation to belonging 262–4
turning points and emergence of the professional self 264–7
words of wisdom 270
Theraplay® 27, 142
Trauma Focused-Cognitive Behavior Therapy (TF-CBT) 139
turning points 9–10, 16–18, 273
　Adlerian play therapy 71–81, 153–9
　Flexible Sequential Play Therapy (FSPT) 133–44
　integrative play therapy 90–100, 229–34
　intersubjective and relational psychoanalysis 168–85
　Learn to Play Therapy 50–6
　Play Therapy Dimensions Model—Revised (PTDM–R) 194–204
　prescriptive play therapy 114–22
　stuck points 212–21
　therapeutic relationship 241–52
　therapist decision-making 274–8
　turning point type 1 18–19
　turning point type 2 19–21
　turning point type 3 21–2
　turning point type 4 23–4
　turning points and emergence of the professional self 264–7
　turning points in supervision 278–81

Window of Tolerance (WOT) 188–90, 191–2, 193–5, 197–9, 276

Author Index

Achenbach, T.M. 151
Adler, A. 60, 61
Allan, J. 194, 198
Allen, J. 239
American Psychiatric Association 43
Ansbacher, H. 148
Ansbacher, R. 148
Aron, L. 164
Ashby, J. 63, 148
Atwood, G. 164
Axline, V. 46, 84, 227, 238
Ayduk, O. 23

Badenoch, B. 150
Baldwin, M. 15
Bates, E. 16, 19
Bath, H. 225
Beebe, B. 164, 165, 167
Beeghly, M. 190
Bergman, A. 242
Berk, L. 46
Berrol, C.F. 194
Bettner, B.L. 148
Booth, P.B. 132
Bowlby, J. 210
Bragan, K. 15
Bratton, S.C. 47, 188, 226, 227
Brody, V. 218
Bromberg, P. 165
Bronfenbrenner, U. 228

Caporino, N. 238
Carey, L. 248
Carmody, D. 48, 49
Casey, S. 48, 50
Cloitre, M. 193
Cohn, T.J. 258

Cook, A. 189
Cooper, R. 48
Corrigan, F.M. 129
Courtois, C.A. 193
Cozolino, L. 127, 190, 197, 239
Crowley, R. 31
Cuskelly, M. 228

Dalai Lama Center (Producer) 191
Damasio, A. 128
De Leo, D. 9
Deblinger, E. 220
Delworth, U. 279
Divecha, D. 239
D'Mello, S. 128
Donald, G. 48
Dreikurs, R. 148
Drewes, A.A. 53, 84, 106, 107, 188, 226, 234, 280

Eberle, S.G. 48, 50
Edge, A.M. 48, 241
Elias, C. 46
Emblen, T. 48
Erwin, E. 15
Eth, S. 29
Evans, J. 226

Falender, C.A. 278
Ferenczi, S. 165
Fisher, J.J. 129, 150, 153
Flückiger, C. 238
Ford, J.D. 193
Fosha, D. 167
Frankiel, R. 242
Friedrich, W. 151

Author Index

Gadamer, H.G. 163
Gallese, V. 261, 264
Gardner, K. 9, 25, 28, 29, 47, 62, 63, 89, 90, 91, 93, 94, 130, 135, 149, 152, 153, 154, 156, 158, 167, 188, 212, 231, 238, 243, 245, 247, 248, 256, 264, 278, 279, 280, 281
Garfield, S.L. 24
Gaskill, R. 48, 50, 127
Geller, S.M. 245
Gergen, K. 15
Gigerenzer, G. 25
Gil, E. 86, 110, 129, 188, 246
Goengian, A. 218
Golding, K.S. 191
Goodyear-Brown, P. 10, 112, 126, 129, 132, 188, 190, 191, 193, 198
Graesser, A. 128
Greenberg, J.R. 163
Greenspan, S.I. 32
Grencavage, L.M. 107
Guerney, L. 27, 248
Gyurak, A. 23

Ham, J. 191
Hambrick, E.P. 110, 112, 127
Hammond, S. 45
Harter, S. 10, 15, 16, 23, 45, 52, 94, 95, 98, 181, 241, 246, 249
Hastings, S.L. 258
Herman, J.L. 211, 212, 238–9
Hill, D. 189, 190
Hobson, R.F. 15
Hoffmann, J. 46
Hogan, L. 190
Hong, R. 240
Horowitz, M. 210
Hughes, C. 45
Hughes, D.A. 191
Husserl, E. 163

Ilgaz, H. 46
Israelievitch, G. 242

James, B. 225–6
James, W. 15, 19
Jennings, S. 10, 87, 246
Jernberg, A.M. 132
Jester, M. 43
Johnson, C.J. 43
Johnson, K. 218
Jordan, J.F. 163

Karver, M.S. 238
Kelly, R. 45
Kestly, T.A. 90, 243
Kendall, J. 109
Khan, M. 15
Kidd, E. 46
King, S.A. 201
Kirkham, J. 46
Kline, M. 141
Knell, S.M. 27
Kottman, T. 27, 30, 60, 61, 62, 63, 64, 65, 66, 75, 79, 148, 149, 275
Krystal, J.H. 218
Kuhbandner, C. 261
Kuhn-Popp, N. 48

Lachmann, F. 164, 165, 167
Landreth, G. 17, 27, 227
Leblanc, M. 227
Leekam, S. 45
Leslie, A. 45
Levine, P.A. 141
Levy, A.J. 197
Levy, T.M. 210
Lew, A. 148
Lewis, F.M. 46, 47
Lewis, M. 48, 49
Lin, Y.-W. 47, 227
Luerssen, A. 23

MacLean, P.D. 127
Maier, M.A. 261
March, J. 218
Marshall, R.J. 261, 264
Marlin, S.J. 190
Mason, C.M. 240
McNeill, B. 279
Meany-Walen, K. 60, 61, 62, 63, 64, 65, 66, 275
Middleton, W. 211
Miller, P.J. 16, 19
Mills, J. 31
Minton, K. 129, 150, 154, 189
Mitchell, S.A. 163
Morin, A. 256, 257, 260, 264
Mullen, J.A. 280
Munns, E. 27
Munsch, R. 231, 232

Nader, K. 218
Nelson, K. 15, 16
Newen, A. 256, 259
Nicolopoulou, A. 46

Norcross, J.C. 24, 106, 107, 238
Norton, B.E. 89, 98, 141
Norton, C.C. 89, 98, 141
Nutt, D.J. 129

OACYC (Ontario Association of Child and Youth Care) 223
Oaklander, V. 27, 194, 197
O'Connor, C. 46
O'Connor, K. 27, 31
Ogden, P. 129, 150, 153, 154, 189, 190, 197
Olejniczak, K. 188, 193
Orange, D.M. 163
Orlans, M. 210
Ornitz, E. 218
O'Sullivan, L. 46

Pain, C. 129, 189
Panksepp, J. 90, 91
Parks, C. 211
Peery, C. 31
Pekrun, R. 261
Perry, B.D. 48, 50, 84, 85, 110, 112, 127, 150, 190, 196, 209, 210, 225, 227, 231–2, 238, 239, 240, 241
Petersen, N. 75
Porges, S.W. 84, 90, 129, 150, 189, 190, 196, 240
Poulsen, A.A. 228
Powell, B. 128
Prendiville, E. 86, 87, 89, 90, 96
Prichard, N. 240
Pynoos, R. 29, 218

Rabe, T. 196
Reidbord, S. 210
Rescorla, L.A. 151
Ritchie, M. 227
Riviere, S. 220
Roelofs, K. 226
Rogers, C. 92
Rose, R. 200
Rothschild, B. 141
Russ, S. 46
Ryan, V. 27, 48, 241, 248

Schaefer, C.E. 24, 27, 53, 84, 107, 188, 226, 234
Schoenewolf, G. 9, 17
Schore, A.N. 127, 165, 166, 190, 191, 194
Shafranske, E.P. 278
Sherratt, D. 48
Siegel, D.J. 84, 86, 95, 127, 150, 189, 211
Simpson, R. 261
Smith, D. 25
Sniscak, C. 27
Soltz, V. 148
Stagnitti, K. 10, 44, 45, 46, 47, 48, 50, 274
Stein, P.T. 109
Steinberg, A. 218
Stewart, A. 46
Stolorow, R. 164
Stoltenberg, C. 279
Stone, M.H. 17
Sunderland, M. 36, 47, 50, 55
Sywulak, A. 27
Szalavitz, M. 150, 227

Terr, L. 86, 246
Tessier, V.P. 45
Tronick, E. 190, 191

van der Kolk, B. 110, 129, 150, 165, 237, 238
VanFleet, R. 27
Vogeley, K. 256, 259
Vygotsky, L. 46

Wallace, C. 46
Westby, C. 46, 49
Whitebread, D. 46
Whitehead, C. 48
Wilson, K. 27
Winnicott, D.W. 17, 165, 183, 193
Wosket, V. 15

Yasenik, L. 9, 25, 28, 29, 47, 62, 63, 89, 90, 91, 93, 94, 130, 135, 149, 152, 153, 154, 156, 158, 167, 188, 212, 231, 238, 243, 245, 247, 248, 256, 264, 278, 279, 280, 281

Ziviani, J. 228